GANGSTERS OF BOSTON

GEORGE HASSETT

STRATEGIC MEDIA BOOKS

13-digit ISBN 978-0-9852440-3-3

10-digit ISBM 0-9852440-3-8

This book is dedicated to the memory of my father, George Hassett Sr., (1953-2012), the best criminal defense lawyer in New England and, more importantly, a great Dad.

CONTENTS

PROLOGUE

WHITEY'S BACK

On June 23 2011, James (Whitey) Bulger walked across the Logan airport tarmac in Boston, shackled and hustled along by federal agents. Dressed in an orange jumpsuit, Bulger was a blast from the city's criminal past. By now, he might have looked like an ancient relic, but he could still solve the most vexing gangland mysteries.

Multimillion dollar art heists, massacres and dozens of forgotten murders – Bulger might be able to solve them all. Bulger might even implicate the half dozen FBI agents he corrupted over the years in his murderous schemes.

After Bulger, the questions shifted to Catherine Grieg, the woman who hid him out the last fifteen years – a quiet, dental hygienist who had fallen for the bad boy and left her middle class family.

In her home neighborhood of Southie, no one expected Grieg to be a gunman's moll. She was a bookish schoolgirl and later a dental hygienist. How the girl voted best looking in her class ended up on the run with a killer wanted by the FBI, and with a $100,000 bounty on her head, is still the subject of speculation on Broadway, the boulevard that splices Southie's heart.

Maybe Boston should not have been so quick to judge Whitey's devoted girl. Hadn't this city fallen for the "good bad guy" for decades? In Southie especially Whitey was revered as the benevolent godfather who kept drugs out - even as he flooded the neighborhood with cocaine and started an epidemic. At the State House his brother, the Senate President, spread the myth to the highest level of state government as Whitey killed dozens.

Bulger even enlisted the Boston office of the FBI in his fatal schemes, corrupting as many as six agents. In return, he worked as an informant – violating the underworld's code of honor but receiving protection from federal agents for his crime empire.

The corrupt agents in the FBI's Boston office and Bulger were a natural match – they had all survived the Irish Gang Wars and wanted to rule the underworld with no competition. Together, they successfully overtook the Mafia to control drug profits, extortion and murder in Boston.

In other cities such an arrangement – the FBI essentially became Bulger's strong-arm men – might be unthinkable. But in Boston the "good guys" and "bad guys" have always been difficult to tell apart. Here, Joe Kennedy turned a liquor business forged in Prohibition into a political dynasty that landed his son Jack in the White House.

Boston's volatile mix of street gangs and dubious politics has made its underworld infamous – enshrined in mob memoirs and Hollywood hits. Boston gangsters are more than seedy characters out of the past – the city's underworld has shaped the American identity and experience all the way back to its founding when a ragtag gang of thugs sparked a revolution.

CHAPTER ONE

HOW BOSTON'S STREET GANGS SPARKED THE AMERICAN REVOLUTION

WEDNESDAY, AUGUST 14, 1765.

THE PATRIOTS HAD waited long enough. After weeks of planning they would strike as the sun came up.

To prepare, they worked frantically – buzzing around a grand old elm tree on a darkened Boston street corner. As the crowd swelled to thousands, one man was looked upon as the undisputed leader.

It wasn't a future founding father; instead, a red-faced gang chief was calling the shots. At various times imprisoned and deemed a drunkard, today Ebeneezer Mackintosh finally had the chance to prove his dedication to liberty.

To attack the British crown, he summoned the laborers, fishermen and seamen from the rough and tumble ranks of the town's waterfront community. Also, members of the town's perpetually warring street gangs were there. Each of them, however, respected Mackintosh and followed his command as the night wore on. Mackintosh even accepted the extravagant title "First Captain General of the Liberty Tree" in recognition of the tree they toiled under.

As dawn broke, the shocking scene was finally revealed: hanging from the tree was an effigy of a man. The effigy was labeled "AO" for Andrew Oliver, the British official appointed to oversee the hated new tax plan in the colonies. Attached was a verse: "A godlier sight who e'er did see/ A Stamp-Man hanging on a tree!"

The tax, referred to as the Stamp Act, was considered an economic attack on Boston's port. Now, Boston's rowdy waterfront laborers were fighting back. Mackintosh directed the crowd to Kilby Street to demolish Andrew Oliver's nearly completed office building. They ransacked and plundered the building, salvaging only wooden planks to build a massive bonfire.

Next, they attacked the home of a customs official and "liberated" cases of wine from his basement. By dinnertime the mob was at Governor Thomas Hutchinson's mansion, beating on the doors with bars and axes, demanding to be heard.

Mackintosh, already very drunk, raised his voice again as the undisputed leader: the family must leave. Though Governor Hutchinson initially stood his ground, his daughter finally persuaded him to flee with the rest of the family. The "Mob was so general and so supported that all Power ceased in an instant," Hutchinson later wrote back to England.

Acting with a disciplined frenzy, rioters labored until three o'clock in the morning to reduce one of New England's grandest houses to a naked shell, missing its walls, floors, and certainly its most valuable contents.

In *A People's History of the United States*, historian Howard Zinn identified the Stamp Act riots as the moment Boston's elite began to wonder if class hatred could be focused against the British. The people now, at this intoxicating moment, seemed really to be considering the prospect of anarchy.

In the following days, loyalists to Britain set their first priority: move against the chief of the mobs, Mackintosh. Sheriff Greenleaf was ordered to arrest Mackintosh, who he soon spotted on the corner of Green Street. Mackintosh gave himself up without a struggle, confident his stay behind bars would be brief. He was right: at day's end, a number of men arrived at the jail and instructed Greenleaf to hand over his keys so they could free the prisoner.

The sheriff, caught in between powers beyond his comprehension, could only agree with those who seemed to be in charge at the moment. Power had been shifted to the citizens and in their moment of authority they chose to rescue their hero Mackintosh.

In the streets, Mackintosh was seen as the boss, thanks to a reputation built not on words but bold action. When he was freed by Sheriff Greenleaf, it became clear that the American people themselves would produce and choose their own leaders. Before he was betrayed he would give the cause of liberty all he had.

The history of Boston gangsters starts at the water's edge where a busy port hardened the town's character forever. In the seventeenth century, Boston had been the quaint refuge of Puritans but a generation after the *Mayflower* landed, the struggling town was forced to turn to the ocean for economic survival. Fishermen, seamen and waterfront laborers would break Boston out of the tight framework of Puritan governance and forever lend the city its rugged character.

From the moment commercial ships began sailing in and out of Boston's port, smugglers made sure there were unrecorded items on board. On the other end of the social spectrum than the rowdy waterfront laborers, Boston's smugglers included some of the most successful merchants and radical political figures in town.

William Molineux may have been the port's most successful smuggler. His anger at the customs regulations he openly ignored later led to his role as a key organizer of the Boston Tea Party. Among the other sly merchants in those pre-Revolutionary years was the smuggler Thomas Hancock. Hancock rose from impoverished beginnings to build the greatest fortune in Boston. [His nephew John Hancock continued the smuggling tradition and was referred to as the "Idol of the Mob."]

Vice flourished too; prostitution was a constant presence in colonial Boston. In a 1650 journal entry, visiting Englishman Walter Muir Whitehill noted, "there's perhaps no town of its size cou'd turn out more whores than this could." By the mid-1700s, the western side of Beacon Hill was designated on several maps as "Mount Whoredom" for its plethora of prostitutes. Men of this generation might have visited the house of one of the town's bawdiest women, Alice Thomas, a tavern owner known as the "Massachusetts Bay Madam."

The elite class was just as likely to indulge in vice. John Hancock continued a long relationship with a woman, said to be "a common prostitute," whom he kept as his mistress prior to marrying Dorothy Quincy.

Piracy also flourished in Boston's maritime culture in the early and mid-eighteenth century. Widely accepted among the waterfront mobs, no seaman or fishermen dismissed the possibility of the pirate's life. A short tour of duty under the skull and crossbones might help get his family through a period of unemployment.

A big heist could buy a spot among the town's most prestigious social and political circles, as was the case with the Quincy family. Their ship, the *Bethel*, carried twenty-four guns and 110 men; a "letter of marquee" authorized her captain to seize perceived enemies as prizes and to divide the spoils among officers and men. In 1748, the *Bethel* came upon a Spanish treasure ship bound for home in Cadiz. After a bloody contest, the Americans triumphed, bringing back to Boston a reputed hundred thousand pounds of gold. It was enough to buy the Quincy family admission to Boston's most elite class. Boston's underworld was beginning its unlikely alliance with the city's wealthy elite.

Boston's 'Mobbish' Spirit is Born

With the influx of irreverent seafaring types, Boston was losing its reputation as a quaint, pious town. Instead of Puritans, waterfront laborers were shaping the events of the day. In 1690, a violent mob chased Governor Edmund Andros after he cracked down on smugglers. Between that time and 1765, Boston's maritime crowds provoked and participated in twenty-eight riots and illegal actions compared to just four and six in the comparable ports of New York and Philadelphia. The city was singled out in the press for its "mobbish spirit."

However, the port continued to stand as the colonies' busiest: more than five hundred vessels sailed out of its harbor to distant lands each year. As business boomed, a unique streetwise mentality continued to develop at all levels of the community, particularly in regards to tipsters and informants.

The lowest category of vermin on the waterfront was the tipsters, local seamen who for various reasons (usually money) informed on their smuggling skippers. In 1701, a tip from a sailor alerted customs officials to an illegal cargo on the ship *Bean and Cole*. The owners were convicted and fined but after the trial, the presiding judge caught up with the tipster in the street and berated him for being a snitch.

Far more humiliating for accused informants was the practice of tarring and feathering. To put a "Yankee jacket" on a snitch was a cruel and inhumane practice but it served its brutal purpose. Historian Ben Irvin describes how it worked:

Having captured an official or informant, the crowd would first apply the tar... Some victims were fortunate enough to be tarred over their clothes or protected by a frock or sheet. Others were stripped, and the tar was brushed, poured, or "bedawbed" over their bare skin...After the tar came the feathers.

Then came the traditional process of throwing the victim up on a "one-horse cart" and parading him through the streets while crowds of people cheered, sang, and made rough music with pots and pans.

In October 1769, a tipster for the British named George Gailer informed authorities of John Hancock's smuggling activities. Gailer received a brutal tarring and feathering from a relentless crowd of hundreds. He later tried to get back at his attackers by filing suit against two merchants and five seamen. His suit was denied: the punishment had been sanctioned and approved by the public.

The cutthroat culture of the waterfront was not just changing Boston: in the 1760s mob actions led by Boston gang leaders would plant the seeds for riots and a revolution.

The Ballad of Ebeneezer Mackintosh: Gang Leader to Founding Father

At the top of Boston's wild mobs stood – well, sometimes stood, sometimes slumped and sometimes fell drunkenly – Ebeneezer Mackintosh.

Tracing his heritage to a ship of Scottish prisoners captured in battle then shipped to the New World as bonded servants, Mackintosh was born to a family living at the lowest levels of colonial society. His father,

Moses, was kicked out of Boston in 1753 as a nonself-supporting individual, having failed to find a living for himself and his son (his wife died two years earlier). When Moses left town as an outcast, his ambitious son stayed behind.

Ebeneezer, described as "slight of build, of sandy complexion and a nervous temperament" first came to the town's attention in March 1760 during a terrifying fire. Raging through the wooden structures of the waterfront, the blaze destroyed hundreds of homes, warehouses and taverns.

Mackintosh, in particular, earned praise from the authorities for his energetic work. Even Sheriff Stephen Greenleaf, who would later throw him into jail, recognized Mackintosh's bravery and tapped him to lead a volunteer firefighting unit.

Mackintosh was a natural leader with a knack for survival, qualities he honed in a punishing tour of duty in the French Indian war. But he would be tested in Boston's underworld of gangs and mobs where deep divisions separated warring neighborhoods.

There had always been a split between the North End and the South End inhabitants – the latter resenting the more established neighborhood for its superior attitude. To straighten out the divisions, neighborhood gangs clashed in mob violence and large-scale gang fighting. Mill Creek, the border line between the two districts, became the usual spot for moonlit battles of Boston's angry and disconnected seamen and landsmen.

The two gangs, known as South End Forever and North End Forever, met formally for battles each November 5 as part of so-called Pope's Day. The celebration honored the plot against Parliament staged by Guy Fawkes and others on behalf of Spain, which was foiled on that date in 1605.

Typically, the violent celebrations began with two competitive parades marching at each other from the rival ends of Boston, and reached a climax with a massive bonfire and brawl at the town's center. There, the North End and the South End gangs each sought to topple and make away with the effigy of the Pope that the other had prepared.

Pope's Day in 1764 loomed as particularly menacing with the town more divided than ever. For Ebeneezer Mackintosh, however, the day promised to be grand: an opportunity to lead his South End gang to long-sought victory and for him to demonstrate his hard-won leadership.

The celebration spun out of control early in the North End when that gang's cart ran over the head of a five year-old boy, killing the lad instantly. Sherriffs, ordered to close things down, began destroying the effigies of the Popes from both the North and South End.

Although the officials succeeded in grabbing the North End effigy and pulling it to pieces, the South Enders, led by Mackintosh, fought back ferociously and kept their effigy intact. Winning that battle and demonstrating that authority no longer belonged to the sheriffs but to the people, Mackintosh led his crew northward and encountered their rival at Mill Bridge. There the battle became bloody; one account reported "many were hurt and bruised."

Mackintosh led his gang to victory but the glory was short lived as he was later arrested. With the powerful weight of the gangs pressing on the authorities, he was quickly released. His men seized what was left of North End Forever's dummy and burned it in a bonfire. The crowd of several thousand cheered and hailed Mackintosh and his men. Mackintosh, in the town of his birth and his father's disgrace, was savoring the salutes and feeling a special triumph as he looked over the adoring crowds.

Nine months later, when Mackintosh led the Stamp Act riots, his rise from gang leader to radical political figure was near complete. After the riots, he was appointed a "sealer of leather" – inspecting and approving the quality of material on behalf of the town – a move that signaled approval from the town's political elite. Although he had come a long way, Mackintosh still had his most shocking move against the British in store.

The Triumph of Ebeneezer Mackintosh and the birth of the United States of America

With the anarchy and destruction of the summer's Stamp Act riots still fresh in the minds of authorities and the gangs, the town prepared for a bloody Pope's Day in fall 1765. The hated Stamp Act was scheduled to go into effect just four days before the annual violent celebration and fear reached all levels of the town.

Then on the morning of November 5, effigies appeared hanging once again on the Liberty Tree. A crowd rapidly assembled and, not long after noon, the people could hear the sounds of trumpets and drums. But then, to their surprise, down the streets leading to the town center came into view two beautifully disciplined teams, led by the old rivals Mackintosh and Swift. Loyalist Peter Oliver was among those to express his amazement that these two men were not leading armed men against one another. He described how Mackintosh

Paraded the town with a mob of armed Men in Two Files, and passed by the State House when the General Assembly were sitting to display his Power...when he had fully displayed his Authority, he marched his Men to the first Rendezvous, & ordered them to retire peacefully to their several Homes and was punctually obeyed.

"What happened here?" Oliver and other British officials must have asked themselves. How did these two gangs who had gone at each other's throats (with sticks and knives) each year for as long as anyone could remember, come together peacefully without conflict?

Unknown to them, the answer lay in the "Union Feast" that many of the gang members had shared in the night before. Arranged by Samuel Adams and John Hancock, the feast had succeeded in uniting the divided town. This rolling event, a series of dinners at Boston's most popular taverns, allowed all classes of men to come together with, "Heart and hand in flowing Bowls and bumping Glasses."

So when the two files of marchers came together on this Pope's Day, Ebenezer Mackintosh and Henry Swift bowed to each other with great formality under the Liberty Tree, the violent mobs easily avoided any conflict.

But was Mackintosh selling out? The staged event could be viewed as mob bosses Mackintosh and Swift, betraying the real intentions of the mobs and giving them over as dupes to the more powerful Hancock and Adams.

However, Mackintosh was no fool. He had brought the people into the American political picture and never again could they be totally excluded. In the political debates to come in the American Revolution, his symbolic voice – and the roar of the mob behind him – had to be heard. As Andrew Oliver ruefully put it, "The People, even to the lowest Ranks, have become more attentive to their liberties."

In fact, the last dramatic scene in the Stamp Act belonged to Mackintosh, with Andrew Oliver playing a degrading role. Oliver, the man who seemed to epitomize the hated tax, promised to resign after the Stamp Act riots in August but by winter he had yet to step aside.

On December 17, during a bone chilling rainstorm, Oliver was forcibly led to the Liberty Tree by none other than Ebenezer Mackintosh. Before a throng of more than two thousand soaked but jubilant spectators, Oliver swore to take no steps "for enforcing the Stamp Act in America."

This performance at the end of 1765 was a thoroughly humiliating personal experience not only for Oliver but also his entire species. To bend to the will of the crowd, a crowd led by a lowly, red faced shoemaker such as Mackintosh, was an unprecedented development in an age of deference to the higher born.

In the summer of 1774, Mackintosh crossed the Neck and left Boston behind, a widower trudging inland with his two young children. As they walked to New Hampshire, they marched in company with others – Boston was no longer a safe place for poor, unemployed families – particularly when the father was a known rioter, possibly with a price on his head.

In one sense Mackintosh was a retreating hero: a lower class leader of rebellion who served a useful purpose only during certain crisis, after which he was regarded by upper class Bostonians as an untrustworthy, riotous blabbermouth. His influence, however would be felt in Boston as Patriots declared their liberty. The rage of Boston's toughest crowds – the angry gang members, seamen and fishermen - had been transformed into a push for change in the order of human affairs, a theme for the American Revolution that would follow soon.

CHAPTER TWO

ADAM WORTH: THE BOSTON BANK ROBBER WHO INSPIRED SHERLOCK HOLMES' GREATEST RIVAL

SUNDAY, NOVEMBER 21, 1869.

A SMALL MAN WRIGGLES his way through an eighteen by twelve inch hole in the steel vault of Boston's biggest bank. Inside, he lights a candle and surveys the loot. The treasure, in 30 tin trunks, is handed to his two partners one by one. The trunks are pried open, examined, and what is valuable pocketed. After a few hours, as dawn breaks over Boston, the three thieves pack their score and hail a carriage to the station to board the early train to New York. Their total haul is almost $1 million; an incredible sum equal to more than $20 million today.

At nine o'clock that morning, twenty four hours after the break-in, bank officials opened the safe and were "thunderstruck at the scene which met their gaze." The entire contents of the vault, and with it the reputation of the Boylston National Bank, were gone.

For the next week, the Boylston Bank robbery was the biggest news in Boston. The Boston Post compared the job to a work of art. "Everyone continues to talk about the robbery of Boylston Bank," the paper reported. "On all sides it is admitted to be a very neat job."

Investigators from the Pinkerton Detective agency – a private investigation agency and forerunner to the FBI - traced the thieves and their spoils to New York, thanks to some loose talk in criminal circles. They were not surprised by the men's identities.

Adam Worth, the small man who climbed into the bank vault, was a disciplined thief with a reputation for hard work and non-violence in his jobs. His criminal legend was still only beginning but within a few years, he would be known as the world's most successful thief.

Charles Bullard was a criminal playboy better known as Piano Charley. "Bullard is a man of good education," recorded one police report, "speaks English, French and German fluently and plays on the piano with the skill of a professional." Bullard had three passions in life which he indulged to the limit: women, music and gambling. With the skill he developed on the piano, he could learn the combination of a safe simply by spinning the dial. Big Ike Marsh was the last, and least, of the crew. A big, dim witted Irishman, he was Bullard's loyal sidekick, ready to do the heavy lifting any job required.

After learning they were suspects, the men made frantic plans to escape the country. "Those damned detectives will get on to us within a week," Bullard warned Worth. "I don't want to be playing the piano in Ludlow Street [jail]." So Worth and Bullard took off for Europe, where wealthy Americans faced few questions when spending their money.

For Worth and Bullard, Europe was a new challenge. In their criminal schemes, they would always be loyal to one another. But when they met and fell for the same woman, their criminal empire was threatened for the first time.

Adam Worth pulled off legendary heists across three continents, but it was Boston that shaped him. Despite living in crushing poverty as a child in Cambridge, he had many opportunities to witness staggering wealth he observed students at nearby Harvard parade by. The hand dealt to Worth didn't contain the aces these Harvard students had but with a peerless criminal instinct and energy, he resolved to mark the deck himself and join them anyway he could.

That meant robbing banks. After a stint in the Union Army fighting in the Civil War, Worth was introduced to the criminal world when he drifted to New York City and came under the influence of Marm Mandelbaum and her criminal society.

Marm's nickname was the result of her maternal attitude toward criminals of all types, she ran a crime school where small boys and girls were taught to be expert pickpockets and sneak thieves. At her dinner party's crooked judges, corrupt cops, and politicians for sale mixed with criminal notables.

At these soirees, Worth met two bank robbers who would play crucial, if different, roles in his rise and fall. The first was his friend Piano Charley Bullard. The second was Max Shinburn. According to an investigator's files, Shinburn was "a bank burglar of distinction who complained that he was at heart an aristocrat and that he detested the crooks with whom he was compelled to associate." Worth admired Shinburn's dress and reputation but found his huge ego unbearable.

Still, Worth was desperate to join this elite circle of bank robbers. He was just in time. The 1860s and 1870s were the boom years for large scale bank robbery and slick burglaries. Locks and safes were almost always made of brittle iron and as the country's wealth increased, these safes held greater treasures. In the right expert hands, the best burglar's tools were capable of bypassing any lock.

"Such operations as bank burglary were held in much higher esteem during the 'sixties and 'seventies than at present, and the most distinguished members of the craft were known by sight and pointed out to strangers," said bank robber James L. Ford.

No robbery pupil was as eager as Adam Worth though. He took notes on larceny from his mentor, Piano Charley Bullard. Often outrageously drunk, but always charming, Bullard had the easy cultural veneer that Worth wanted so badly. Worth was clever and calculating, qualities the daring Bullard lacked.

When Bullard and Big Ike Marsh were imprisoned for robbing a safe of $100,000, their friends – including Worth – dug through the wall of the jail to set him free. The immediate effect of the successful jail break was to cement the friendship between Bullard and Worth. They decided to form a partnership. Within months, they pulled off the biggest heist Boston had ever seen.

After the Boylston Bank robbery, the trio of thieves hit Europe. Big Ike Marsh returned to Ireland where he was received by adoring crowds and ceremony. In the end though, the Irishman "gambled, drank and did everything he should not have done, and eventually returned to America for more funds," according to an investigator's report. Poor Ike was arrested while trying to rob another bank and sentenced to twenty years' solitary confinement in eastern Pennsylvania.

Worth and Bullard had a far different experience on the continent. Within minutes after their arrival at a Liverpool hotel, the two men fell in love with the same woman. Kitty Flynn was a seventeen year old Irish colleen with thick blond hair, enticing dimples and an expression that hovered between flirtatious and wicked. "Bullard and Worth both fell madly in love with her," Sophie Lyons, a friend and criminal accomplice of the two crooks, noted in her memoir. Suddenly Flynn, born into poverty in Dublin, found herself being wined and dined on a scale beyond her most extravagant dreams.

In spite of their romantic rivalry, Worth and Bullard remained friends as they swept Kitty from one expensive, candlelit dinner to another. "The race for her favor was a close one," wrote friend and criminal associate Sophie Lyons. Finally Kitty gave in to Piano Charley's charm and agreed to marry him. Yet Worth would always have a place in her heart – and her bed; Kitty's two daughters born during her marriage to Bullard were likely Worth's children. The arrangement apparently did not bother the open minded Bullard.

While Kitty and Charley enjoyed a short honeymoon, Worth passed his time profitably by robbing Liverpool's largest pawnshop of $25,000 in jewelry. Worth showered Kitty with the stolen gems, bought her expensive clothes and encouraged her to leave her past of poverty behind. He remade her just as he was remaking himself – a thief and bank robber who could now pass in aristocratic circles. But grimy Liverpool was no place for aspiring socialites. At the end of 1870, the two socially ambitious crooks and their shared moll packed up their belongings and headed for Paris.

With the remains of the money from the Boylston robbery, Worth and Bullard purchased a building and spent $75,000 to refurbish it "in palatial splendor" with oil paintings, mirrors, and expensive glassware. They christened it the American Bar and imported bartenders to mix cocktails popular in New York but unknown in Europe. In the upper floors of the house Worth and Bullard set up an illegal gambling operation.

From the day it opened, the American Bar became the headquarters for American gamblers and criminals in Europe. While gorgeous Kitty presided, the affable Bullard played the piano and Worth carefully monitored the clientele. An alarm button was discretely installed behind the bar "which the bar tender touched and which rung a buzzer in the gambling rooms above whenever the police or any suspicious party came in." Within seconds a den of iniquity became respectable. The Paris police "made two or three raids on the house, but never succeeded in finding anything upstairs, except a lot of men sitting around reading papers, and no gambling in sight."

For three years the American Bar prospered and the peculiar threesome of Worth, Bullard and Kitty Flynn continued without a hitch. Kitty became the gracious grande dame she always wanted to be. Bullard happily drank cocktails from the moment he opened his eyes in the afternoon until he passed out face down on his piano. Two American detectives reported that in Paris he was a well-known gambler and wealthy rogue – which was all Piano Charley ever really wanted to be.

The fun wouldn't last though. In 1873 the good times started to unravel when William Pinkerton, detective for Worth's greatest rival the Pinkerton Agency, walked into the American Bar and ordered a drink. The scrutiny of officials soon proved bad for business. "The respectable people did not patronize it, and it soon went to the dog," Pinkerton recorded triumphantly.

The failure of the American Bar, however, did not really upset Worth who was still a wealthy man at age thirty-one. His friend Piano Charley, however, was spiraling downward. He was no longer the carefree, dashing figure Kitty had fallen for in Liverpool. Now he vanished for long periods in seamy neighborhoods and returned hungover and wracked with guilt playing sad songs on the piano for hours. Conversely, Worth was laying the groundwork for the greatest phase of his criminal career.

Worth's phenomenal success in this period is best described by his rivals, the Pinkerton Detectives who considered him "the most dangerous professional criminal known to modern times." In an official history of the detective agency published many decades later, the detectives recalled that "for years he perpetrated every form of theft – check forging, swindling, larceny, safe cracking, diamond robbery, mail robbery, burglary of every degree, 'hold ups' on the road and bank robbery – with complete immunity."

Sober, industrious and loyal, Worth was a criminal of principle which he imposed on his gang of thieves with rigid discipline. With the exception of his old friend Piano Charley, drunks were excluded and violence forbidden. "A man with brains has no right to carry firearms," he told his crew. Robberies were to be inflicted only on those who could afford them, and the division of spoils was to be fair. The Pinkerton detectives who chased Worth across the world grudgingly admitted that he "never forsook a friend or accomplice."

Yet there was not much he could do for his friend Piano Charley, who went on one of his boozy jaunts and ended up in New York, where he was arrested for the Boylston Bank robbery. He was tried and sentenced to twenty years.

Kitty too would soon be out of Worth's life as she moved to New York, pawned some of the jewelry he had lavished on her and opened a boarding house for fashionable gentlemen. Worth was devastated by Kitty's departure but soon he would have his sights set on a different woman. To win her, he would have to pull off his biggest heist yet.

In the spring of 1876 Worth, like everyone else who opened a newspaper, read of the mounting excitement surrounding the sale of Thomas Gainsborough's celebrated portrait of Georgiana Spencer, the Duchess of Devonshire.

The celebrated painting was loved for its depiction of the controversial Spencer. Poets praised her to the heavens but her detractors saw her as a scandalous aristocrat whose hats were too tall and morals too low.

Gainsborough's painting appeared to capture both sides of Spencer as she smirked both playful and suggestive.

Junius Morgan was an art connoisseur who bought the Duchess of Devonshire as a "princely gift" for his son, J.P. Morgan. Morgan agreed to pay $50,000 (the equivalent of some $620,000 today) for the painting to dealer William Agnew.

So, in a technical sense, the Duchess was the property of J.P. Morgan when, at around midnight on May 27, 1876, Adam Worth set out in his best clothes to, as he later said, elope with the Duchess. Worth initially eyed the painting as a way to bribe his brother out of jail but when his brother was released shortly after the heist he had no reason to give up his prize possession.

Without his former partners, Kitty Flynn and Piano Charley Bullard, Worth developed a bizarre relationship with the painting over the next twenty years. Once he learned Kitty had married a wealthy man, he cut off negotiations for the painting's return and vowed to keep his duchess. The painting became his permanent companion and he literally slept with her, the Duchess pinned beneath his mattress. She became the ultimate testament to his crimes and a reminder that the poor boy from Cambridge had stolen what the wealthiest aristocrats could not hold onto.

By 1890, most of Worth's criminal contemporaries were dead or in jail. His best friend Piano Charley Bullard had died in a Belgium prison before Worth could get there to break him out. Maybe it was the emotional trauma of Bullard's death that caused Worth to carry out his next reckless heist. On October 5, 1892, Worth was arrested in Belgium as he stole a strongbox from an unoccupied coach used to make cash drop-offs around town.

Belgian authorities didn't know they had caught the world's most famous criminal until Max Shinburn, Worth's old rival from Marm Mandelbaum's dinner parties, read about the unknown man in a newspaper article. Shinburn, who had always resented Worth's unblemished success in robbery, informed to authorities the true identity of the prisoner.

Worth was sentenced to seven years hard labor in a Belgian prison. He could have exchanged his Duchess of Devonshire portrait for his freedom but he chose to stay in jail rather than let go of his prize, stored discretely somewhere in Boston.

In December 1893, just five months after Worth's crimes made international news, Professor James Moriaty, one of the most memorable villains in literature, came into the world. There is no doubt that Sir Arthur Conan Doyle based his portrait of Professor Moriaty, the evil genius and bitter foe of Sherlock Holmes, principally on the career of Adam Worth.

Doyle met Worth's great adversary William Pinkerton just once but used their conversation about the bank robber to create Moriaty – proving that like Worth he was ready to "appropriate" what he wanted.

In one of Doyle's stories, Detective Holmes captures Worth's status in the criminal underworld when he describes Moriaty to his long-suffering assistant. "He is the Napoleon of crime, Watson. He is the organizer of half that is evil and of nearly all that is undetected in this great city. He is a genius, a philosopher, an abstract thinker."

At the end of Conan Doyle's "The Final Problem" Holmes and Professor Moriaty meet, fight and fall to their apparent deaths, "locked in each other's arms." Holmes came back to life; Moriaty did not. But Conan Doyle observed, "Everything comes in circles, even Professor Moriaty... The old wheel turns and the same spoke comes up. It's all been done before, and it will again."

When the Belgian prison authorities released Worth in 1897 after five years of barbaric punishment, there was no one at the gates of the Prison de Louvain to greet the fifty-three-year-old felon. Piano Charley and Kitty were dead. Professor Moriaty was a household name but Worth's own name was all but forgotten by the world.

Later that year, he robbed London's largest diamond merchants, Smith's, of L15,000 worth of jewelry. Worth was aging though and he had trouble finding a reliable crew of thieves to match his old team. For his final score, he enlisted an unlikely figure - his old rival William Pinkerton. The two men had built a grudging respect for one another after years of Pinkerton chasing Worth across the world. When they finally met, Worth confessed to stealing four million dollars over thirty years.

They were not there to reminisce though – Worth and Pinkerton agreed that Worth would return the Duchess of Devonshire portrait he had stolen two decades earlier. In return, Worth received twenty-five thousand dollars in cash.

Four days after J.P. Morgan finally took possession of the Duchess of Devonshire portrait, Adam Worth, the man who kept her for twenty five years, died in Camden, New Jersey. Newspapers competed to pay tribute to a man who had robbed, forged, and conned his way through life. "Adam Worth is dead," proclaimed The New York Journal. "His demise marks the closing of a singular modern romance."

Adam Worth's impact on popular culture did not end with Professor Moriaty. In 1939, T.S. Eliot published *Old Possum's Book of Cats*, one of whom is Macavity, the Mystery Cat. Here, metamorphosed into cat form, is Adam Worth. Conan Doyle took his inspiration from Worth's life, and T.S. Eliot took his from Conan Doyle. Completing the trail, the composer Andrew Lloyd Weber based *Cats*, the popular musical, on Eliot's work. Adam Worth, after his humble beginnings and law breaking entry into high society, had made it all the way to Broadway – his brilliant criminal legacy kept alive forever.

CHAPTER THREE

PROHIBITION: CORRUPT COPS, A KENNEDY, AND THE GANGSTER 'KING'

SPRING 1922, CAPE COD BEACH PARTY, HARVARD COLLEGE, TEN-YEAR REUNION.

TWO YEARS INTO the so-called Dry Era and the nation is thirsty. The Volstead Act outlawing the sale and use of alcohol passed with the understanding it was prohibiting everyone else's drinking - not the boozing of the people found here, wealthy wasps at a ten-year Harvard class reunion.

Still, the law had its intended effect in the days leading up to the party – no one could procure any liquor. That is, until they remembered that their classmate, Joseph P. Kennedy, boasted many connections to the liquor business. In fact, Kennedy was able to arrange for the overseas delivery of bootleg Scotch on the day of the party.

He didn't do it alone. Notorious gangster Frank Costello, who would take over the New York Mafia twenty years later, helped Kennedy deliver the whiskey for the Harvard class reunion. "We were together in the liquor business," Costello said of Kennedy before his death.

Within months, Kennedy organized the importation of another major shipment to Carson Beach in South Boston, believed to be the biggest single shipment of whiskey in Boston Prohibition history. His profits were staggering; on a $325,000 investment he could make a net profit of $525,000.

In accounts of his life Joe Kennedy is sometimes called a bootlegger which is not precisely accurate. During the outset of Prohibition Kennedy was a rum runner or whiskey baron – an importer or wholesaler. He purchased large quantities of alcohol, mostly Scotch, from England or Canada and facilitated its shipment along Rum Row. The booze was usually transferred from Novia Scotia to coastlines along Massachusetts and Rhode Island.

To distribute his liquor he turned to the most notorious killers and crime figures in the nation. Owney Madden, in particular, worked closely with Kennedy. A sadistic killer in his youth, Madden emerged in the 1920s as a sophisticated racketeer who mixed with corrupt judges and politicians.

"Owney and Joe Kennedy were partners in the bootleg business for a number of years," Q. Bynum Hurst, Madden's attorney and a former Arkansas state senator, told investigative reporter Seymour Hersh. "I discussed the Kennedy partnership with him many times...Owney controlled all the nightclubs in New York then. He ran New York more than anyone in the 1920s, and Joe wanted the outlets for his liquor. [Madden] told me he valued Kennedy's business judgment. He recognized Kennedy's brains."

Kennedy was always looking for ways to expand his empire and increase profits; in the bootlegging business in the 1920s that led to Al Capone. By 1926, Capone was firmly in control of the liquor business in Chicago and much of the Midwest. He'd rubbed out his major rivals and expanded into adjoining states like Indiana, Missouri and Wisconsin. Kennedy wanted Big Al's business and the two men allegedly met over dinner at Capone's home to hammer out the details.

The meeting was overheard by a young piano tuner named John Kohlert. Capone was a jazz lover who sometimes invited musicians to his place for after hour jam sessions. Kohlert kept the piano tuned on a monthly basis. On this night, he was invited to stay for a spaghetti dinner, also attended by Kennedy. The young piano tuner listened while Kennedy and Capone struck a deal in which Capone traded his whiskey for a shipment of Kennedy's Seagram brand.

In a 1926 Canadian government investigation into Canadian alcohol being exported to the United States, by way of Detroit and Chicago, one name came up time and again. Joe Kennedy had been buying up liquor from Canadian facilities that increased their production 400 percent to meet his demands. In records seized by investigators, Kennedy's name appears alongside Al Capone's and other U.S. bootleggers.

Other Kennedy's were involved in the sale of liquor at the time too; Joe's father owned at least three taverns in Boston and a liquor importing business and two of his wife's uncles were active in the bootleg liquor business during Prohibition. The family connections gave Kennedy an inside track to seize a dominant position during the first days of Prohibition.

In the early 1920s as huge shipments of illicit liquor were making their way into the United States, money began to "flood into the [Kennedy] family," according to one biographer. Investigative reporter Seymour Hersh interviewed former high level government officials of the

1950s and 1960s, including Justice Department prosecutors, CIA operatives, and FBI agents who each insisted that Joe Kennedy had been prominent in the illegal liquor business during Prohibition.

"I do know that he had associates in organized crime who respected him," Cartha D. DeLoach, a deputy director of the FBI under J. Edgar Hoover, told Hersh. "I only knew him through Mr. Hoover. He had considerable experience in the bygone era of smuggling, and that's how he made his fortune, according to Mr. Hoover."

The extent of his fortune was exhibited in 1925, when Fortune magazine estimated Joe Kennedy's wealth at $2 million, equal to roughly $20 million today. Kennedy built that fortune despite leaving his job as a stock broker in 1922. Only his role as the country's preeminent whiskey baron could account for such sudden and fabulous wealth.

The fortune Joe Kennedy made during Prohibition eventually built a path to the White House for his son. For the others who profited from the illegal sale of liquor in Boston, such lofty goals may have been out of reach. But in the anything-goes era of the 1920s that wasn't important to the city's most feared kingpins – the only thing that mattered was their street reputation, political muscle and the cash in their pocket.

Boston was not ready for Prohibition. It all happened so quickly. City politicians didn't put up much of a fight; the issue was seen to lack bite and relevance to their constituents.

The public in Boston had other matters to worry about in 1919 anyway. Boston Police patrolmen went on strike after Governor Calvin Coolidge refused to allow them to unionize – leaving the city entirely without police presence. Over the next four days, a third of a million dollars in property was damaged and eight people died in the rioting.

Also distracting the public was a bizarre tragedy in the North End. A huge storage tank with over two million gallons of molasses burst on the outer edge of the neighborhood. A fifteen-foot tidal wave of goo swept aside everything in its path, drowning twenty-one people, destroying a fire station and pushing horse drawn wagons into the harbor.

But if citizens were slow to catch on, gangsters quickly recognized the significance of the Eighteenth Amendment and the rich opportunities it offered for a new type of crime: bootlegging, or supplying beer and booze to a clientele that was law abiding but thirsty. Overnight in apartments, in sheds, in the backrooms of stores, primitive stills or distilleries dubbed "alky cookers" sprouted in the city's slums and working class neighborhoods. Prohibition would be organized crime's "golden goose" transforming small time pimps and dope dealers to millionaires in a few short years.

Encouraged by lax law enforcement, Boston gangs and bootleggers soon abandoned the primitive, rot gut alky cookers. They developed more sophisticated and profitable techniques, smuggling quality liquor from Britain and Canada and opening their own secret breweries.

Charles "King" Solomon was the undisputed king of Boston's underworld during Prohibition. In fact, he was called King Solomon for good reason: the round faced thug ran liquor and dope smuggling operations in the city with little competition. He made millions but couldn't give up the street life in time to enjoy the riches.

Born in Russia in 1883 to Joseph and Sarah Blum Solomon, his family immigrated to Massachusetts along with about seventy five thousand other Russian Jews between 1880 and 1914. Young Solomon's early arrests in Boston included several charges of keeping a house of prostitution and "breaking and entering and stealing some 1700 yards of cloth."

Even as Prohibition created unprecedented criminal opportunities, Jewish gangsters such as Solomon were forced to prove themselves more often than Irish or Italian bootleggers. Within Jewish communities, negligible consumers of alcohol, there was no huge market to tap. To capture his big shot, Solomon had to secure a foothold elsewhere in neighborhoods of varying race and ethnicity and soon Italians and Jews had prominent roles in his gang.

His power was due to his ability to peacefully resolve gang quarrels. Years later a longtime crime reporter said, "the fact that newspapers outside Boston didn't know of Solomon...showed the quiet efficiency of his machine as compared to the noisy, shooting mob of Capone in Chicago at the same time." If peace negotiations failed, Solomon's connections to the Murder Incorporated team of hitmen in New York City protected his interest.

Solomon was a vain man who disliked the label "The Dope King" claiming that he had nothing to do with drug traffic even as he "taxed" smugglers and dealers. He could often be seen in the company of government officials and was dubbed "the Capone of the east" by federal agents.

Solomon eventually commanded a fleet of boats guided by secret radio stations along the coast of New Jersey and Long Island that brought booze in from Central America. He owned legitimate businesses too; he bought at least three Boston theaters, several nightclubs, a beauty parlor and restaurants in outlying cities; he owned hotels in New York, a factory in Brooklyn and a nightclub in Montreal.

In 1931, for ten thousand dollars, Solomon bought the city's hottest nightspot the Cocoanut Grove. The club was the crown jewel in Solomon's criminal empire. Austen Lake of the *Boston Evening American* newspaper described Solomon as he "sat on his lobby throne, or with assorted society, and flashed his $500 store teeth, occasionally excusing himself at the discrete eye-wink of some private courtier to 'see a certain party about a certain matter which concerns you know what.'"

Lake reported that he planned for the club to be his personal showcase at a time when he was "at the peak of his crime renaissance, with a complete sideline of alki-cooking, morphine, heroin, cocaine and the dandruff-like little granules which produce delirious uproar. He hogged the bail-bond market, owned a large loan shark company at usurious rate, held full partnership in the white slave industry, a cut in a growing lottery racket and drivers and [other schemes] built on human mischief." Authorities estimated his crooked fortune to be worth $14 million.

The best of vaudeville came to the Cocoanut Grove stage and pretty girls were always seated at Solomon's table. Stars that lit up the club included Jimmy Durante, Rudy Vallee, and Guy Lombardo. It was Solomon's paranoia, however, that would be his darkest legacy at the Cocoanut Grove – and doom hundreds of patrons years later.

He made sure exit doors to the club were locked inside and out. No one could sneak in on him and no one-neither patron nor employee-could run out on a bill. On the night of November 28, 1942 those locked doors and a raging fire caused the deaths of 491 people – the worst nightclub fire in American history.

But that awful incident was still a decade away. Solomon had his court, a legion of admirers and millions of dollars at his disposal. A police captain once asked him, "Charlie, you've got millions. Why don't you get out of the racket?" Solomon waved him off, saying, "Don't be silly." Two years later, a crew of stick-up men in an after-hours club wouldn't ask so nicely.

The Gustin Gang

The Gustin Gang was known as the toughest street gang in Boston – one witness in a Gustin case was so afraid of their vengeance he cut his own throat. Named after a street in South Boston and led by a crew of brothers named Wallace they were a violent crew that tore through Southie, afraid of no one.

In one incident, gang members cracked a police officer's skull. In another, they attacked hometown hero and heavyweight boxing contender Jim Maloney – beating him up and stealing a safe he kept in the lunch cart diner he owned.

Originally known as the "Tailboard Thieves" the Gustins first came to the attention of authorities when they began hijacking and looting delivery trucks stopped at intersections. Their underworld rise was momentarily halted in 1928 when Frank and Stephen Wallace along with five other men, pulled off a deadly heist in Detroit.

The gang entered the building of the Detroit News newspaper with guns firing and held about 150 hostages captive as they looted the office. They burst into the cashier's office and scooped up $40,000 in cash that had been placed in pay envelopes. A dozen shots were fired during the heist killing a traffic officer. Frank Wallace was later charged with the slaying but he was acquitted and returned to Boston.

Frank's next venture was bootlegging. On September 10, 1930, he was arrested after a wild car chase through Southie's side streets, with a gallon of whiskey in his trunk. For that offense he received no serious jail time.

The Gustins run ended on December 21, 1931 in a watershed moment in Boston Mafia history when Frankie Wallace was killed by a firing squad of Mafia hitmen. The murder would forever alter the balance of power in Boston's gangland. The immediate effect was an open spot at the top of Southie rackets as surviving Gustin gang members descended into street crime and drunkenness.

In their place was the more diplomatic Daniel Carroll. An ex-Boston police officer fired in the 1919 strike, Carroll kept a framed portrait of the man who fired him, Governor Calvin Coolidge, on his office wall. He said the firing was the best thing that ever happened to him.

Unlike Frank Wallace and the Gustins, Carroll worked well with the city's other gangsters. He made fight deals with King Solomon and Italian gangsters such as Phil Buccola and boasted a link to legitimate society in his brother, a respected state senator.

Phil Buccola

Filippo "Phil" Buccola was the Italian mobster who rounded out Boston's ethnic triumvirate of Jewish, Irish and Italian kingpins. When Buccola's name appeared in the Boston newspapers – and it wasn't too often

– he was referred to as a local sportsman, a boxing manager and promoter who also owned racehorses. His dream was to manage an Italian fighter to a world championship. The closest he came was having one of his fighters, Odonne Piazzo, fight unsuccessfully in 1932 for the middleweight title.

Born in Palermo, Buccola was an educated man and an adventurer who attended the Universita degli Studi in Palermo and another school in Switzerland and who traveled to Russia before the Revolution. He was believed to have been forced to flee from vengeful rivals in Sicily after a murder in Palermo, arriving in Boston with impressive credentials and persuasive old world ties. After he came to the United States in 1920, he had a meteoric rise.

Buccola's timing could not have been better. He was an experienced leader arriving at the age of thirty-four on the eve of the criminal bonanza of Prohibition. He was head man within a few years and was formally sanctioned as head of the New England Mafia by the newly formed Luciano Commission in 1932, according to an FBI summary of a bugged conversation. Most other Mafia leaders, in contrast, had immigrated as much younger men from impoverished families and fought their way up the ranks. Buccola treated his power casually; he was used to it.

By all accounts, Buccola was a savvy man who never overplayed his hand or stayed too long in the game. He was flexible as long as you didn't push him in a corner. He even looked the part of a harmless businessman; he wore suits and bow ties and rimless glasses. From his men he got the ultimate accolade for a crime boss: "A man you could talk to."

Buccola was the godfather of the second chance who told repentant offenders, go and sin no more. In leading the Boston Mafia to record profits, Buccola built an organization that would survive past Prohibition.

Oliver Garrett and the corrupt Boston liquor squad

Corrupt Boston Police officers may have profited more than gangsters during the 'Dry Era.' In fact, a myth developed in Boston that the police organized the liquor trade before the criminals could and, as a result, nobody died from bad booze and bootleggers never flourished.

In reality, Boston Police liquor squad agents amassed personal fortunes by extorting the four thousand speakeasies in the city. Further, there was plenty of cheap product around including "near beer" sold by Anheuser Busch which was closer to dishwater than alcohol. To raise money to pay off corrupt liquor squad detectives many bar owners rented rooms to prostitutes. Huntington Avenue in the Back Bay was lined with speakeasies cum bordellos, and streetwalkers elsewhere in the city were a common sight.

Oliver Garrett was the top officer in the liquor squad. Said to have run away from an unhappy childhood in Maine, Garrett was a $40 a week patrolman who joined the liquor squad in the first days of Prohibition. By the time the era was over, he had built up a fortune of at least $250,000 by strong arming saloon owners into paying protection fees and selling liquor himself.

Saloon owners soon learned even a bribe was not enough to keep Garrett's agents from raiding their clubs – they would take the bribe, sure, but then they'd still knock down the doors. When word got around that certain clubs were paying Garrett off, a warrantless raid was executed the next day and great quantities of liquor poured down the sinks. Garrett was said to have made twenty-five thousand such raids, almost all without warrants, as head of the liquor squad.

However, the liquor poured down those sinks was saved by "the Garrett system." Each speakeasy that had been paying off (and providing free drinks for cops) had a special sink system installed. When raiders disposed of the liquor, the rye was poured down one sink, the gin down another and the beer down a third. Underneath the sinks were barrels to catch the liquor and prepare it for rebottling.

Garrett owned two prize horses and was known to take lavish vacations with his wife. John F. Sullivan, the owner of the Ritz Hotel on Columbus Avenue, must have felt like he was the one footing the bill for Garrett's lifestyle. Each month, Sullivan was paying $100 to Garrett, $20 each to two other officers and a traffic officer $120 to look the other way while liquor shipments arrived at the hotel. Sullivan had initially tried to run his hotel and club without serving alcohol but after six months he was losing too much money to obey the law.

Solomon was addicted to the guns and glamour. "It means everything to me. I've had enough of the hard and the rotten and the miserable. I was always a bum to nice people. Now, when I put on those evening clothes and step through the door of the Cocoanut Grove, I'm a gentleman. I'm not a heel, you understand, I'm their host."

As soon as Sullivan started serving cocktails he was raided by Garrett's liquor squad. "You're making a lot of money here," Garrett said to him. "You'll have to come across with some of it." From then on, Sullivan would receive a phone call thirty minutes before a planned raid – enough time to hide the booze from federal agents.

The Ritz was only one small piece in Garrett's empire of payoffs and bribes. Each morning a milk truck left the dairy farm owned by Garrett and his wife and stopped at the biggest speakeasies in the city selling gallons of milk at the wildly inflated price of $1.25 while picking up that week's protection pay off.

Sometimes, Garrett cut out the middleman and sold the liquor himself on these milk routes. He was a partner in a speakeasy located in the backroom of the Dudley Pharmacy at 233 Dudley Street and both his brother and father were well known bootleggers.

As his domination of the Boston bootlegging business came to a close having squeezed almost half a million dollars out of bootleggers, Garrett was done in by trying to get money that was rightfully his: a $19,000 disability pension. Without that request, Garrett might have gotten away clean. Instead, he would be at the center of Boston's greatest Dry Era scandal.

Garrett's pension request prompted state legislators to order the attorney general to investigate his finances. His bank accounts revealed more than a quarter of a million dollars – a staggering sum for the time. In safe deposit boxes, detectives found even more cash along with expensive jewels.

Garrett, however, refused to go quietly. He promised to "blow the lid off" the department and expose further corruption. The only people he was hurting though were his colleagues and criminal associates. State investigators were examining the bank accounts of twenty-five other officers connected to the liquor squad and a friend of Garrett's – a reputed bootlegger - collapsed and died as he was being questioned at Garrett's hearing.

Garrett never did expose other corrupt officers but at a packed hearing in the State House he added to the theatrics. From his seat in the audience, in the midst of proceedings, Garrett jumped up and shouted, "They're liars. They're all liars!" According to the next day's papers, Garrett – pale and shaking – pushed his way through the throng up to the chair of Attorney General Joseph E. Warner and yelled, "What is this, Russia?"

On the eve of his trial for extortion he skipped town. For almost six months Garrett wandered as far south as Mexico. He was nearly apprehended in North Attleboro and he had been recognized and called by name in Providence. He lived for weeks in New York and walked the streets, went to boxing matches, barrooms, nightclubs and was never recognized.

Back in Boston, the controversy swirled. In the legislature outspoken politicians pressured Governor Frank G. Allen for action. Citizens charged that the police didn't dare find Garrett in fear that he would expose more corruption. "There isn't a square man in the whole department," street corner discussions proclaimed.

After five months of speculation and front page headlines, Garrett decided to turn himself in. He wrote to Lawrence R. Goldberg, a crime reporter for the Boston Post to make the arrangements. On Nov. 30, 1930, the Post splashed its front page with the headline, "Garrett Returns Home; All Ready to Surrender." The run on the Post presses was the largest in the paper's history. Goldberg, the crime reporter, turned Garrett over to Lt. James F. Daley of the Boston Police at the Charles Street jail. The surrender was made at deadline so that other papers could not get the story on the streets themselves.

After two sensational trials in which the juries failed to reach a verdict, Garrett pled guilty to extortion charges and was sentenced to two years in jail.

Prohibition Epilogue

Of all the ambitious schemers of Prohibition, Joe Kennedy made the most graceful, and lucrative,' exit. Although he likely left the racket by 1926 when violent gangs began to take control, Kennedy swooped back in during the last days of the Dry Era to make millions. By this time he was an ambassador in President Roosevelt's administration and, through inside government contacts, learned that Prohibition would soon be repealed.

He immediately began buying up huge quantities of Scotch fraudulently by claiming it was for medicinal purposes. The Scotch, mostly Haig & Haig and Dewars, was stockpiled in warehouses near the Canadian border. When Prohibition was finally repealed, Kennedy became overnight the largest single distributor of Scotch in the United States. He remained on top of the business until 1946, when he sold his interest in Somerset Importers for $8 million and a huge personal profit.

The fate of Charles "King" Solomon was Prohibition's most dramatic ending. On January 24, 1933 at three a.m., Solomon arrived at the Cotton Club speakeasy with two dancers and the bandleader from his Cocoanut Grove nightclub. With $4,600 in his pocket, he danced twice before he had the waitress break a $50 bill. Across the dance floor were six Irish toughs in a booth, nursing their drinks. After an hour, one of the men went to Solomon's table and told him a friend wanted to see him in the men's room.

When Solomon got up and headed for the bathroom, four of the men followed him, one saying, "Keep going we've got you covered." In the bathroom, Solomon was heard to say, "You've got my roll. Now what do you want?" James "Skeets" Coyne, a twenty-eight year old petty thief, replied, "You've been asking for this," followed by gunshots. Coyne and his accomplices crashed into and fell over one another as they stumbled out of the club. Solomon staggered out of the bathroom, shot four times in the chest, abdomen and neck. "The dirty rats got me," he grunted as he crashed on top of a nightclub table.

It was an over the top end to an era of excess. With the imprisonment of Garrett on Deer Island and the murder of Solomon, Prohibition in Boston had come to an end. The repeal of the Eighteenth Amendment a short time later seemed a mere formality.

CHAPTER FOUR

DADDY BLACK AND THE STORY OF THE NUMBERS GAME

MONDAY, SEPTEMBER 28, 1932.

THOUSANDS OF MOURNERS crowd the streets of Providence to say goodbye to Arthur "Daddy" Black, the legendary Number King of Rhode Island. In the days leading up to the procession, more than 20,000 paid emotional final respects to the fallen gangster inside Montgomery Funeral Home. It was an extraordinary sight for its era — thousands of white men and women crying over the casket of a dead black man — but Daddy Black had led an extraordinary life.

As the procession traveled down Broadway and Courtland Street, the crowd swelled around Hoyle Square. For a decade, Black looked out for the neighborhood when City Hall would not. His number pool provided the employment, capital, and social services that consistently bypassed Providence's black community. "No black man will go hungry as long as I am making money," was Daddy Black's famous boast. Today, residents would repay Black's loyalty with a show of their own.

Inside Church of the Saviour, every bit of available space was taken. The reverend described Black as "a friend to humanity and a brother to us all . . . His many acts of kindness were done without a flourish of trumpets. Many poor people will miss him during the coming winter months."

A reporter for the Boston Chronicle described the sad march of mourners that passed by Black's coffin. "Women cried and in some cases strong men broke down and wept — and some of these men were white — as they looked on Daddy's face for the last time."

Black's murder made the front pages of black newspapers across the country. In Providence, his funeral procession marked the end of the numbers game as a black-owned business and source of racial pride.

Caught just a few hours after the shooting, Black's killers claimed it was a robbery that went bad when a New York gunman "got jumpy" and accidentally fired. Officials and media accepted that version but around Hoyle Square, black residents believed differently: Daddy Black may have been killed by a black gunman, but he was targeted because he had resisted the demands of white men.

From Tuffy to Daddy

Arthur Black was born in Charleston, South Carolina on July 24, 1880. He arrived in Providence a short time later with his mother. "He was a regular boy and earned the nickname Tuffy from his companions," a newspaper article noted.

Eventually he enlisted in the United States Navy where he served for 20 years. He saw active service in Cuba in the Spanish-American War, in China during the Boxer Rebellion, and was cited twice for bravery in World War I. He also worked as a machinist on the Panama Canal. "It is said only his color prevented him from rising to a higher rank," according to the Boston Chronicle, New England's leading black publication.

After mistakenly being credited with 30 years of service instead of 20, he returned to Providence and started his number pool. In 1923, the game was black America's glamour business — a testament to black innovation and entrepreneurship during a time of pervasive racism. With unemployment rates more than double for blacks what they were for whites, the numbers provided jobs for average, upstanding citizens.

In Providence, the pool became a part of the community's everyday life; bettors discussed their luck at the game on street corners. Just as importantly, the game injected capital into a black community ignored by white financial institutions. Two white men invested money they earned from the bootlegging business in Daddy Black's pool and became his partners.

For the typical player the game held the promise of a dime and a dream. With a 600-to-1 payout, a dime bet would win $60, a small fortune for a family in those Depression years. Bettors placed their wager with collectors around Hoyle Square and checked daily horse race results in the local newspaper to find the winning number — always whatever the final three digits in the total handle at a local racetrack happened to be.

Even for the pool's losers, Daddy Black could be of help. Ed Kelly, the Providence police chief during Black's reign, said Black was fond of telling the story of how one woman's losing bet changed her life for the better.

According to legend, the woman had three cents to her name when Black convinced her to place it on a number. The next day Black delivered the woman $15 and told her she won. In reality, she hadn't; Black paid the money from his own pocket and told her to spread the word to her friends and neighbors about her good fortune. Soon "there was a shower of pennies, nickels and dimes from people who would never have played the game if the bolt of luck had not struck within their own circle," read a Providence Journal account.

The loose change added up to piles of cash for Daddy Black. He was referred to in the press as "Providence's richest Negro." Daily receipts for the pool reached almost $5000. "Daddy Black was known for handling big money, big, big money," says a 90-year-old local who remembers Black from his childhood.

Politically, Black was a key figure in turning out the black vote at a time when blacks were solidly Republican. His leadership role in fraternal organizations such as the Otha Boone Elks Lodge and the Veterans of Foreign Wars put him in an advantageous position to "encourage" voting for selected candidates.

Black was a major player in New England professional sports — in black and white leagues alike. In 1926, he purchased an all-white baseball team called the Monarchs and later he held a controlling interest in an all-white basketball team, the Cardinals. In 1931, he joined one of the most prestigious black business circles when he bought an independent professional black team, the Providence Colored Giants. Black put his squad up against quality opponents such as the Black Yankees owned by celebrity tap dancer and actor Bill "Bojangles" Robinson.

He transformed the Giants from a perennial loser to an elite organization and his ownership tenure is viewed as the high point of New England black professional baseball. "In baseball circles Black was always known as a free spender," the Providence Journal reported.

As Black was cultivating contacts in politics and sports he maintained his underworld ties. He was usually accompanied by armed bodyguard Lonnie Williams and he employed a young Raymond Patriarca, then considered a dangerous wild card in Providence's black community. A decade later, Patriarca would begin his rapid rise in the New England Mafia.

Black's most visible link to organized crime was his plum job as an official for a local labor union — a position that signaled approval from higher echelons of the mob. The job and feared gunmen such as Williams and Patriarca may have made Black feel secure but they were no protection from the forces of history conspiring against him.

Daddy's Downfall

In 1932, with Black at the height of his power, Italian gangsters aggressively moved to take over his racket. It was hardly a rare occurrence — black Number Kings and Queens across the country were under siege from violent and politically connected white gangs.

The Mafia, anticipating a loss of revenue with the end of Prohibition, was able to move in on the numbers up and down the East Coast using official corruption and violence. In Providence, Daddy Black fought back.

To resist white gangs, Black placed his "soldiers in the field" and "drove the outsiders outside his territory," according to a contemporary newspaper account. The pressure continued, however, and some of Black's men were roughed up and beaten by Italian thugs.

On September 24, 1932, it seems, the feud turned deadly and the numbers changed forever. Black and bodyguard Lonnie Williams were on the third floor of Black's home at 160 Cranston Street. Black, his wife Louella, and daughter lived on the first floor. On the second floor, the front apartment housed the medical office of Dr. James A. Gilbert, one of the few black physicians in Providence, and in the rear flat lived a woman and her young daughter.

At 7 pm, as Black, Williams, and a couple of employees counted the receipts from the day's pool, five men quietly crept up the stairway. They were led by a 31-year-old New York man named Webster Barnwell. Following were Fred Harris-Bowe, 26, from New York, and Weston Qualls, 25, Edward Sutton, 26, and Edward Gray, 32, all from Rhode Island. William Shepard, a number runner for Black who was in on the scheme, stood guard on the second floor.

"Stick 'em up," Barnwell said, after entering the counting room. When one number runner hesitated, Barnwell hit him in the face. Black's bodyguard Williams ducked behind a desk and drew his gun. Barnwell saw him and began firing. Shots were exchanged and a bullet pierced Daddy Black's heart.

Black stumbled to a secret stairwell connecting the third floor to the basement. He had it built knowing one day he may need it to make a quick exit. But once down the steps all he could do was slump next to the furnace. Black's second floor tenant rushed to the basement where she found him dead. In hysterics, she ran out to Cranston Street and screamed, "They killed Daddy Black! They killed Daddy Black!"

The shooters rushed downstairs to the getaway car. Barnwell's wife Flo Sullivan was in the driver's seat and sped off with tires squealing. Witnesses told police they noticed the getaway car had a broken tail light. A few hours later a state trooper in Portsmouth noticed the car and pulled it over for the light violation.

The men confessed to the shooting that night. They claimed it was accidental. Two months later, a jury deliberated for less than an hour before returning a guilty verdict. The six men were each sentenced to life in prison. The case appeared to be closed, but Hoyle Square residents still had their doubts.

Black Out

Police officials and the Providence Journal quickly accepted the robbery-gone-bad scenario. Little attention was given to the ongoing power struggle in Providence and across the country between black numbers innovators and the Italian thugs trying to move in. However, the Boston Chronicle reported that "On the street it is thought that revenge, and a desire to 'get' Black, and put him out of the number business, so that others might 'muscle in' was the real motive for the shooting."

The streets may have been onto something. There was and continues to be compelling evidence that the assassination of Daddy Black was ordered by Italian gangsters who manipulated his inner circle to bring him down.

According to the testimony of the killers, Shepard — the inside man in the conspiracy — was the one who brought Barnwell and Harris-Bowe in from New York. Before the murder, the gang met at Shepard's house on Bank Street to arm themselves. When they walked the four blocks to Black's home, it was probably Shepard — the known face — who got the crew in the door and past Black's wife without raising suspicion.

It is unlikely that Shepard, a low-level employee, could have imported New York gunmen by himself. Indeed, the presence of two sharply dressed New York gangsters signals a conspiracy organized by higher ranking thugs than a local number runner. As Black lay in his casket, his number pool continued with one major difference — black number runners had been replaced by agents with Italian names like Rao and Cacchione. In police files they were identified as successors to the Daddy Black organization.

Seeing Italian gangsters take over the pool, locals became more dubious of the botched robbery theory. The messages of Daddy Black's murder were clear — when a black man reaches too high he will be taken down, violently if necessary; and you can't trust what white authorities say.

CHAPTER FIVE

GANGSTERS IN BLUE UNIFORMS: CORRUPT POLICE AND AN UPSTART BLACK MOB

JUNE 17, 1932, OUTSIDE A TREMONT STREET MALT SHOP IN THE SOUTH END.

GUY PERELLI WAS on the attack. Perelli, a Mafia thug and numbers man, was a constant menace to black citizens on this South End block. Working with corrupt police, he had been one of the architects of the Boston Mafia's takeover of the numbers game from black operators.

This day, Perelli was accosting two black women outside the malt shop that doubled as his headquarters. When the women objected, Perelli slapped one with a newspaper and kicked the other in the stomach. His bodyguard, a professional boxer, joined in and assaulted both women, badly hurting one.

Immediately, about forty black men came on the scene "with the intensity and suddenness of an erupting volcano." Perelli and his bodyguard retreated behind the locked door of the malt shop, revolvers in hand. In the presence of police, the women were offered $200 and told to forget about it.

It was a familiar scenario – white gangsters and police officers routinely worked together in Boston's black neighborhoods. Their tools were violence and intimidation. In fact, conventional wisdom of the day held that black women were not safe to walk the streets of Boston without attack from white gangsters and policemen. In one publicized case a white police officer was suspended after a court found probable cause that he attempted to rape and rob a black woman. When a grand jury refused to indict, the incident was derided as "southern justice."

The most brutal white officer, George L. Smith, was given the nickname Hard Boiled for his viciousness. One summer night in 1932, with his breath smelling of liquor, Hard Boiled went on a violent rampage. He hit a well-known black comedian from behind with a blackjack and severely beat a blind man. "Also, it is common knowledge that Smith on every possible occasion refers to colored people in the most insulting language," the Boston Chronicle reported.

When he was found guilty of the assaults, Hard Boiled's reaction reflected the surprise of a white man – a police officer, at that - being held responsible for assaulting black people in 1930s Boston: he fainted.

A team of FBI agents got an even more shocking response a year later when they stormed into a black-owned night club on Columbus Avenue in the South End without identifying themselves and demanded money. Customers, thinking the agents were stick up men, pounced, sending them out of the neighborhood "nursing cracked heads," The Chronicle reported.

Despite occasional vindications and triumphs, the extreme racism in Boston stifled black advancement, even in the field of organized crime. One nightclub, in particular, embodied the era's embrace of segregation, gangsters and violence.

The Cotton Club

It was not easy for anyone to just walk into the Cotton Club, Boston's most notorious speakeasy; potential patrons had to pass through a maze of doors and discriminating doormen - but the exclusion of black patrons was particularly insulting. The club lured its gangster clientele with the best black jazz musicians of the day, it employed blacks in service capacities and was located in the heart of the city's black community. No black patrons were to be admitted though.

The club "was located in this district merely for color but not for colored patronage," said a "Cotton Club Must Go" editorial in the city's weekly black newspaper, the Boston Chronicle. The Cotton Club rejected black customers while catering to a gangster clientele –"notorious characters of both sexes, drug addicts, murder suspects and other undesirables went there regularly," The Chronicle said.

The club's most famous gangland murder was typical of the spot African Americans occupied in the Boston underworld. On January 24, 1933 when Charles King Solomon, the Jewish kingpin, was killed by small time Irish thugs possibly on order from the Italian Mafia, only innocent black musicians were detained by police and subjected to media speculation in the immediate aftermath. A black employee of the club who helped police identify one of the gunmen was harassed and threatened by gangsters and corrupt police officers. Just as in the Cotton Club, blacks in Boston's gangland were shut out of the inner most worlds while their neighborhoods suffered the consequences. To black residents, the Cotton Club stood on Tremont Street as a symbol of the era's hypocrisy.

"We are constantly exhorted about the virtues of good citizenship and still on our very doorsteps are dumped those undesirable institutions and practices conducive to vice and violation of the law," the Boston Chronicle wrote after the Solomon murder. "Policemen have been shot, women beaten in the streets and innocent men set upon and partially blinded or beaten unmercifully by policemen, while protests are answered by a rustle of papers and the click of typewriters as they belch forth effusive apologies."

Boston's black underworld was forced to overcome many disadvantages in building a powerful organized crime group; lack of political power, a corrupt and racist police force and an encroaching Italian Mafia. Despite those obstacles, a Boston number runner known as Homeboy was about to push the country toward its multicultural destiny.

CHAPTER SIX

MALCOLM X AND THE LEGEND OF DETROIT RED

ROXBURY, 1940S.

ALTHOUGH THE MAFIA wrestled control of the numbers game from black operators by the mid-1930s, many blacks continued to work at the lower and middle levels of the business. One such number runner in Boston was Malcolm Little, a teenager who would one day be known to the world as civil rights leader Malcolm X.

When Malcolm arrived in Boston, there were around 23,000 black people in the city mostly living in the South End and Lower Roxbury. Malcolm moved in with his sister Ella Collins who lived among a growing cluster of black homeowners and renters on Dale Street.

Exposure to the harder aspects of city life was shocking to Malcolm. Raised in the Midwest, he was a naive country bumpkin when he first arrived in Roxbury: "I had never tasted a sip of liquor, never even smoked a cigarette, and here I saw little black children, ten and twelve years old, shooting craps, and playing cards."

One night at a local Boston pool hall, a "dark, stubby conked headed fellow" approached him and introduced himself as "Shorty." The two teenagers were pleased to discover that they were both from Lansing, Michigan and Shorty immediately dubbed his new friend "Homeboy."

This was Malcolm "Shorty" Jarvis – two years older, he was already a minor figure in Boston's black nightlife. He would soon become "Malcolm's guide and companion in the Boston street life and nightclub scene," according to Ella's son Rodnell Collins. Shorty was an accomplished trumpet player, sitting in for big bands, and he gave his young friend a tour of the city's underworld, pointing out the hustlers, gamblers and pimps. Malcolm proved a quick study – he was soon engaged in smoking "reefer", hustling, petty thievery, and seducing fast women.

Even in his dress, Malcolm was showing his loyalty to the street life. At Shorty's insistence, he purchased his first colorful "zoot suit" on credit and "conked" his hair using a "jellylike starchy-looking glop" produced from lye, several potatoes, and two eggs. The mixture burned intensely, but the final product, viewed from a mirror, transformed Malcolm into the street hustler he wanted to be.

Though he eventually came to disdain the practice, the conk was the emblem of the hippest, street savvy black man at the time, the choice of hustlers, pimps, professional gamblers, and criminals. It was directly influenced by wavy haired Latinos not straight haired whites. Malcolm's obsession with jazz, zoot suits and illegal hustling were symbols of the divide between urban black youth and the black middle class – and he was making it clear he was on the side of the street hustlers.

Malcolm fell deeper into thug life after a job as a train cook brought him to Harlem. As soon as he arrived in the fabled black Mecca, he was sizing up criminal opportunities. With the street savvy he honed in Boston, "I was going to become one of the most depraved parasitical hustlers among New York's eight million people," he said.

Malcolm began supplementing his income by peddling marijuana, casually at first, then more aggressively. Bea Caragulian – his older, white girlfriend from Boston – visited frequently and Malcolm showed her off at his favorite nightspots. He was now a mid-level drug dealer with a gift for dodging narcotics detectives. With an older white woman on his arm, he had arrived as a serious player to the world of street criminals. For a boy just reaching his seventeenth birthday, barely more than a year after settling in Roxbury, his reinvention as a streetwise hustler was remarkable.

Malcolm was now using his railroad jobs to transport and sell marijuana across the country. He would return from long hauls "with two of the biggest suitcases you ever saw, full of that stuff…marijuana pressed into bricks you know…but they would pay him a thousand dollars a trip," his brother Wilfred said. Malcolm's slick style influenced by city streets in Roxbury and Harlem helped him meet and learn from the jazz musicians who were his marijuana customers. "After selling reefers with the bands as they traveled, I was known to almost every popular Negro musician around New York in 1944 [and] 1945," he boasted.

Malcolm, now known as Detroit Red to other hustlers, continued his criminal apprenticeship when he got a job at the legendary Harlem club Small's Paradise. He met more experienced criminals, legendary "bad Negroes" who treated crime more professionally than the "various hot-headed, wild young hustlers out trying to make a name for themselves for being crazy with a pistol trigger or a knife," Malcolm said. "The old heads that I'm talking about were… Black Sammy, Bub Hewlett, King Padmore and West Indian Archie." He also met pimps such as Cadillac Drake and Sammy the Pimp.

"I was thus schooled well, by experts in such hustles as the numbers, pimping, con games of many kinds, peddling dope, and thievery of all sorts, including armed robbery," he said. "I couldn't have been in a more educational situation. Some of the ablest of New York's black hustlers took a liking to me, and knowing that I still was green by their terms, soon began in a paternal way to "straighten Red out."

These professional criminals made Malcolm think about the intelligence needed in the rackets. He was particularly impressed by West Indian Archie. A legendary Harlem badman who worked as muscle for the era's toughest gangsters, West Indian Archie had a photographic memory that allowed him to store the numbers customers played in his head and avoid paper evidence. "I've often reflected upon such black veteran numbers men as West Indian Archie," he said decades later. "If they had lived in another kind of society, their exceptional mathematical talents might have been better used. But they were black."

Meanwhile, Malcolm was developing a cocaine addiction and getting involved with more serious crimes. Over a six to eight month period he and Sammy the Pimp pulled a series of robberies and burglaries outside New York City. During one heist, the robbery encountered "some bad luck. A bullet grazed Sammy. We just barely escaped."

The close brush didn't discourage Malcolm from getting deeper into crime, in particular the numbers game. This was a different racket from the era of Daddy Black, however, with more suspicion, violence and white men. "My job now was to ride a bus across the George Washington Bridge where a fellow was waiting for me to hand him a bag of betting slips. We never spoke...You didn't ask questions in the rackets." He also worked as a "steerer" in Times Square, making connections with white johns and placing them with mostly black prostitutes working out of Harlem apartments. Through these criminal activities, Malcolm was witnessing what he viewed as the filth and hypocrisy of the white man.

By early December 1945, Malcolm was back in Boston after a falling out with West Indian Archie. He quickly found his old friend Shorty Jarvis, who complained to him about money problems. Within several days, Malcolm organized a gang, with the goal of robbing homes in Boston's affluent suburbs. Early in the evening of December 14, 1945, the gang robbed a Brookline home, absconding with $2,400 worth of fur coats, silverware, jewelry and other items. The next night they hit a second Brookline home, stealing several rugs and silverware valued at nearly $400, in addition to liquer, jewelry and linen.

For these break-ins, the gang followed a general pattern. One would jimmy the home's rear door then open the front door for Malcolm and Shorty. The premises was quickly looted, with a focus on items that could be sold on the black market. The women stayed outside acting as lookouts. The gang made errors no veteran burglars would have ever made: some of the loot was split among members after they drove to New York City and only sold part of their merchandise.

When they returned to Boston, they pulled off one of their most lucrative hauls. Breaking into a home in Newton, a wealthy Boston suburb, they managed to grab merchandise with a total value estimated by police at $6,275. The next month they robbed eight more homes.

When they were finally caught, Malcolm was primarily responsible for their downfall. He gave a watch to a relative as a Christmas gift; the relative sold it to a Boston jeweler, who, suspecting it had been stolen, contacted the police. The authorities bided their time. In early January 1946, Malcolm took another stolen watch to the repair shop. When he returned for it, local police were on hand to arrest him. Malcolm was carrying a loaded .32 caliber pistol at the time.

During his interrogation, detectives lied and promised not to prosecute him on the gun charge if he agreed to give up his accomplices. He readily complied, naming his whole crew who were each promptly arrested – a detail he later left out of his autobiography.

Malcolm was charged with the illegal possession of a firearm in Roxbury court on January 15. The next day, at the Quincy court, charges of larceny and breaking and entering were added. Shorty Jarvis' account provides a vivid description of he and Malcolm's ordeal: "We were urged by the district attorney and our white lawyers to plead guilty as charged; we were also told if we did things would go real easy and well in our favor [in sentencing]."

Both men had been "damn fools" not to have anticipated a legal double cross, Shorty said. Malcolm's white girlfriend Bea – the woman he showed off so proudly in Roxbury and Harlem - was subpoenaed and turned state's evidence against him, reading from the script prosecutors wrote for her.

Jarvis claimed the district attorney even tried unsuccessfully "to get the girls to testify that we had raped them; this was so he could ask the judge for a fifteen to twenty year sentence or life in prison." The prime motivation for the prosecution seemed racial. "As long as I live," Shorty said, "I will never forget how the judge told me I had no business associating with white women." Ella's son Rodnell said: "In court Ella said, the men were described by one lawyer as 'schvartze bastards' and by another as minor Al Capones. The arresting officer meanwhile referred to [the women] as 'poor, unfortunate, friendless, scared lost girls.'"

Both Malcolm and Shorty pled guilty and were sentenced in a Middlesex County court to four concurrent eight-to-ten year sentences, to be served in prison. While this was read out they were confined behind bars in a steel cage in the courtroom. Shorty snapped, shaking the bars and screaming at the presiding judge, "Why don't you kill me? Why don't you kill me? I would rather be dead than do 10 years."

Malcolm was transported to Norfolk State Prison where he would undergo another reinvention; this time a spiritual awakening would lead to a transformation from street hustler to civil rights icon. Yet even as a religious, disciplined intellectual figure, he would continually draw on – and sometimes exaggerate – his street exploits. The autobiography he wrote with Alex Haley transformed Detroit Red from a young man who turned to petty crime to survive into a criminal kingpin, according to biographer and scholar Manning Marable.

"In his lengthy conversations with Haley, Malcolm deliberately exaggerated his gangster exploits – the number of his burglaries, the amount of marijuana he sold to musicians and the like – to illustrate how depraved he had become," Marable wrote in the Pulitzer Prize winning biography Malcolm X: A Life of Reinvention. "Malcolm told Haley stories about himself as being more illiterate and backward than he really was. Malcolm's overriding mission was to show himself in the worst possible light which would illustrate the power of Muhammad's message in changing people's lives."

The outlaw myth Malcolm created for himself served an important purpose though. Marable compared Detroit Red to famous black anti-heroes such as Nat Turner, Robert Johnson, Stagger Lee and Tupac Shakur.

"What these black outlaws all had in common was a cool contempt for the bourgeois status quo, the system of white supremacy and its law and courts. More significantly, the tradition of the black outlaw was to transgress the established moral order," Marable said. "In this respect, Detroit Red as Malcolm constructed him was the antihero, the hepcat who laughed at conventional mores, who used illegal drugs and engaged in illicit sex, who broke all the rules.

A close examination of the Autobiography illustrates that many of the elements of Detroit Red's narrative are fictive; despite this, the character's experiences resonate with black audiences because the contexts of racism, crime, and violence are integral aspects of ghetto life."

In 1952, Malcolm was released from prison and embarked on a Civil Rights career with the Nation of Islam. It is an understatement to say this ex-number runner from Roxbury changed the direction of the United States.

At the time though, Boston was still the provincial, stubborn city it had always been. The old school ethic was epitomized in a sensational crime drama sweeping the city and the nation around the same time Malcolm was released. The Brink's robbery saga was still front page news two years after the heist as authorities couldn't pin enough evidence on infamous suspects Tony Pino and Specs O'Keefe.

If Malcolm was a sign of the future, the ragtag crooks who pulled of the record-setting Brink's heist were signs of the times. By 1950, Boston was growing shabby and decrepit and had drifted toward a financial crisis. Its financial status was rated lowest of any large American city. Downtown was beginning to feel the pinch of suburban shopping plazas. From two years before the Great Depression until thirteen years after World War II, not one new office building was constructed in downtown Boston.

Boston's working class identity was formed in these years and it was represented by the small-time crooks who pulled off the biggest heist in history. The Brink's robbers not only stole $2.7 million from the number one name in security, with their local allegiances, disputes and quirks, they made off with the hearts of Bostonians.

CHAPTER SEVEN

TONY PINO AND THE BRINK'S ROBBERY: A $3 MILLION LOVE AFFAIR

TONY PINO COULD make anyone laugh. The mastermind of the Brink's heist had that indefinable power that marks a good comedian. Maybe it was timing but whatever it was, Pino could make the toughest cop or meanest hood laugh.

Pino was a storyteller, blessed with a gift of gab that got him out of many a tough spot with both lawmen and the lawless. His friends thought he was funnier than professional comedians. Pino's jovial appearance hid a deeper and darker personality. His brother-in-law Vincent Costa said, "He was the best goddamn thief I ever met. The best. And he was the world's biggest liar too as far as I was concerned." Pino was also a double-crosser, a pathological liar, and maybe even a killer. But he could tell a joke and he dreamed big – in Boston maybe that would be enough.

Anthony Pino was born May 10, 1907, in Sicily, and was brought to the United States with his parents when he was eight months old. He never became an American citizen. The family settled in South Boston, and Tony grew up among members of a large, tightly knit clan, many of whom continued to arrive from Italy. He learned English from fighting with Irish kids in the neighborhood.

Young Tony was an accomplished thief from the age of six. He started by stealing coal for his impoverished family. By age eight he was detained by police for hitching rides on trolley cars. At nine he was caught breaking and entering.

The incident that would dog him all his life came in 1928, when he was arrested for abuse of a child who was allegedly held in a West End house. Pino would always maintain he was framed for the abuse but some accounts imply that while he was innocent, he had protected the real culprit. Nonetheless, Pino spent March 29, 1928, to November 29, 1930, in jail. The morals charge would one day become a legal albatross for the career crook.

The stint did little to reform Pino; in fact he met other young men who would become his partners in crime and started to learn the art of safecracking. On Thanksgiving Day 1937 Pino and four other men were nabbed in the basement of Rhodes Brothers store in the Back Bay, just as they were breaking into a safe. At age thirty-one, Pino was sentenced to two consecutive three to four year terms in the state prison in Charlestown. The "police were confident they had broken up Greater Boston's most prolific crew of strong-box yeggs," the Boston American announced.

When Pino was released in September 1944 he was given a huge coming-home party by his parents and his fiancée. He promised them he would go straight this time but soon returned to his old habits. He was shoplifting but it was penny-ante stuff. He needed a crew and little by little he put one together.

The Robbers

Vincent James "Vinnie" Costa was born February 8, 1914 and grew up in South Boston. By his teens Costa was living the gangster lifestyle, committing crimes and wearing the double breasted suits and soft hats that fashionable hoodlums favored. He always had a scam going but Pino wasn't impressed. Costa had married Pino's sister when he was seventeen and they eventually had five children. Pino would later describe Costa as a "brother in law who thinks he's a crook but ain't ever been pinched for nothing respectable in his life." But family was family for Pino – throughout his life he would support his parents and siblings - and Costa was soon his right hand man.

More capable was Thomas Francis Richardson, better known as Sandy. He was born March 22, 1907, in South Boston. He'd met Pino when they were both nineteen and they soon crime partners. When Pino got out of jail, they continued to do jobs together with the help of another longshoreman, James Ignatius Faherty.

Sandy and "Jimma" Faherty, born on April 19, 1911, grew up together in South Boston and became inseparable friends. Jimma was said to be a member of the notorious Gustin Gang. Police would later describe him as a man who "likes filter-tipped cigarettes, prize fights and is fond of wide, grey hats with turned up brims. He talks slowly and enunciates carefully."

In 1930 Richardson introduced Pino to Michael Vincent "Vinnie" Geagan. Geagan, born on September 22, 1908, had been continually in trouble with the law since childhood. But two years of high school at Charlestown High made him the most educated member of the crew.

Sandy Richardson brought another new face around Pino when he introduced Adolph "Jazz" Maffie, a local bookie. A smooth dresser, he earned his nickname for his snazzy style. Despite his affectations, the gang agreed: Maffie's alright.

Not everyone in the crew had that support. Around the corner from Pino's home in Egleston Square was the J.A. Café. A poor man's night-club, the dingy café served watered down liquor and featured nude dancing. It was owned by Joseph F. McGinnis, described as "sadistic, bull-shouldered, vile tempered, penny pinching, a one-time professional fist fighter and possessed of a super inflated built-in ego."

However, this tough guy harbored an odd secret. Born on August 19, 1903, he was raised in Rhode Island, the son of a Providence policeman and a kind but troubled woman. His mother had dressed him as a daughter when he was a boy. McGinnis kept a photo of himself at age seven or eight, dressed in a black velvet dress with a white lace collar. By contrast, his father regularly used his fists on his young son to toughen him up. To Pino, McGinnis was arrogant, but he was also a businessman with contacts throughout the city which Pino admired greatly.

One of the young hoods who often came to the J.A. Café was Stanley Albert Gusciora known to his friends as Gus. Described as a "handsome son of a gun" by the late 1940s Gus was fresh out of prison but had drifted back into crime and hooked up with the man who would become his best friend, Specky O'Keefe.

Joseph James "Specky" O'Keefe got his nickname when, as a child in South Boston, he begged for bananas from the local produce sellers. The merchants usually gave him old, "speckled" bananas and he was often seen eating them. The name Specky – later shortened to Specs – stuck with him.

He was born on March 30, 1908, the seventh child of a large Irish family; of sixteen children, ten – seven boys and three girls – survived infancy. At eight he was caught robbing a candy store; at nine he stole a horse and wagon. He hung around with a group called the C Street Gang and was caught stealing eight watches from a jewelry store. His crimes grew more serious, and in December 1927 he was convicted of breaking and entering and sentenced to five years in the Concord Reformatory, where he got to know Pino, Faherty, and a safecracker named Henry Baker.

"Robbery was his business," a lawyer later told Boston Post columnist Grace Davidson. "Yet if you gave him your wallet to guard, he'd return it intact. For him to rob, it had to be a 'job' something impersonal like Brink's, something, something challenging."

With his impoverished and deprived childhood, O'Keefe believed he was entitled to the good life, but he seemed unable to figure out how to achieve it. "What he wanted out of life," Davidson wrote, "is what lots of men want-good clothes, fast cars, plenty of money to spend for steaks and drinks and cafes and bars that are frequented by girls described in his vernacular as dolls."

In Boston's underworld the crew was near the top of local rackets. Pino, however, was dealing with a new set of troubles. As a young man, he never got around to applying for American citizenship. While he was in prison in the 1940s, immigration authorities deemed him a menace to American society and he was ordered deported. The cost of obtaining a pardon – in legal fees and "other costs" was put at $30,000 by his lawyer. Shoplifting, his only expertise - was not going to cover that expense.

Then Pino stumbled on something that would change history. While walking through the narrow, twisting streets of Boston's Financial District, he noted an armored vehicle marked "Brink's." The car drove into the Chamber of Commerce building, which was bordered by Federal, Congress, Milk, and Franklin Streets. Curious, he watched the outside of the building and saw more armored trucks pulling inside. Old men were unloading bags of cash and hauling them into the building. Despite the Brink's reputation, the guards looked like they could be easily convinced to hand over the loot: a .38 in the face would do the trick. Pino described the moment as:

"Mother of God, I couldn't believe what I was seeing. There was all them money trucks standing there and once they started loading up, I knew they was mine. I damn near shouted, 'Hey you

fellas, go easy with that merchandise. It belongs to me.' I don't know how I ever got home. But I musta been jumping up and down on the train seat all the way. And when I got home, I was all perspired thinking about it. I had maybe four belts of whiskey and a hot bath, trying to stop thinking about it but I was beyond help. I was electrified...Now I was rehabilitated, too, understand? I wasn't going to steal a cent more than I needed for my deportation and moderate living. But when a man walks right up to you and says, 'Here, take all my money,' it would be bad manners to turn your back on him. The terrible thing was I had nobody to tell it to 'cause I didn't have a phone and if I did, it wasn't any good. Here Mr. Brink's was going to make me a millionaire and the whole goddamn world was fast asleep."

One day he followed a Brink's truck to a garage in Cambridge. "Bang, there I seen 'em all lined up. Brink's trucks. I know I got their garage. And I'm watching this janitor they got. This fella's mopping up in between the trucks. He goes into the back, and fast, I open the door and sneak in. The first thing I see is a board nailed up on the wall with the keys on it." When the garage was closed for the evening, Pino broke in, picked up the keys, had copies made, and returned them. Pino now had a copy of a key for every Brink's truck in Boston.

On January 7, 1949, the crew put the plan into action. The men were dropped off by Pino, who was driving the getaway truck. But Pino quickly noticed that the men were moving out of their assigned positions and weren't moving according to the carefully designed plan. Fuming, Pino picked them up. They had bad news. Brink's was gone! The office was no longer located on Federal Street. Pino's three years of observations and meticulous planning wasted.

He was not about to give up though. When Pino next spotted a Brink's truck, he followed it until it pulled into the North Terminal Garage in the North End. Pino returned after dark and circled the garage by foot. On Hull Street he could see Brink's trucks lined up in the garage. He walked nonchalantly down Prince Street. On a door at number 165 he saw the distinct shield of Brink's Inc. "Gotcha," he said quietly to himself.

He walked into the brick playground that bordered the garage. Making sure no one was nearby, he scaled the wall and found himself on a terrace from which he could see straight into the windows of the second floor. On his hands and knees, Pino crept forward until he realized he was staring right into Brink's offices, where he could see the men sorting and counting stacks of money.

As his eyes swept over the five large windows, he could see, behind the fifth window, a small room and in the back corner – Mother of God! – the vault. For Pino – who had worked for years to find a way to crack Brink's – it was a transcendent moment. "I spent all them years over at Congress [Street] trying everything to peek into their pete and now by climbing on some rotten fence, I'm staring right into her face."

Pino's obsession with Brink's intensified. He was going to take the company in a way no one had ever dreamed of. To begin, he bought a seventy five dollar telescope and assigned Costa to help with the observations. As he had on Federal Street, Pino soon learned every detail of the company's daily routines. Costa and Pino even knew the schedules of the guards' bathroom breaks. The Brink's job is back on, Pino announced.

Now the crew was visiting the Brink's garage each day. According to Specs, the group made at least a dozen forays into the building. The trips took on a surreal quality as the men began to act like playful children. Once Gus hid behind a desk and, when Jazz walked by, yelled, "Stick 'em up, I got ya." They became careless about being heard; they used the phone and the bathrooms. They smoked cigarette after cigarette. When a sign on the company bulletin board solicited contributions for a wedding present for one of the drivers, Gus and Costa each put a dollar in the cup. Specs O'Keefe even brought in a girlfriend one night.

Now that the burglars could come and go as they pleased in Brink's they were within a few feet of more money than any crook could dream of. However, between them and the money stood plates of steel that no one with their minor league ability could crack. The gang considered blowing up the vault but rejected that as too risky.

To break the vault, Pino tapped Henry Baker, one of the region's best safecrackers. On August 22, 1949, Baker was paroled from the state prison in Charlestown. Pino drove him home on the day of his release and probably talked to him about the new enterprise he had planned. Finally, Joseph (Barney) Banfield of Charlestown was brought in to drive the getaway car. Banfield was drunk most of the time but he was considered one of the best "wheelmen" in the business.

Some days before January 17, 1950, O'Keefe, Pino and some of the others finished dinner and were leaving a restaurant when a Brink's armored truck drove by with a banner proclaiming "Brink's celebrates its 90th birthday next month." Pino took the toothpick out of his mouth and said, "They'll never make it."

The Big Stick-Up

Starting at about 6:15 p.m. on January 17, 1950 Pino's grand plan finally went into motion. Sandy Richardson picked up eight of the robbers at a string of locations from Dorchester to the

North End. The men were absolutely silent as they slipped on the peacoats, placed the masks, rolled up, on the top of their heads, and donned the chauffers' hats over the masks.

In a separate car, Vinnie Costa was traveling alone to Prince Street and parked. He hopped out, carrying binoculars, a flashlight, and a .45. He slipped into the building at 109 Prince Street and climbed the stairs to the roof to take his assigned position. Costa trained his binoculars on the second floor of the building. He could see that the vault door was wide open. He also saw the line of men in peacoats walking slowly into the building.

The robbers quickly slipped inside and closed the door behind them. They pulled the masks over their faces, climbed the stairs to the second floor, and opened the locked door into the Brink's suite. From his vantage point on the roof, Costa could see all seven men move into position outside the mesh fence of the vault room. That was a mistake – Pino's plan called for five men to cover the five Brink's employees while two stayed in the hallway.

Yet the Brink's men kept on working, unaware of the robbers standing just feet away. Someone, maybe Specky O'Keefe, finally spoke. "All right, boys, put them in the air."

The Brink's men slowly raised their arms. One man gasped, "Oh my God." Specs snapped, "Come on, come on. Get them up. It's a stickup. You, get over here and open up."

Brink's guard Charles Grell paused, his hand hovering above the gun in his holster. "Better not reach for it, mister," Specs said, as another guard cried out, "Take it easy. Let's not have any trouble." Grell slowly raised his hands. He glanced at Lloyd who nodded and said, "Do as he says." Grell walked to the gate and slid it open.

The robbers slid into the vault and filled their bags with packages of cash. Baker pulled a pry bar from his bag and began to work on the metal General Electric lockbox standing in the room. Each man filled a bag, then another, and another. The months of planning had come to this, a mad, chaotic scramble to grab all the cash they could. Every few minutes Richardson would grab one of the filled bags and run out of the vault room and through the corridors down to the door.

In the middle of the chaos, the buzzer at the front door went off.

The robbers paused. What the hell was that?

"It means somebody wants to come in," a Brink's employee said.

"What happens if nobody answers?"

"He might get suspicious and notify the police."

After a few moments, the garageman who rang the buzzer figured the men were too busy to respond and turned away from the door. But the robbers knew their time was running out. Gus and Jazz Maffie rushed back into the vault room and grabbed money bags for the last run before everyone huddled back at the Prince Street door.

Geagan carefully pushed it open. That was the signal. The Ford truck's idling motor came alive, and Costa, who had left the roof, revved his car. Bags crammed with Brink's swag were tossed into the back of the waiting truck. Geagan and Pino had a brief, violent exchange over the GE payroll box, which had been left behind. "I been dreaming of that box for years," Pino wailed. He was brushed aside by the others, who threw themselves into the truck. Getaway driver Joseph Banfield took off, tires squealing around the corner. In less than twenty minutes, Pino and his gang had made a mockery of the great Brink's security system.

The truck with the loot pulled up to a modest house in the Mission Hill neighborhood, the home of Jazz Maffie's parents. Maffie shooed his parents upstairs and the money was hauled inside. "You never saw people working faster in your life," Maffie recalled. Sacks of money were dumped out and one of the men threw bills in the air but soon they were quietly counting.

Of the $2.7 million in checks and cash stolen, there was more than $1 million in untraceable bills. The gang, after establishing various alibis - Pino "accidentally" bumped into a police officer - wandered back to the Maffie home. But no one wanted to take their share – the heat was still too great.

Even as typesetters in newspaper composing rooms were rolling out their biggest type to describe the heist, Pino was cursing the bad luck of choosing the night of January 17. Two million dollars was nothing compared to the $9 million and $10 million logged on other nights. In the end, the take per participant came to roughly $100,000, which they would collect over the next few days.

As a well known thief, Pino knew he might be hauled in for questioning. So he went to Filene's Department Store and boosted two pairs of jockey shorts. He wanted to be prepared for a strip search.

****

Brink's President John B. Allen arrived in Boston soon after to assess the situation. In announcing a $100,000 reward for the capture of the stick-up men, Allen said it was for the capture of the robbers, dead or alive, adding, "We'd rather have them dead." It was a sensational statement for a sensational case, but it ran up against public opinion: the daring bandits hadn't harmed anyone and the ill-prepared Brink's was just begging to be hit.

On Sunday night, during Ed Sullivan's popular TV show, The Toast of the Town, the audience roared when nine men clad in peacoats, hats, and Halloween masks joined the deadpan host onstage. "We want you to recommend a good strong bank for this money," one of the fake robbers said. A Boston café even offered a "Brink's special" cocktail: "It's one in a million (and a half)" the menu read.

Sipping their morning coffee, or nursing a whiskey after work, Bostonians were in fact whispering, "I hope they get away with it." As the years passed without an arrest, it look they actually might.

****

The Saga of Specs O'Keefe

For the next four years, even after Pino, O'Keefe and others, were publicly identified as suspects, Boston Police and the FBI were clearly frustrated. By 1954 they knew who was behind the Brink's job, but nothing could be proven in court. The bandits had not only succeeded in executing the heist, they had pulled off a second perfect act in the crime of the century; maintaining a code of silence that kept them free.

Pino had finally cleared up his immigration status. With the help of two lawyers, he fought his deportation all the way to the U.S. Supreme Court. The court ruled in his favor and he could stay. Had Pino been deported – had he set up shop in Italy with his money – his fate may have been quite different. But he was as devoted to Boston as he was to stealing.

Specks O'Keefe, on the other hand, was the most miserable of the gang. A few months after the heist, he and another bandit Stanley (Gus) Gusciora, hit the road. They traveled from Jefferson City, Missouri to St. Louis to Chicago, spending as much money as they wanted. A break-in at a gun store and a haberdashery in northern Pennsylvania, however, landed Specs and Gus in prison for three years.

Then, Specs started saying he'd been swindled out of his share of the loot. Before he left for the road trip he pocketed only $5,000 and left the rest - $93,000 – with Jazz Maffie, thinking he could trust the friendly bookie to hold it for a short time. When he got out of prison he went to see Maffie. Jazz broke down and gave him the news: O'Keefe's money was gone. Jazz had spent it on horses, dice games, and the numbers. His own $100,000 was gone too. He sobbed as he told the story begging for forgiveness.

O'Keefe thought about killing Jazz but he couldn't do it. Instead he demanded his full share minus the legal fees for his Pennsylvania case - $59,000. To get it, he decided on radical action. On the night of May 19, 1954, he trailed another Brink's bandit, Vincent Costa, jumped into his car, put a gun to his head, and told him to drive to an isolated tenement. The kidnapped Costa would be released for $25,000, he told Pino. Pino agreed on a $2,500 down payment. O'Keefe let Costa go the next day.

Pino was furious with O'Keefe. He had never liked the Irishman. He hadn't wanted Specs, a heavy drinker, on the job in the first place. The previously bloodless Brink's job was about to take a violent turn.

On the night of June 5, 1954, Specs was driving home alone when machine gun fire raked his vehicle. He was shaken and furious. The next day he confronted Pino who denied knowing anything about the incident.

Specs tried another approach. He called on Henry Baker, the expert safecracker of the gang, and told Baker he should chip in and pay his share of the Brink's loot. Baker responded by pulling his gun. Specs pulled out his. The former colleagues cursed at each other, then started shooting. They were lousy shots, hitting only nearby cars. When a cop ran over to investigate, they fled in opposite directions.

O'Keefe was a marked man. About 3:00 A.M. on June 16, 1954, he was walking near his apartment when he saw a car pull out and come toward him. He started to run just as machine-gun fire exploded around him. He ducked behind the hood of a car and fired back. Bullets smashed the walls around him. One hit his wristwatch, tearing it from his wrist and cutting his flesh. Another bullet hit him in the chest but it was deflected from his heart by a leather bound notebook he carried. Specs fired again, and ran leaping over a fence. He hid in the shadows as the neighborhood woke up and the police cars started to arrive. A stray bullet had gone through a wall and narrowly missed a sleeping girl.

Specs hightailed it to New Hampshire. When he called an underworld source the next day he was surprised to hear police actually made an arrest. The man arrested was well known to Specky and the Boston underworld, a cold-blooded, psychotic hit man known as Trigger Burke. New York Police alerted Boston Police that Burke, wanted in connection with at least six murders, was in their city provided photos of the slightly built killer. A day later a rookie cop recognized Burke in the Back Bay and took him in for questioning. A search of Burke's room on St. Botolph Street revealed an arsenal of weapons, including a submachine gun. Burke thought he had killed O'Keefe. He boasted that he was brought in for the murder, then denied it and refused to say who hired him. Investigators suspected Burke was called to Boston by Pino.

Trigger Burke would not have to stay in the Charles Street jail too long. Two months later on August 28, three men, including one dressed as a woman, helped him escape in a brazen daylight breakout. The man dressed as a woman was probably Pino, who by now was determined to get Specky.

For his part, Specky was in awful shape. He was stuck in jail in Springfield, Massachusetts. He was still hassling his fellow gang members for his full share of the loot. Worse, Trigger Burke was free, possibly coming for another whack at him. Two FBI agents John Kehoe and John Larkin started hearing stories that Specky was unhappy in Springfield. Technically, the federal statute had run out, but the FBI continued to investigate, hoping for a break before the state statute ran out in January 1956.

In December 1955 the agents, John Kehoe and John Larkin, visited Specky. They told him how Pino was building a new ranch house, Vinnie Costa was prospering in the automobile business, and Joe McGinnis seemed to be living fat too. The agents knew to turn the pressure on slowly; to ask Specky to rat went against the grain of O'Keefe's entire life.

But the feds needed something. The state statute of limitations ran out in a month and then the robbers might forever be out of the reach of the law. Soon, O'Keefe began to reveal details about the robbery, talking about his role in the case in the third person.

On January 6, O'Keefe finally came to a decision. "All right," he said. "What do you want to know?" In the days that followed, O'Keefe described the details of the crime to the agents, naming McGinnis and Pino as the planners and Baker, Maffie, Banfield (who had since died), Geagan, Costa, Richardson and Faherty as accomplices. On January 11, 1956, six days before the statute of limitations ran out, complaints against each of the robbers were issued.

The next day, six of the eight surviving robbers were arrested. Joseph Banfield had died and Sandy Richardson and Jimma Faherty eluded authorities for four months until they were nabbed in a Dorchester apartment. It would be thirteen years before any of them were out of prison.

The Fabulous Brink's Job

In Boston, the term Brink's has become synonymous with large wads of cash, the type of money that could make every dream come true. "Perhaps it was ingenious planning, perhaps the flawless execution or maybe the complete lack of violence. But whatever it was it seemed to produce a public reaction of almost envious admiration. 'Positively a beautiful job' people still

say. 'And no one got hurt,'" exulted the Globe scribe Jerome Sullivan in one of his anniversary stories.

And yet, as author Stephanie Schorow points out in her definitive account of the robbery *The Crime of the Century*, all of Sullivan's assertions are wrong. The planning was flawed (the robbers missed a potential windfall of $9 to $10 million) and the case was later marked by murders, shoot-outs and disappearances. It was a big robbery-a very big robbery-but still just a robbery.

Nonetheless, the Brink's caper will always engage the imagination. It is a crime saga, a comedy, a morality tale and a mystery wrapped into one.

It was a beautiful job.

CHAPTER EIGHT

RAYMOND PATRIARCA AND JERRY ANGIULO: DONS OF THE NEW ENGLAND MAFIA

DECEMBER 21, 1931. TESTA BUILDING, 317 HANOVER STREET, THE NORTH END.

GUSTIN GANG LEADER **Frankie Wallace** has been called to the office of Joseph Lombardo. Arriving with bodyguards **Barney (Dodo) Walsh** and **Timothy Coffey**, Wallace was there to settle a dispute over his gang's recent hijacking of a truck filled with $50,000 in liquor. He didn't know it but he had sealed his fate earlier that day when he ruled out any compromise with Lombardo's Italian mob.

Gustin was leader of the city's toughest gang, from the Irish stronghold of South Boston. He was there to run things not split up the pie. The Irishmen expected trouble – guns were loaded – but were still caught off guard.

As war veterans packed Christmas baskets for the poor children of the North End on the floor above, Wallace banged on the door to Lombardo's office. Seven mafiosi were behind it and when they started to fire, their guns roared for several seconds. Dodo Walsh tried to escape down the stairwell but was shot down and died on his face on the second floor landing. The other bodyguard, Coffey survived by hiding in an office down the hall, not coming out until police arrived to mop up the blood. Boss Frankie Wallace staggered down the hall to a law office and careened through the door, landing like a ragdoll on an office chair and toppling to the floor.

The audacious execution of the city's biggest Irish mobster on foreign turf at high noon meant Boston's underworld would stay segregated. The Mafia won because it didn't lose. There would be no one reigning Boston crime boss, and the fighting factions would retreat to their own neighborhoods where they would stay for decades.

After the Wallace murder, Lombardo disappeared for nine days. He then surrendered on his own terms - he knew the only evidence to put him at the scene was an Irish policeman who tried to sell Lombardo tickets to the policeman's ball two hours before the guns went off.

Questioned on his activities the day of the murders, the 36-year-old Lombardo apologized for his lack of cooperation – but firmly declined to answer. "I don't want you to think I'm sassy, Superintendent," he said, "but I'm not going to answer any questions." He never did, not one, and was released for good in March.

Lombardo worked with Phil Buccola to protect and expand the Mafia's footprint in the flagrantly Irish city of Boston. With criminal cunning and a willingness to kill, they never took a backward step.

Before the Wallace murder, the Boston Mafia had been the puny pushcart peddlers of organized crime – dwarfed by the Chicago and New York factions. However small, though, the Boston Mafia had been growing steadily in profits and reputation since the beginning of the century. (*Underboss* by Dick Lehr and Gerard O'Neill is the definitive account of the New England Mafia.)

In 1905, in the North End, on sidewalks leading to a labyrinth of brick tenements, Gaspare Messina founded the Boston faction of the Mafia. He ruled during the early years of Prohibition, hooking up with Frank Cucchiara and Paolo Pagnotta to form G. Messina & Co., a wholesale grocery business on Prince Street.

Messina symbolized the old guard of the Mafia's "Moustache Pete's" – immigrants who confined small time schemes to their own neighborhoods. In 1930, Messina was appointed to resolve a New York dispute that eventually became the Castellammarese War. Eager to end the bloodshed, Messina called a grand council meeting in Boston but his efforts were futile.

The bloody power struggle over control of the Mafia continued until 1932, when Messina's generation was largely wiped out by a more aggressive and more ambitious regime led by Charles (Lucky) Luciano. In Boston that meant Messina was out and Filipo "Phil" Buccola and his second-in-command, Joseph Lombardo, were in charge.

During the Depression era and World War II, the Mafia was able to expand slightly its loansharking and gambling network into other small pockets throughout the city, most prominently in East Boston, another former Irish stronghold that became an Italian neighborhood after World War I, and the neighboring city of Revere. In this time, the uneducated but stately Lombardo became a major figure in the mob, a consigliere and then an eminent elder statesman.

According to *Underboss*, Lombardo became an almost mystical figure, a man of respect who could settle the childish squabbles among his underlings over money and territory. Known as J.L., he had the bearing and manner of leadership, a combination of street toughness and old world gentility.

Lombardo's importing business was on the North End's main thoroughfare, historic Hanover Street. By the time of the Gustin Gang ambush, Hanover Street was a bustling, congested and dangerous section of town dominated by the violence of Prohibition. Gunfights were so common on this street of saloons and small businesses that it had become known as the "shooting gallery."

On these streets, Lombardo would run gambling and the satellite industry of loansharking for decades as second in command to Filippo Buccola until 1954. Small and lean, the group was able to prosper without the constant feuds and violence of New York and Chicago and Detroit. In other waterfront cities, the Mafia families had larger numbers, control of pier pilferage, and far less competition from rivals. In Boston, they would remain in their own neighborhood but the dark narrow streets of the North End would be an effective cover for organized crime.

The real power behind the Boston mafia, however, was found one state over in Rhode Island. There, an old school Mafia don with a combination of finesse and murderous strength ruled Boston's entire underworld from afar.

The Raymond Patriarca Story

Born on Plum Street in Worcester on St. Patrick's Day, 1908, the son of Eleuterio and Mary Jane Patriarca, Raymond Patriarca lived in Providence since 1911. His rise was similar to many of the Mafia dons of the same era; born in the United States to parents from hardscrabble villages in Sicily or southern Italy who left around the turn of the century for lack of food and work.

He would take his mother's maiden name as his alias in crime. Over the years, he would identify himself on occasion as John DeNubile, John Romma, Frank Bruno or Ellis Ronca. But as his power and reputation grew, he would be known in State Houses, bookie joints and police headquarters simply as Raymond.

A few months after his father's death Patriarca's criminal record began. His lifetime nemesis Col. Walter Stone of the Rhode Island State Police said that career began with a double cross. Hired to guard an illegal shipment of booze "he ended up hijacking the liquor he was supposed to be guarding," Stone said. He was arrested at Greenwich, Connecticut for violation of Prohibition laws and was fined $250 and sentenced to a month in jail.

On Dec. 30, 1930, after an arrest with his brother in a prostitution operation, he was sentenced to one year in federal prison. His criminal activities won him the title of "Public Enemy" in Rhode Island. In the same year he allegedly masterminded an escape and riot on Easter at the Rhode Island State Prison where a guard and trusty were killed by gunfire.

Soon he would be known across New England. In 1938 he was sentenced in Norfolk Superior Court to three to five years in state prison for the armed robbery of a Brookline jewelry firm. Four days before Christmas that year, during a week traditionally quiet at the State House, Patriarca was granted a pardon by the Governor's Council and hustled across the state line into Rhode Island. He had served only 84 days of a three to five year sentence. The ensuing scandal would reach the highest levels of state government.

Eventually it became clear that Governor's Councilor Daniel Coakley had handed the pardon to Gov. Charles Hurley and then used a parliamentary trick to push it through. Coakley was a notoriously corrupt figure in Boston politics who initially built his power by supporting and delivering votes for Honey Fitz, John F. Kennedy's grandfather. As a defense attorney he worked with two district attorney's offices to fix cases and blackmail prominent citizens. Despite a string of public scandals and the loss of his law license, Coakley was elected to the Governor's Council by a landslide.

Under his leadership, pardons were essentially for sale. In the petition for Patriarca's release, Coakley clipped eight years from the thirty-two year old Patriarca and forged the signatures of three priests – one of whom was completely fabricated. A letter sent to the governor endorsing the pardon and purportedly signed by Patriarca's victim was actually dictated by Coakley.

Coakley defended the pardon by telling reporters, "Some idiots think that because a man is arrested he is a criminal." A reporter reminded him that Patriarca had spent time in a federal prison and he replied: "Oh I wonder if that's so terrible?" The Patriarca case led to a legislative investigation that found money was the primary basis for procuring a pardon in Massachusetts.

Even as Patriarca's name was in the headlines daily – his marriage made front page news – he still appeared to be just another armed robber and three time loser. In fact, he was a rising star in the Mafia whose street smarts and toughness had made him a favorite among New York bosses – particularly in the Genovese and Profaci families. He was their "can do" man in New England.

In 1944, Patriarca was transferred to Phil Buccola's crew as heir apparent. The Boston and Providence mob factions had merged a decade earlier to create one New England crime family. The merger was engineered by Buccola and Frank Morelli, who headed a powerful gang that controlled bootlegging and gambling in Providence. (Morelli's gang is also suspected of being responsible for the 1920 payroll robbery and murders in Braintree, Massachusetts that were pinned on innocent Italian anarchists Nicola Sacco and Bartolomeo Vanzetti.)

By 1950 Patriarca had eclipsed Buccola. His trademark would be murder and political influence. Contributions and payoffs gave him access to governors, legislators and judges in Rhode Island and Massachusetts.

Patriarca would bring the New England Mafia to a place Buccola could never go and the axis of New England mob power would tilt toward Providence forever. There, Patriarca had advantages Buccola and other Boston mobsters never had – strong New York connections and a small, largely Italian city as his base. By the mid-1950s nothing east of the Connecticut River moved without an okay from "Raymond."

Safely in his office and off the front lines of crime, Patriarca became the classic Godfather, with nothing too minor for his consideration if it involved someone who would remember the favor when the time came.

For all his sinister looks and sullen attitude with cops and reporters, Patriarca had a deft sense of public relations. While he might duck the press he always had a smile and wave for neighbors on his nightly walk. Patriarca had the paradoxical personality of the most feared leaders: friendly but fatal. His smoothness made people forget how vicious he really was. His snap decisions on death contracts were one of the reasons he drove home alone each day at the same time without fear for his safety.

A Day in the Life of Raymond Patriarca

On a typical day Patriarca might arrive at his office on Atwells Avenue at 8:45 a.m. By 9:25 a.m., a visitor tells him about a Dorchester bookie who owes The Office $3,100. He wants Patriarca's advice. Patriarca says he does not want to get involved but the visitor should grab the number runner by the neck and get his money.

Five minutes later a second man comes in after the first leaves. He has been trying to line up someone for a "hit." He explains all the difficulties involved. "It's impossible to get this guy alone. He knows he is going to go, he just doesn't know when," the visitor says. "Providence is so small he'll stick out like a sore thumb though." Patriarca tells the man to use his own judgment.

On less criminal matters that other mobsters would have sneered at, people felt free to petition Patriarca. He regularly sorted out domestic and family disputes in his Providence office, patching up such things as a feud between brothers that was threatening to ruin their auto body shop.

Most days the parade into his office was a procession of faithful bearing tithes – cold cash for the middle drawer. He completely controlled some markets – especially gambling, loansharking and pornography, and dabbled in others such as truck hijacking and drug trafficking in which free lancers negotiated fees to do business. As a member of the ruling Mafia commission in New York, he also had some national investments, holding hidden interests in two Las Vegas casinos and pieces of deals in Florida and Philadelphia.

Patriarca's frequent contact with Genovese family leaders concerned jurisdictional matters, with New England divided along the Connecticut River. The Genovese family controlled such major cities as Hartford, Springfield and Albany, while Patriarca had most of Worcester and exclusive control in Boston, Revere and Maine.

The final obstacle to absolute power was eliminated with the shooting death in 1952 of the only real rival left – the tough and defiant Carlton O'Brien, a major bootlegging figure from the Prohibition days who didn't want to fall in line with Patriarca's new order. When he died of two shotgun blasts walking home one morning, Patriarca had an open field.

Patriarca had paid his dues. With the O'Brien murder he was at the top of a New England crime empire. The respect he earned came from the violence he used to get there.

Jerry Angiulo: The Mafia's Little Man in Charge

That wasn't the case with Jerry Angiulo – the Boston mob boss never even "made his bones." In an organization where entry requires prospective members to "get dirty" – to commit a murder – Angiulo bought his way into the Mafia. While both he and Patriarca shared the same background of poor immigrant parents from southern Italy, Angiulo was a pint sized gangster who would make it on smarts rather than strength.

After serving in the Navy in World War II where he won some battle awards for duty in the Pacific, he found his way quickly into the North End's gambling network. He drove a truck days and worked as a clerk in Joe Lombardo's horse room at night, taking bets and saving his money.

But his ambition got the best of him in the late 1940s. Some of Lombardo's money failed to turn up and Angiulo had to go on the lam for a while until his parents could make good on the debt. When all was forgiven and Angiulo could walk the streets of the North End without fear, he pledged never to be the sucker again. He immediately began devising schemes, using his knowledge of fixed horse races to stack a big bankroll. He graduated from the horse room to the job of runner for bookies in Roxbury and the North End.

In 1950, he would get his chance for the big time from an obscure U.S. senator from Tennessee. Estes Kefauver began seeking a national audience by taking on organized crime in televised hearings that year. It was the first hard look at the Mafia and it terrified Boston's old-timers such as Buccola and Lombardo. They overreacted to the announcement of Kefauver hearings in Boston – hearings that were scheduled but never took place. Lombardo ordered the gambling shut down and Buccola, at his wife's urging, retired to Sicily.

The Kefauver scare would prove to make the New England Mafia stronger. It pushed aside the old, tamer leadership, leaving Raymond Patriarca firmly at the helm and giving Angiulo the opportunity to take gambling in Boston from a petty cash game into the big time - he made gambling a full-time, streamlined business in Boston for the first time.

In 1950, after Lombardo ordered all Mafia and independent books to shut down, Angiulo went to him with a simple proposition: Let me run your books and take the fall if there's trouble. Lombardo gave him the nod. The Kefauver plague passed when the congressional hearings focused on bigger names in more established Mafia cities such as New York and Chicago, giving an inadvertent boost to Boston – and especially Angiulo.

Under Angiulo's rule, independent bookies viewed him as a scheming dictator always looking for ways to squeeze them for more money. The old regime's philosophy had been more hands off with the only harsh penalties being for cheating. Lombardo had been tough but fair, treating bookies with respect.

But in the post-Kefauver era, Angiulo moved quickly, picking up the business of some dropouts and slowly encroaching on Irish, Italian and Jewish independents. One of Angiulo's innovations was ingenious in its simplicity: He turned casual bettors into small-time bookies by offering them a quarter back on each dollar bet they placed, providing an incentive to collect and deliver bets to a central spot for reimbursement. Older Mafia leaders never really understood the intricacies of the numbers business, but Angiulo did. He figured out ways to monitor heavy betting on certain numbers and how best to lay off bets to avoid large payouts.

In addition to the numbers game, he ran two other betting operations. At night, he had a boiler-room type system in the North End that handled dog race betting, with about fifteen men taking bets on eight races at fifty cents a race. A similar operation ran during the day for horse races.

With the help of his brothers, Angiulo had about fifty office workers taking bets.

There was still one final hurdle for Angiulo, however – he didn't "have his button." Though he was at the top of Boston's gambling hierarchy, he was still considered "a freelancer" – not a made member of the Mafia. That made him fair game for one of Boston's toughest hoodlums.

Larry Zannino was Patriarca's favorite leg breaker. A hardnosed thug from the South End, he was the ultimate company man in the Boston mafia, reveling in what he saw as the codes and honor of the organization. Born on June 15, 1920, he was a member of a youth gang called Let's Go in his teens. Operating a "pay or die" loansharking ring earned him a four year prison stint a short time later; he was later convicted in the 1965 murder of a waiter he stabbed to death at a South End restaurant because the service was too slow. When he was released he earned his way up the ranks through a "can do" attitude toward murder and intimidation that impressed Patriarca.

Now, he was preying on the vulnerable Angiulo, shaking him down constantly, even roughing him up when he refused to pay. Angiulo's solution was to stuff $50,000 in cash in an envelope and bring it to Patriarca in Providence, promising him at least $100,000 a year for the right to run Boston – free of Zannino's strong arm tactics. It would be Angiulo's shrewdest deal yet. Zannino, would become his top enforcer and the pair would run Boston for two decades.

Although it is unclear when Angiulo became a made member of La Cosa Nostra, it was likely before he turned forty. In 1959, Angiulo joined Patriarca at a meeting in New York with Vito Genovese, the reigning strongman of the national Mafia, shortly before Genovese went off to jail for good. Decades later, Angiulo trembled at the memory of Genovese. "Right now I got a fucking knot in my stomach," he told a visitor.

By 1961, Angiulo had extensive investments in real estate, owned a small hospital in Boston, and had interests in two car dealerships in Lynn and a country club in Worcester County. He had two business addresses, adding his new lounge in Boston's Combat Zone district to the longstanding Prince Street office. He named the lounge Jay's after himself and used a basement room as an office for most of the 1960s. With Patriarca on his side and Zannino behind him, Angiulo moved strongly against the independent bookies, setting up a system in which Mafia enforcers were assigned to bookies, collecting half their profits as the price of letting them operate and, in turn, giving half to Angiulo who gave half to Patriarca.

About a year after Angiulo opened Jay's Lounge, the downstairs office was illegally bugged by the FBI, which was racing to get intelligence on the Mafia after denying its existence for decades. In 1963, the cocky street kid was publicly identified in congressional hearings as Patriarca's underboss.

The illegal bugs also revealed the vital role of political corruption in protecting the New England Mafia. Through bribes and favors, Patriarca influenced state legislation and won favorable treatment from courts for his soldiers. He was on a first name basis with high ranking Rhode Island officials, had fast access to a handful of judges in Rhode Island, Massachusetts, and New York, and dealt regularly with politicians on legislation and overtures to parole boards.

In Boston, Angiulo cultivated Boston police with the objective of protecting his gambling ring from raids that cost him money and manpower. Building on existing access to Boston police, Angiulo had strengthened the network of official corruption in a short time. Angiulo's police pad included a major in the state police and a high ranking Boston police official.

Angiulo used his power mostly to suck more money from those he deemed "suckers" – non-Mafia employees who took most of the risks and did the dirty work for the family. Angiulo's brutal leadership methods were the main reason that Boston became both bonanza and rat's nest. It made the most money per capita of Mafia cities, but it also had the highest number of informers. Single handedly, Angiulo had turned Boston into one of the most lucrative – and dangerous – places for the Mafia to operate in the country.

For much of the 1960s, he was in and out of trouble with Patriarca for making waves in the Boston gambling scene. He slapped an IRS agent with two bodyguards present and had to serve a month in jail for it – the first time he was incarcerated in a lifetime of hustling bets and numbers.

He had become Little Caesar, a short, scrappy thug who used his active mind as a weapon in a world of slow-witted brutes. But he was a poser who would glare at jurors and berate his lawyers. His rapid rise, based on his business skills, left him hopelessly insecure about his physical prowess in the ultimate macho world.

Yet he was on top of Boston's Mafia ranks by the 1960s with his gambling empire now firmly in place in the North End, West End, East Boston and parts of Roxbury and the South End. Independents in and around Boston paid rising contributions to get strong arm men off their backs and win access to Patriarca's monopoly over racing results and layoff banks. The Angiulo gambling network had also followed the exodus of

Italians to suburbs such as Medford, Watertown, Waltham and Newton.

Boston's Mafia had fought off Irish thugs just to survive in a city where they started off hopelessly outnumbered and outgunned. The 1950s and 60s, however, had been good to Angiulo and Patriarca as they secured power and expanded their interests. Now that they had a foothold, Angiulo was determined to get as much as he could.

CHAPTER NINE

THE KENNEDY'S: WHISKEY BARONS IN THE WHITE HOUSE

AS THE ITALIAN MAFIA rose in power across the country, a less organized but just as powerful underworld of Irish corruption was beginning to take shape. At the top of this hierarchy of politics and payoffs was an unlikely figure – a man celebrated as the patriarch of America's greatest political dynasty. Joe Kennedy may have led his family to the White House but the way he got there revealed his status as the Godfather of an entirely different kind of family.

"The flower may look different, but the roots are the same," was how mobster Sam Giancana once put it to his brother, describing how the Kennedys were operating within the same corrupt universe as the Mafia.

Joe Kennedy's overwhelming ambition to succeed frequently placed him outside the law. He stole elections, manipulated private financial markets and government agencies, and formed alliances with the most notorious killers and crime bosses in the country when it suited his interest. Even in the most elite circles, however, his unsavory reputation only increased his power.

Despite his days as a notorious stock fixer, President Franklin Delano Roosevelt tapped Kennedy to lead the newly formed Securities and Exchange Commission, a New Deal agency set up to reform and regulate the financial markets. Roosevelt was said to have explained the odd choice by repeating, with a laugh, an old saw – "It takes a thief to catch a thief."

Thomas G. Corcoran, one of Roosevelt's senior political advisers, depicted Joe Kennedy, with grudging admiration, as having staged a "remarkable coup d'etat" in putting his son Jack into the presidency. "You have to look at this piece of energy adapting itself to its time. A man not afraid to think in a daring way. He had imperial instinct. He knew what he wanted – money and status for his family. What other end is there but power?" Corcoran said. "These are not the attributes of the philosopher, the humanitarian, educators or priests. These are the attributes of those in command."

Papa Joe's willingness to cheat and steal would one day land his son in the White House, but it all began in Boston and its tradition of dirty ward politics. Joseph Patrick Kennedy was born on September 6, 1888. His father, Patrick Joseph "P.J." Kennedy was a ward boss from East Boston who rose to the state senate with the support of the Boston liquor lobby. After graduating from Harvard and becoming the youngest bank president in the country at age twenty-five, Joe Kennedy entered the political world himself.

Joe married Rose Fitzgerald in October 1914. With the vows, he entered into Boston political royalty – her father, John "Honey" Fitzgerald, was in the midst of a legendary career. Fitzgerald was the consummate Irish pol - he is still remembered fondly for his tireless campaigning and singing "Sweet Adeline" at political events. He was said to be the first politician to campaign by automobile: dramatically speeding across Boston, he preached his message at twenty-eight rallies on the last night of his successful 1905 campaign for mayor. But there was another side of Honey Fitz' two terms as mayor of Boston, one marked by sworn testimony of payoffs and cronyism. Like other big city politicians at the time Fitzgerald relied heavily on alcohol, prostitution, and violence to win elections.

In 1918, Joe Kennedy was part of Honey Fitz's last winning election, a victory over incumbent Massachusetts congressman Peter F. Tague. As a key strategist, Joe acquainted himself with the city's growing Italian immigrant population. In his old neighborhood of East Boston, Kennedy recruited and paid Italian thugs to intimidate potential Tague voters sending them into election precincts with instructions to use threats and physical violence. A few professional boxers were also hired. Kennedy achieved his goal; his father in law defeated the incumbent by a mere 238 votes.

But one year later, after a congressional investigation into the campaign, Fitzgerald was formally accused of voter fraud and his election was overturned. House investigators determined that at least one-third of the votes in East Boston were fraudulent. Other Fitzgerald votes were determined to have been cast by men who had been killed in combat or were still stationed overseas in World War I.

The investigators suspected Kennedy of playing a major organizational role in the fraud, including illicit campaign financing. Fitzgerald was unseated and ended his career in humiliation but, as would happen again, Joe Kennedy escaped the scandal unscathed.

Hollywood Dreams of Murder

In 1927, Joe Kennedy was out of the increasingly dangerous liquor business and looking for a new adventure. That year he took his fortune to Hollywood where his stint as a budding movie mogul spanned the end of the Silent Era and the beginning of the talkies. Gangsters were already calling the movie business "the new booze" and Kennedy was ready to exploit it for his own profit.

In Hollywood, Kennedy felt a freedom to indulge. Far away from Boston, he carried on affairs with movie starlets and a mob widow. He also met more openly with organized crime figures than he ever had during his bootlegging days, including Johnny Roselli, the underworld's main representative in the movie business. Years later, before a U.S. Senate Committee Roselli testified that Joe Kennedy had begun courting him almost as soon as he arrived in town.

Known as the underworld's Mister Smooth for his good looks and slick dress, Roselli was born in Italy and raised in East Boston, the same area where Kennedy's Irish immigrant grandfather had first settled and been a ward boss. He was still living in Boston in 1918 when young Joe Kennedy showered the neighborhood with money, hiring thugs on behalf of Honey Fitz.

By that time, Roselli was a skinny thug looking for an opportunity. By the age of seventeen, he'd been arrested twice for narcotics trafficking, once due to a sting operation involving an informant. After spending six months in jail, Roselli was released and the informant was found dead. When local police came looking for him, Roselli fled to Chicago where he landed a criminal's dream job as Al Capone's personal driver.

Kennedy used Roselli's influence with Hollywood trade unions to avoid costly strikes but he didn't need any help to make a dishonest buck. He made his most ethically questionable profits at Pathe, the newsreel company that had been around since the beginning of motion pictures. Kennedy plundered the stock there after being brought in as a special advisor. The insider deals he made at Pathe were corporate robbery that would be punishable by a jail sentence today.

In his biggest scheme, Kennedy arranged to pay himself eighty dollars a share, while the average stockholder received a dollar-fifty share. Since he acquired his stock at thirty dollars a share he more than doubled his investments and made a fortune. Stockholders felt swindled and filed suit but nothing came of it. One stockholder who lost her life savings to Kennedy in the scheme wrote to him: "This seems hardly Christian-like, fair, or just for a man of your character. I wish you would think of the poor working women who had so much faith in you as to give their money to your Pathe."

Kennedy learned to truly make a killing in the movie business he needed to control distribution by owning his own theater chain. In 1929, Kennedy's attempt to purchase the Pantages Theatre Chain was rejected by the company's owner Alexander Pantages, an illiterate Greek immigrant. The chain was the second biggest on the West Coast and its primary showcase was an elegant Art Deco movie palace at the corner of Hollywood and Vine. After several bullying maneuvers against Pantages failed, Kennedy resorted to a more sinister plan.

On the evening of August 9, seventeen-year-old Eunice Pringle, wearing a low cut red dress, went to Pantages' office inside his theater on South Hill Street in downtown Los Angeles. Several minutes later, she ran screaming into the lobby, collapsing into a man's arm and screaming, "There he is – the beast. Don't let him get at me." She pointed at Alexander Pantages. A cop arrived on the scene and she told him Pantages tried to rape her. "It's a lie," protested Pantages, who spoke little English.

The trial was a Hollywood sensation. The girl, Pringle, was described by one newspaper as "the sweetest seventeen since Clara Bow." Pantages, on the witness stand, broke into tears and repeated over and over in halting English, "I did not. I did not." He came off as a crude, paranoid foreigner. A jury found him guilty and he was sentenced to fifty years in prison.

Pantages appealed the verdict and a team of private investigators found evidence that Eunice Pringle was a professional con artist, and likely a prostitute. At a second trial, Pantages was acquitted but the scandal crippled his business. In November 1931, he finally cut his losses and sold to Joe Kennedy for less than half what Kennedy offered a few months before.

Two years after the acquittal, Eunice Pringle told her lawyer she wanted to tell the truth. Rumors began to circulate that she was ready to name names. Suddenly, she died of unknown causes. On her deathbed she confessed to her mother that men representing Joe Kennedy had paid her to set up Pantages. For her perjured testimony she and a boyfriend/agent were paid $10,000 with a promise that studio boss Joe Kennedy would make her a star. The night she died she showed signs of cyanide poisoning.

Whether or not Kennedy had Pringle killed to silence her, no one would ever know. For one thing no autopsy was conducted. It might seem farfetched that Kennedy would resort to murder but he had been leading a double life ever since he entered the public sphere. While the press promoted him as a business genius and family man, he was on a first name basis with some of the most ruthless gangsters alive. In *Paddy Whacked* author T.J. English provides a thorough account of Joe Kennedy's underworld deeds and he does not rule out the possibility of Kennedy ordering Pringle's death: "Blackmailing Alexander Pantages, a stubborn business competitor who refused to submit to his will, was not inconsistent with tactics Kennedy used throughout his life. The silencing of Eunice Pringle was, perhaps, a regrettable but unavoidable consequence."

Kennedy, gangster

The strongest evidence connecting Joe Kennedy to organized crime can be found in the Senate hearings chaired by Estes Kefauver, a Democrat of Tennessee. This was the government probe that caused Boston's old time Mafioso to close down business and retreat while opening the way for Raymond Patriarca and Gennaro Angiulo to rise in the ranks. The Kefauver hearings never made it to Boston, the committee's appearance was cancelled without explanation, but in their Miami hearings they learned indirectly of Kennedy ties to gangsters.

The hearings focused, in part, on the influx of gambling and racketeering in the Miami area in the 1940s. One of the most important front men in that era was Thomas J. Cassara, a mobbed up lawyer who owned hotels with organized crime families led by Al Capone's successors in Chicago and Frank Costello in New York. A few years later Cassara took over the leases of two more mob affiliated hotels, the Grand and the Wofford.

Daniel P. Sullivan, a former FBI agent who became operating director of the Crime Commission of Greater Miami, told Kefauver's committee that the area around the Cassara-operated hotels in Miami Beach "became nationally known as a meeting place probably for more nationally known racketeers and gangsters than any one local area in the United States."

Within three years of leaving Miami, according to testimony before the Kefauver Committee, Cassara was working full time for Joe Kennedy's Somerset Importers. Joseph Fusco, a former bootlegger and a strong-arm man for Al Capone in Chicago, testified before the Kefauver Committee in a closed door hearing and was asked, among other things, about his dealings with Cassara. Fusco didn't hesitate: "When he first came to Chicago, I think [it] was in 1944, he was working for Kennedy, the Somerset Import Company. He was their representative here...We knew Tom Cassara's working for Somerset in Chicago."

The reference to Kennedy's company was fleeting and, although the committee knew who Fusco was talking about, his name does not appear in any of the Kefauver transcripts. The important organized crime link to Kennedy's liquor business escaped public notice until discovered by investigative reporter Seymour Hersh for his book *The Dark Side of Camelot.* Hersh's reporting on Kennedy family ties to organized crime is the most fully researched and realized account of Kennedy and underworld ties.

Cassara was shot in the head, gangland style, in front of a mob-dominated Chicago nightspot in January 1946 and Joe Kennedy began negotiating his exit from the liquor business within months. Both men were soon out of the liquor industry; Cassara survived but moved to Los Angeles where he once again was a front man for mob families from New York and Chicago; Kennedy sold Somerset to a New York firm controlled by gangsters.

With that sale, Kennedy cut his last known tie to the liquor trade. His links to organized, crime, however, continued. In 1945 Kennedy bought the Merchandise Mart in Chicago, then the world's largest building and a center of organized crime in the Windy City. The Mart brought Kennedy directly into contact with the Outfit, the Chicago based mob crucial to the creation of Las Vegas, the plundering of the Teamsters Union pension fund and other major rackets.

Kennedy joined the long list of businessmen making monthly payoffs to the Outfit to keep the Mart in business. But the real payoff, as it always seemed to, went to Kennedy. Even at the price of 12.5 million, the Mart was considered to be a steal and valued at $75 million two decades later. It "became the basis for a whole new Kennedy fortune," said his wife Rose.

Joe rarely showed his face in the area and didn't need to. With control of the Mart, he was at the center of corruption in Chicago. Few businessmen had Kennedy's understanding of the intricate relationship between politics, unions, and organized crime that dominated major American cities after World War II. It was a nexus he would come to rely on in later years, especially in the 1960 presidential election, an election stolen, by Kennedy and the Mafia, from Richard Nixon.

How the Kennedy's Stole the 1960 Presidential Election

By the mid-1950s Joe Kennedy had virtually disappeared from public life. A millionaire many times over, Joe the Patriarch was content to stay in the background and pull the levers of power on behalf of his children, particularly sons John and Robert. John F. (Jack) Kennedy was the golden boy in the mid-1950s emerging as an attractive, well-spoken senator with serious potential as a national candidate. Robert, on the other hand, was trying to keep up. In late 1956, after Jack's name was briefly floated as a possible presidential candidate, Bobby jumped at the chance to work on a major senate investigation into organized crime led by Arkansas Senator John J. McClellan. As chief counsel, Bobby would be squaring off with the country's most notorious mobsters.

When Bobby told his father the news, Joe Kennedy was livid. According to Bobby's sister Jean Kennedy Smith, the argument that ensued at the family's annual Christmas gathering at Hyannis Port was bitter, "the worst one we ever witnessed."

Joe Kennedy's main argument against Bobby's mafia crusade was that it would turn organized labor against Senator John Kennedy, damaging his quest for the presidency. Ever since the death of his first son Joe Jr. – a fighter pilot whose plane blew up while transporting explosives during World War II – Papa Joe's greatest ambition was to see J.F.K. elected as the first Irish Catholic president of the United States.

Of course, Papa Joe had other reasons to keep his son away from an organized crime investigation. His own dirty little secret might be exposed: the fact that he had dealt with organized crime for nearly all his adult life and made millions through underworld alliances. He couldn't fully express that to Bobby however and he fumed.

Bobby held his ground. Even among family and friends he was known at times to be a "stubborn bastard." Although he had a more privileged upbringing than his father, he had served under and learned from Senator Joe McCarthy and his lead counsel Roy Cohn during their vicious and unethical pursuit of phantom communists and subversives. Bobby's decision to proceed as planned caused a rift between father and son that continued over the next two years as Joe increasingly made plans – sometimes with gangsters – for JFK's presidential run.

The McClellan Committee turned out to be one of the longest and most expensive senatorial investigations in history. Alongside the Kefauver hearings of nine years earlier, it was an early look at the inner workings of organized crime and featured an all-star cast. Most of the dominant Mafiosi in America were dragged before the committee, including Papa Joe's old pal from East Boston Johnny Roselli, Carlos Marcello of New Orleans, and Sam Giancana of Chicago. During his testimony, Giancana smirked at Bobby Kennedy from the witness stand and famously received this rebuke from the feisty young lawyer: "I thought only little girls giggled, Mr. Giancana."

Throughout the hearings, Bobby Kennedy badgered and ridiculed powerful gangsters in his shrill, Hyannis Port-by-way-of-Harvard manner of speech. One riveting encounter was between Kennedy and forty-nine-year-old Carlos Marcello, who oozed disdain as he invoked his Fifth Amendment privilege no less than sixty-six times and refused to tell the committee where he was born.

Bobby seemed determined to establish "the Mafia" and mobsters with Italian roots as the primary source of organized crime in America. To the mobsters he was grilling, he was the embodiment of the bullying Irish cop and his emphasis on the fraternal Italian nature of organized crime was an effort to shift the focus away from others (like his own father) who profited from the underworld.

After fifteen hundred witnesses, the McClellan Committee finally began to wind down in early 1959. Joe knew Bobby had ruffled feathers in the underworld but there was no time to waste in enlisting organized crime's help in J.F.K.'s presidential campaign. For decades, Joe had helped powerful criminal figures make money through bootlegging, stock scams and influence peddling. Now was the time to call in the favors.

In February 1960, Papa Kennedy reached out to his old friend, Johnny

Roselli and arranged for a sit-down with high ranking mobsters to discuss J.F.K.'s candidacy. The meeting took place at Felix Young's Restaurant in Manhattan. One of the people in attendance was attorney Mario Brod, who revealed the details of the powwow to historian Richard Mahoney; he said that many of the mob bosses Kennedy asked Roselli to invite failed to show up, however, a fair number did. Kennedy got right to the point; he asked for a large campaign contribution and, more importantly, for the mob's help in ensuring that organized labor support his son's campaign. A number of Mafioso at the table objected, reminding Papa Joe of Bobby's recent crusade. "The elder Kennedy replied that it was Jack who was running for president, not Bobby, and that this was business, not politics."

After making his case, Kennedy left the restaurant and the mobsters discussed Kennedy's overture. Most were suspicious, but Roselli reminded the men that Kennedy had come to them, which was significant, and asked his associates at least to consider the Kennedy alliance.

Joe Kennedy wasn't about to wait around for answers. Papa Joe had carefully studied Jack's prospects and identified two areas of concern: the West Virginia primary in May, which J.F.K. desperately needed to win, and the state of Illinois which would be crucial in the general election. In April 1960, Papa Joe invited entertainer Frank Sinatra to the Kennedy compound at Hyannis Port. Joe Kennedy knew Sinatra through his son-in-law, actor Peter Lawford, a Sinatra hanger-on. He also knew Sinatra had a close relationship with Sam Giancana, boss of the Outfit syndicate.

Giancana, born in 1908 and known as Mooney to those closest to him, began his criminal career as a hit man for Al Capone in the area known as Little Italy or The Patch, just west of downtown Chicago. By age twenty, Giancana had reportedly murdered dozens of men on his way to gaining control of the Chicago Mafia, known as the Outfit. A reporter who covered organized crime in Chicago for twenty years recalled Giancana's leadership style: "As a boss, if there was a problem, he'd listen to a very brief description and then say, 'Hit him! Hit him!' There were a lot of hits."

Through their man in Hollywood, Johnny Roselli, the Outfit had helped boost Frank Sinatra's career repeatedly. The singer was forever grateful and even closed his live shows by singing "My Kind of Town (Chicago Is)" as a tribute to Giancana. For decades, Sinatra remained mum about his initial meeting with Joe Kennedy, until 1997, when he authorized his daughter Tina Sinatra to give the following account:

"A meeting was called [between Joe and Frank]. Dad was more than willing to go. It was a private meeting. I remember it was over lunch... Dad was ushered in. He hadn't been to the house before. Over lunch Joe said, 'I believe you can help me in Virginia and Illinois with our friends. I can't approach them but you can.' It gave Dad pause...But it still wasn't anything that he felt he shouldn't do. So off to Sam Giancana he went. Dad calls Sam to make a golf game and told Sam of his belief and support of Jack Kennedy. And I believe that Sam felt the same way."

Once Sinatra broke the ice, Joe Kennedy took matters into his own hands. He asked circuit court judge William J. Tuohy, one of Kennedy's oldest friends in the city to arrange a meeting with Giancana. Tuohy did not know the gangster but a former protégé from his days as the State's Attorney of Cook County, Robert J. McDonnell, was then one of the mob's leading attorneys.

A meeting was arranged and the jittery Judge Tuohy invited McDonnell to attend. McDonnell entered the judge's chambers and was introduced to Joe Kennedy. After twenty minutes or so, McDonnell said, "we heard footsteps come into the courtroom, and in walked Mooney Giancana" and one of his associates.

Behind closed doors, Kennedy made certain assurances that despite his son Bobby's recent crusade, the election of J.F.K. would benefit the mob. Certain gangsters, including Carlos Marcello of New Orleans, facing legal and deportation problems would see those problems disappear. "Any administration led by the Kennedy family will be good for your people," Joe assured Giancana.

Considering the way Giancana had been ridiculed by Bobby Kennedy during the McClellan hearings, the mobster had every right to be skeptical. But he was apparently dazzled by the Irish patriarch; in later months, he was often heard bragging that he was "trying to get that Joe Kennedy's kid elected president."

Many people in Giancana's own organization told him he was crazy. Some mobsters flatly refused to help with Kennedy's election in any way, most notably Carlos Marcello, who later made a personal cash contribution of $500,000 to the campaign of Kennedy's opponent, Richard Nixon.

But Giancana had his reasons. Kennedy was dangling the prospect of an inside track on American political and business affairs unlike anything organized crime had ever experienced before. The two men were following underworld traditions: Kennedy, the Irishman, had infiltrated the mainstream before Giancana and the Italians, and was fulfilling his role as a hatcher of schemes from within the system. Giancana was following the tacit understanding that Italians would carry out criminal enterprises with help from the inside, whether it was a corrupt Irish cop, ward alderman or the president's father.

Meanwhile, J.F.K. was stumbling in the Democratic primary, failing to put away Senator Hubert H. Humphrey in Wisconsin. J.F.K.'s disappointing showing kept the hard working Humphrey alive. Kennedy still had to prove his electability in rural, non-Catholic regions of the country. West Virginia thus became the ultimate battleground for the Democratic nomination, and the Kennedys threw every resource they had, legal and illegal, at defeating Humphrey. At stake was not only Jack's presidency but Papa Joe's dream of a family dynasty: Bobby was to be his brother's successor.

Papa Joe called in his organized crime connections to keep that dream alive. In West Virginia, mob-controlled juke bosses began featuring J.F.K.'s campaign theme song, a reworded version of Sammy Cahn's current hit "High Hopes," sung by Sinatra. A Kennedy aide crossed the state, paying tavern owners twenty dollars each to play the song repeatedly.

Money began to flow. FBI wiretaps later disclosed that Sinatra and Giancana's close friend Paul "Skinny" D'Amato spent two weeks in the state dispensing $50,000 worth of campaign contributions to local politicians. The Kennedy's handled the bribes.

In October 1959, young Teddy Kennedy traveled across the state distributing about $275,000 in cash to the Democratic committeeman in each county. The Kennedy's didn't understand that local committeemen would take bribes but had little power to influence the process. The sheriff was the pivotal local figure to payoff, a local advisor told them.

There is evidence that Bobby Kennedy took over bribing the sheriffs in the hectic weeks before May 10 primary. Multiple West Virginia sheriffs have said in interviews they received payoffs of $5,000 to $40,000 to rally support for Kennedy, providing a pivotal advantage over Humphrey (who was also buying votes) as Kennedy won West Virginia and secured the nomination by August. Just as Papa Joe had predicted, the Nixon-Kennedy race for president would come down to the state of Illinois.

Joe Kennedy was close to getting his son into the White House and now he worked with Chicago Mayor Richard Daley and Giancana to finish the job. At the Ambassador East Hotel in downtown Chicago, over the course of three meetings, Kennedy, Daley and Giancana discussed strategy. It was agreed that certain key districts, including the First Ward, would be delivered on election day by large margins in favor of Kennedy. Mayor Daley, through the Chicago police department, would make sure there was no outside interference. On Election Day, November 8, 1960, everything fell into place. J.F.K. won by the slimmest margin in history, with corrupt Chicago districts proving to be the difference.

Losing candidate Richard Nixon learned a lesson he remembered in future campaigns: "From this point on I had the wisdom and wariness of someone who had been burned by the power of the Kennedys and their money and by the license they were given by the media. I vowed that I would never again enter an election at a disadvantage by being vulnerable to them – or anyone –on the level of political tactics." The lessons learned would lead Nixon to the presidency in 1968 and to the disgrace of a resignation, after the Watergate scandal, in August 1974.

For the winners, the election was a classic Machine-style effort. Irish and Italian criminal forces worked together as they had in so many city, county and state elections since the birth of the underworld. In fact, the 1960 presidential election was little different than the election fraud Joe Kennedy coordinated for his father-in-law, Honey Fitz, in East Boston in 1918, when he used Italian thugs to stuff ballot boxes and intimidate voters. This time, the stakes were much higher. Joe Kennedy had stolen the White House and he had made promises to powerful gangsters who had followed his every command. These were dangerous men and they expected Joe Kennedy to keep his word.

The Kennedy Double Cross

The first sign that the Irishman had lied came with J.F.K.'s naming of his attorney general. The appointment of brother Bobby at the insistence of Papa Joe did not sit well with the gangsters but it was necessary to protect J.F.K. Papa Joe was concerned that FBI Director J. Edgar Hoover might blackmail the President over an affair J.F.K. was carrying on with a woman named Judith Campbell, who was at the same time having an affair with Sam Giancana. Papa Joe believed Bobby's appointment would provide protection against internal government attacks on the President.

At his first press conference as attorney general, Bobby announced that dismantling organized crime would be the Justice Department's highest priority, and added that he had his brother's full support. Bobby Kennedy's war on organized crime was unprecedented. The number of attorneys in the Department's Organized Crime and Racketeering Section ballooned from seventeen to sixty-three; the number of illegal bugs and wiretaps grew from only a few to more than eight hundred nationwide; Bobby even drew up a hit list of mob targets – a list that included Johnny Roselli and Sam Giancana, the same men whom Papa Joe leaned on to get J.F.K. elected. To the gangsters, Bobby's anti-mob crusade seemed highly personal and inexplicable given his father's ties.

One of the most explosive acts undertaken by the Kennedy Administration against the underworld was the "kidnapping" of Carlos Marcello, the New Orleans crime boss and top name on Bobby's hit list. On April

4, 1961, under pressure from the Justice Department, Marcello was literally snatched off the streets of New Orleans by federal agents, put in an airplane, and dropped off in Guatemala.

Outraged and hysterical, Marcello snuck back into the United States two months later and filed suit against Attorney General Bobby Kennedy. Down in New Orleans, the volatile Marcello seethed and cursed the Kennedy name. When an associate made the mistake of bringing up Bobby Kennedy, Marcello exploded. "You know what they say in Sicily: If you want to kill a dog, you don't cut off the tail, you cut off the head." The Kennedys, explained Carlos, were like a mad dog; the president was the head and the attorney general was the tail. "That dog will keep biting you if you only cut off its tail. But if the dog's head is cut off, the dog will die –tail and all."

Marcello continued ranting and explained that the death of the attorney general would not solve anything, since his brother, the president, would go after Bobby's enemies with a vengeance. The president himself would have to go, and it would have to be done in such a way that it could not be directly linked to the organization. He said they should set up some nut to take the blame, "the way they do it in Sicily."

To Marcello, the Kennedy's were "Irish bastards" who represented the legitimate world but were as corrupt as any hoodlum. The insult of Bobby's war on organized crime struck at the core of the underworld's twisted code of honor. The mob had been used, manipulated, and played for a fool, and now they were being persecuted. It was a transgression punishable by death.

Death to Giovanni

Joe Kennedy was unable to react much to the events in Dallas on November, 22, 1963. Two years earlier, the patriarch had suffered a massive stroke that rendered him speechless and immobile. Confined to a wheelchair, the once powerful leader of the Kennedy clan retreated into his own private universe. When told of President Kennedy's assassination, he did not cry, although a family assistant claimed later to have seen remnants of tears on his cheeks.

For Carlos Marcello, November 22 was a good day. Almost simultaneously with the announcement that his nemesis had been shot down in Dallas, he was found not guilty in a New Orleans courtroom on conspiracy and perjury charges. Marcello embraced his attorney and hurried home to watch reports of the assassination on television.

Much of the credible evidence of a conspiracy to kill Kennedy leads back to New Orleans and organized crime. Respected criminal defense attorney Frank Ragano related a chilling snippet of conversation he had with his client, mobster Santo Trafficante, Carlos Marcello's closest associate in the underworld. "Carlos fucked up," Trafficante told his lawyer. "We shouldn't have gotten rid of Giovanni. We should have killed Bobby."

One person who was convinced that the Mafia had killed President Kennedy was Bobby Kennedy. Bobby, wracked with guilt, admitted his personal crusade against the Mafia had quite possibly boomeranged with horrible consequences. In the summer of 1967, he told a close friend that he believed his brother was killed by "the guy from New Orleans," meaning Carlos Marcello.

Bobby Kennedy had misjudged the volatile melding of ethnic and underworld forces. The Mafia had been dealing with characters like Joe Kennedy all along – legitimate citizens whose careers were enhanced by gangster alliances. Bobby, however, was from a new generation; either he didn't know the rules, or he was deliberately rebelling against what his father had done. It was a dangerous game and an insult that demanded vengeance.

The Kennedys and the Mafia were engaged in a high stakes game of American social climbing that could be traced back to the earliest maneuverings for power between Irish and Italian immigrants. Irish and Italian gangsters and politicians had been engaged in the same dance for decades as they battled for power on the waterfront and in the streets. The Kennedy hit was merely the loudest shot in an ongoing war.

CHAPTER TEN

JAMES "BUDDY" MCLEAN AND THE STORY OF THE IRISH GANG WAR

ON SEPTEMBER 2, 1961 a group of longshoremen, teamsters, hoodlums and their girls gathered for a party in Salisbury Beach, Massachusetts, a run-down seaside town. After hours of drinking, 22-year-old Georgie McLaughlin was staggering and starting trouble. McLaughlin wasn't an average drunk though; he was the youngest and wildest member of the McLaughlin Brothers gang, a Charlestown outfit that controlled the gambling and loan sharking business in Boston.

The McLaughlins forged strong connections with Italian organizations by carrying out contract murders for the Genovese Family in New York and the Angiulos in Boston. Business, however, was the furthest thing from Georgie's mind that day in Salisbury when he grabbed the breast of Ann Hickey, a woman at the party with her husband Bill, a grocery store employee, and his friend Red Lloyd, a roofer. (In Boston, retellings of the story always note that, to be fair, Ann did have extraordinary breasts). Bill pushed McLaughlin away and became furious, but on the advice of Red, let it go.

The drinking continued and the earlier incident resurfaced when Georgie mouthed off about Ann's amazing breasts. Bill pulled his fist back and punched Georgie in the face, followed by a few more blows for the disrespect of his wife. Georgie swung back wildly but couldn't land a single punch, angering him even more. Across the room, Red sighed and thought he better break it up before they busted up the cottage. He poured a glass of booze for Georgie and motioned for Bill to back off.

"Georgie, that's enough now."

Georgie grabbed the glass out of Red's hand and smashed it in his face. Red was far bigger than Georgie and when he pulled his fist back and landed a right hand into Georgie's nose, McLaughlin was down for good.

"Now what are we going to do?" Bill looked over at Red. Red decided Georgie, unconscious and covered with blood, needed a hospital. But as they drove, Georgie started to make gurgling noises and Red and Bill thought he might not survive. Not wanting to be on the hook for murder but trying to save their victim's life they compromised and left him off on the hospital's front lawn. McLaughlin survived with just a badly broken nose. His gangster brothers, however, wanted revenge – Irish revenge.

The McLaughlins traced their Irish ancestry to County Donegal, bandit country in the far north of Ireland. No one held a grudge quite like the Donegal Irish; they were tough, fearless and refused to back down. The beating of their brother Georgie was an insult to the local crime franchise the McLaughlins built along the docks and at the Charlestown Navy Yard.

So they went to see the gangsters who controlled Somerville, Red and Bill's hometown: James J. "Buddy" McLean, the unofficial Irish godfather of the north side of Boston, and Howard T. Winter. There was no more respected figure in the Boston underworld than McLean, the originator of the Winter Hill Gang. A racketeer and longshoremen, McLean earned his reputation as a tough guy in Somerville's Winter Hill neighborhood – a bustling, working class neighborhood that ran along the city's main thoroughfare, Broadway, and included plenty of dive bars and lounges. Years later then District Attorney John Kerry would call "Howie" Winter "The number two mob boss in New England," but for now he was McLean's most trusted associate.

For one week after the beating the McLaughlins had kept a low profile. According to *Citizen Somerville* by Bobby Martini and Elayne Keratsis, the definitive account of the Irish Gang War, Georgie McLaughlin's brother Bernie finally went to McLean's home and demanded Donegal-style payback. "I want 'em dead Buddy," Bernie McLaughlin screamed as Buddy opened his front door.

Red and Bill were from Somerville but they weren't even in the rackets. Buddy gave his visitor a long look, but did not ask him in. "Is that so?"

Bernie McLaughlin was fuming, red faced. "They gotta go, Buddy, those fuckin' bastards! This ain't right." He was shaking now waiting for Buddy to agree.

"Bernie," Buddy drawled as he leaned against the doorway, "your brother was way out of line. This is one I suggest you let go of, it's not worth it." He shut the door on Bernie.

Next, Bernie sought out McLean's right hand man, Winter. Bernie, his older brother Edward (Punchy) McLaughlin and another thug pulled up alongside Winter as he was walking down the street and invited him into their car. "I got in," Winter said, "but I had a feeling there was a good chance I'd never get out."

As Howie slid into the backseat, Punchy McLaughlin – considered to be the most reasonable and least crazed of the bunch – got to it. What did Howie think of the incident in Salisbury Beach? Howie demurred; he hadn't been there.

Bernie interrupted and pushed for the Somerville group to set up Red and Bill for murder. "We need your help to do this thing," Bernie growled. "You with us?"

Howie paused for a long second. "What did Buddy say?"

"What do you mean, what did Buddy say? I'm asking you now," Bernie said.

Howie carefully replied, "However Buddy feels is the way it is and I'm not going to go against what he's already told you."

"Get out," Bernie finally grumbled and Winter exited, thankful to be alive.

The next night Buddy's wife was watching television and heard their two dogs barking. She looked out the window and saw movement in the shadows. There were men in the driveway. When she screamed to Buddy he grabbed his luger from the closet and burst out of the house. He started firing at the men, one of whom he recognized as Bernie, as they rounded the corner and jumped into a car.

The next morning, a neighbor showed McLean wires hanging from the bottom of McLean's car. Underneath the hood he found a bomb made of plastique wired to the ignition. It was official, Buddy McLean and the Somerville boys were at war with the McLaughlins. The war they spawned – a war that began not over money or territory but over a lot of beers and a single breast – would last 15 years and claim at least 60 lives.

Buddy McLean: 'Face of an Angel But He Fought Like The Devil'

The life of James "Buddy" McLean is a classic rags to riches gangster saga. Born in 1929, he'd been orphaned at a young age and later adopted by immigrant Portuguese parents. By the seventh grade, he met Howie Winter and the two friends soon quit school to work full-time on the docks in Charlestown. Two years later, at age 14, they were both union members at the Teamsters Local 25.

In 1955, Buddy married a local Portuguese nurse, had four children and moved into a modest home on Snow Terrace in the Winter Hill section of Somerville. With a growing family he and Winter started a bookmaking business to supplement their incomes.

McLean was medium-sized with blond hair, boyish good looks, and piercing blue eyes. He was tough and had distinguished himself in many barroom fights. His reputation was that he could fight forever due to his daily run at the Tufts University track.

Despite his fearsome reputation he was well liked in the underworld and his crew spanned ethnic lines. Even Raymond Patriarca revered him. On an FBI wiretap he was caught calling McLean "a real sweet guy" and "a facilitator." With Winter, McLean made biweekly trips to the Federal Hill section of Providence to meet with Patriarca and discuss various deals.

The Winter Hill Gang, as led by McLean, dabbled in everything from numbers and loan sharking to truck hijackings and waterfront pilferage. The gang consisted of some of the most hardened old-school hoods in Somerville including Winter, a former cop turned gangster named Russell Nicholson, a veteran thief from Charlestown named Tommy Ballou, a two-bit thug named Alex "Bobo" Petricone and Joseph "Joe Mac" McDonald, a legendary strong-arm man whom Southie gangster Pat Nee called "probably the toughest guy that ever was. Joe Mac was one of those rare people who was fearless without being a psychopath. He was utterly without fear of anybody or anything or any situation, but he was also a very likable guy." The Winter Hill Gang gathered at a bar known as Tap Royal, at the Winter Hill Athletic Club, or at the 318 Club (later known as Pal Joey's), all on Broadway.

Buddy McLean was the acknowledged leader because he was a man of action. So on the day he found a bomb underneath his car he immediately began stalking Bernie McLaughlin. Then on Halloween day, McLean and two friends – later identified as Bobo Petricone and the corrupt cop Russell Nicholson – sped into City Square, Charlestown just before the noontime whistle.

The car screeched to a halt next to a parked tractor trailer as Bernie exited the Morning Glory Lounge. Buddy jumped out and emptied his gun into Bernie in front of almost one hundred witnesses. He ran back toward the tractor, slipped underneath and emerged to hop into the waiting car. The trio sped back across city lines as McLaughlin lay bleeding. One man even strolled up to the local bully, leaned over him and said, "Bernie you poor bastard, you're dying and the guy who did this should get a medal."

When McLean and his crew got back to Somerville, legendary cop Joe McCain caught a glimpse of Bobo Petricone's black Oldsmobile turning onto a side street in Winter Hill. Just a moment earlier a bulletin had come over the car radio that Bernie McLaughlin had been shot and three assailants had fled the scene in a black Oldsmobile with its trunk open to hide the license plate. McCain told his partner to follow the Oldsmobile saying, "I'll bet we find Bobo's car, and I bet they did Bernie."

Walking up the alley, McCain found Petricone's black Oldsmobile pulled off the street, the engine still warm and its trunk lid in the fully upright position, obscuring the license plate – matching the bulletin's description. Minutes later, backup arrived and McLean, Petricone and

Nicholson were arrested for Bernie McLaughlin's murder. But not one witness at the scene would offer evidence against McLean and he was sentenced to two years on a gun possession charge.

[Bobo Petricone eventually left Boston for Hollywood, changed his name to Alex Rocco and made a career for himself playing tough guys and heavies in the movies, most notably as Moe Greene in The Godfather. When he returned to Boston in 1972 to play a bank robber in the prototypical Boston crime drama The Friends of Eddie Coyle he introduced actor Robert Mitchum to Winter Hill Gang members.]

The very week McLean was released from the penitentiary, Georgie McLaughlin shot and killed a man he heard saying nice things about Buddy at a party in Roxbury. Only Georgie shot the wrong man. When he heard the comment, he left to get a gun, returned, and wrongfully shot Billy Sheridan, an innocent bank teller.

Now the murders came fast and furious. On May 3, 1964, ex-con Frank Benjamin was running his mouth about how he was going to take out the whole Winter Hill Gang, starting with McLean. A gunman loyal to Winter Hill shot him in the head. The killer severed Benjamin's head and wanted to put it on Punchy McLaughlin's doorstep but he decided against it. The next day, Benjamin's body was found in the trunk of a stolen car in South Boston. His head was buried in the woods.

A week later the Charlestown side struck back, killing Russell Nicholson, the six-foot four ex-cop whose gambling and drinking habits got him involved with the Winter Hill Gang. One month later, McLean would get his revenge and the infamous saga of Dottie from Dorchester, the Irish gang war's leading lady, would begin.

Dorothy Barchard was Boston's most infamous gun moll in the 1950s and 60s. Romantically linked to some of the city's best known hoods, Dottie had one foot (and one boyfriend) on each side of the war. In August 1964, she was hosting McLaughlin associates Harold Hannon, a vicious killer, and Wilfred Delaney, his trusted underling. Suddenly Dottie announced she had to leave and told the two men to make themselves at home. Later, there was a knock at the door – it was Buddy McLean, with a deadly grin on his face and a gun in his hand.

Out of respect for Dottie he didn't shoot the men on her doorstep. Instead, he held a blowtorch to their genitals, strangled them both, wrapped them in rugs and dumped the bodies in Boston Harbor. "If this war lasts much longer, maybe we should think about getting' into the rug business," McLean said to a laughing gang member as they rolled the dead men up.

The next time Dottie entered the war though, McLean would be the target. Ron Dermody was a bank robber from Cambridge head over heels in love with Dottie. In the 1950s he was arrested with a young career criminal from Southie named Jimmy (Whitey) Bulger. By 1964, he was fresh out of prison and pining for Dottie who was seeing another hoodlum.

When Dermody bumped into Georgie McLaughlin, McLaughlin suggested a deal: if Dermody could get close enough to McLean to shoot him, then a McLaughlin gang member would eliminate Dermody's romantic rival.

On September 2, Dermody stormed into the Capitol Café on Broadway in Winter Hill and gunned down a man he thought was Buddy McLean. It wasn't, he had shot a petty thief named Charlie Robinson. Even worse, as he fled, he was identified by people connected to Buddy McLean. Soon, he was being tracked by Winter Hill gunmen.

Dermody was frantic. Eventually he decided he had to call one person he figured had to be straight – Agent H. Paul Rico of the FBI. Rico, who lived in Belmont, gave Dermody directions to a secluded suburban street. He told Dermody: Come alone, unarmed. Don't tell anyone where you're going. I'll meet you there just after dark.

Then Rico called McLean. He told him that the guy who'd just tried to shoot him, would be waiting, by himself, unarmed. An hour later, Dermody was shot to death in his car. Buddy McLean soon vanished, waiting for the heat to die down. His hideout was the Belmont basement of his getaway driver, Agent Rico.

By 1965, the feeling among the Winter Hill Gang was that if they could eliminate Punchy McLaughlin and his unquenchable Irish thirst for revenge, maybe the war would end. Buddy McLean turned to a hit team of Cadillac Frank Salemme and Stevie Flemmi. An old-time Roxbury hoodlum named Earl Smith arranged to meet Punchy in a hospital parking lot by mentioning the possibility of an easy payday.

Punchy trusted Smith. He was waiting in his car when suddenly he saw two men dressed as Hasidic rabbis walking rapidly toward him. It was the hit team of Salemme and Flemmi, one armed with a revolver, the other with a shotgun. A blast from the shotgun shattered Bernie's jaw, but they couldn't finish him off and he survived.

The Italians finally had enough. New England Mafia boss Raymond Patriarca was overheard on an FBI wiretap that he was prepared to implement "martial law" if the killing continued. Nobody was making money amidst the carnage. A summit was called at the Ebb Tide in Revere Beach.

Both Winter Hill and the McLaughlins were expected for the meeting, at which Patriarca's top diplomat, Henry Tameleo would try and mediate the dispute. There was only one condition: no guns.

The Somerville crew arrived first, unarmed. A few minutes later, the McLaughlins arrived, carrying their guns in paper bags. Tameleo started screaming and threw them out. From that moment on the entire Boston underworld was against the McLaughlins.

That included H. Paul Rico, the dirty FBI agent who had already helped McLean kill Dermody. Rico was obsessed with taking down the McLaughlins. J. Edgar Hoover had directed his agents to install illegal wiretaps everywhere hoodlums did business. Rico put a wire on a phone in some McLaughlin hangout and heard Punchy McLaughlin give his sneering assessment of Rico's role in Hoover's FBI.

In his testimony before Congress years later, Frank Salemme recounted for a congressional committee what Rico had once told him about the conversation between the McLaughlins. "They were always on the phone, according to him, and...the feds would pick up the McLaughlins [and their top enforcers] the Hughes brothers, casting aspersions on Paul's manhood and his relationship with J. Edgar Hoover, and J. Edgar Hoover was, excuse me again, a fag, and that Paul used to go down there and have a relationship with Colson. They had a ménage a trois with a guy by the name of Colson, I think –"

The prosecutor interrupted: "I believe the name was Tolson," a reference to Hoover's top deputy, Clyde Tolson. Rico often hung out at Salemme and Flemmi's garage in Roxbury railing against the McLaughlins. He swore that if he ever got the right opportunity he would shoot any of them in cold blood.

And by March 1965 the FBI was closing in on Georgie McLaughlin. Rico showed up at the garage and said he needed a throwdown – an untraceable handgun. Flemmi asked why. Rico smiled and said, "Because we know where Georgie is, and when we bust in, we're going to shoot him, but we need a throwdown that we can say he drew on us first." Rico picked up the gun an hour later.

The next day, Georgie was finally captured, alive, hiding in a Mattapan apartment with another gang member, Spike O'Toole (O'Toole later fathered two children by Dottie from Dorchester). The papers said Georgie had been traveling the country as a woman, in drag, "with tight slacks, kerchiefs and the ever present lipstick and makeup."

Flemmi asked Rico why his gang of G-men hadn't killed Georgie McLaughlin. Rico shook his head sadly and said that four of the five agents were on board with the plan but they weren't sure about one guy, so they decided not to take a chance. Georgie was indicted for murder and the McLaughlin gang was down to three soldiers: Punchy and the two Hughes brothers, Steve and Connie.

After a second bungled attempt on Punchy's life - he lost a hand but survived as Stevie Flemmi sprayed gunfire from the top of a tree – Agent Rico showed up at the garage and approached Salemme. In his testimony before congressional investigators, Salemme recalled how Rico referenced the botched hit: "Paul was a very shrewd individual…he'd have the papers and say, 'Boy, what a sloppy piece of work that was, other people could have got hurt.'"

"The problem," said Salemme, "is that we don't know where he's been hiding out; we don't know his address."

Two days later, Agent Rico returned to the garage. Salemme said, "He'd just be patting my shoulder like he usually does, and he hit my hand… he kept walking, and [I saw] there was a piece of paper with an address, and I didn't have to ask anymore. I knew who it was. It was Helen Kronis, Punchy's girlfriend. So I went out and started to work on that."

Meanwhile, Punchy was depressed. He couldn't believe how many had been killed in this feud. "All this," he told a fellow hoodlum, "over a broad." On October 20, 1965, Punchy was boarding a bus for his brother Georgie's trial for the murder of the bank teller. Suddenly, two men in suits approached on foot, drew guns, and began firing at him. Stevie Flemmi was wearing a wig and makeup and carrying a .38-caliber, long barreled handgun. Punchy was shot nine times, twice in the genitals and once in the face.

That day, Agent Rico conveniently took the day off to play a round of golf. The next morning he showed up back at the garage. "Nice shooting," he told Flemmi and Salemme.

Ten days later, Buddy McLean was with two bodyguards, including an ex-boxer, in the back room of Pal Joey's on Marshall Street off Broadway. The men exited the bar and walked across Broadway toward Buddy's car until they were standing in front of the shuttered Capitol Theater. Charlestown gangster Steve Hughes stepped from the shadows, raised an automatic rifle, and fired at Buddy McLean, hitting him in the head. McLean's bodyguards were hit but survived. McLean did not. He was dead at 36.

Howie Winter was now the undisputed leader of the Winter Hill Gang. Winter had a reputation as a negotiator and it was hoped he could broker peace. But the Charlestown boys viewed any type of agreement as a sign of backing down and took pride in the fact they had no "boss" and acted as equal members of the clan. Although they had been reduced to two primary members, after two McLaughlins were killed and Georgie was sent to prison for life, they were the most feared killers in the crew:

the Hughes brothers, Connie and Steve.

The Winter Hill Gang's hit men feared and respected the Hughes brothers. Cadillac Frank Salemme called them "very capable, very dangerous guys." He and Stevie Flemmi stalked the brothers for ten months. In March 1966, the Hugheses were ambushed outside Steve Hughes home in Malden. Just before shots rang out, a male voice screamed: "How do you like that, you motherfuckers?" Connie ran, but Steve was hit and hospitalized for a month. After the shooting, they never appeared publicly together; they would have to be taken out separately.

On May 24, 1966, Connie Hughes was hunting Howie Winter. He took his investigation to a bar on the Charlestown-Somerville line where he stayed for hours drinking. He was spotted by a young thug named Brian Halloran, who quickly called Winter Hill Gang members. By the time Connie Hughes stumbled out of the bar long after last call, a dark sedan picked up his trail. When the car pulled up alongside Hughes, a gunner opened up with an M-1 Army rifle and killed Hughes with two shots.

Four months later Steve Hughes was driving on the highway when a black Lincoln with four people inside pulled alongside him and fired shots at Hughes and a passenger killing both men. The legendary Charlestown crew had been wiped out.

From the day Georgie McLaughlin grabbed the wrong breast at a Labor Day beach party in 1961 to the murders of the Hughes brothers in 1966, the killing in Boston's underworld had not stopped. Ironically, the three men who started the war in a Salisbury Beach cottage survived. Georgie McLaughlin is still alive today in the Massachusetts State Prison system serving a life sentence. Bill Hickey and Red Lloyd, the hapless drinkers who beat Georgie up and started a

war, both left town almost immediately after the brawl. Hickey headed for Texas and Lloyd moved to Cape Cod.

The years of terrifying gang violence they left behind had nothing to do with commerce or territory or ethnic rivalry and everything to do with the concept of revenge in a brutal, inbred, Irish underworld. A deep sense of grievance had left dozens dead but now that the instigators on both sides were almost entirely gone - dead or in prison - the underworld hoped the killings would stop. They did not.

Irish Gang War Part II: A South Boston Story

By 1968, the United States may have been going through rapid changes but in South Boston the old guard was still in control and that meant the Killeen brothers. The Killeen gang was led by three brothers: Donald, Kenneth and Edward. Donald was the boss.

Born in 1924, Donald Killeen was an old school racket boss with most of his profits coming from bookmaking and gambling. His Southie crime roots went all the way back to the Gustin Gang and almost all the old school crooks in the neighborhood were affiliated with the Killeens. They also boasted two younger gunmen – Billy O'Sullivan, better known as Billy O, and James "Whitey" Bulger.

Bulger and O'Sullivan may have been young for the Killeens but they were still in their 40s – ancient compared to a new generation of Southie gangsters rising along the waterfront. No one knows for sure the exact origins of the Mullen Gang. What is known is the gang got its name from an intersection in South Boston at the corner of East Second and O streets that commemorated a war veteran by the name of John Joseph Mullen. The gang adopted the name in the 1940s and took a place in Southie's gang world next to groups such as the Saints, the Red Wings, the Shamrocks and others, some of which dated back to the 1920s.

By the early 1960s the Mullens had supplanted them all, winning legendary street fights and full scale battles where they were outnumbered but came away victorious. They were also developing as thieves. Mullen gang members Paulie McGonagle, Pat Nee and Buddy Roache were skilled stick up artists, B & E men, bank robbers, safecrackers, and hijackers. They usually fenced their stolen goods to Howie Winter in Somerville. There were other Mullens too, including one who would be elected president of the Boston City Council.

As the Mullens rose in Southie's underworld, the Killeens were looking vulnerable. Holed up in the Transit Café, appearing sometimes on West Broadway, bleary-eyed with beer bellies hanging over their belts, the Killeens were an aging bunch of hoods at a time in the U.S. when old timers were being pushed aside. By the summer of 1969, Mullens such as Pat Nee were newly home from Vietnam and the Killeens did not instill as much fear as they once did. The rivalry might have simmered quietly if not for a vicious barroom fight that mixed blood and bruised egos – similar to how the McLaughlin and Winter Hill war started eight years earlier.

In July 1969, one of the Mullens, Mickey Dwyer, was outside the Transit Café. Donald Killeen's brother Kenny stumbled out of the barroom, and Dwyer jumped him. In the ensuing struggle, Kenny Killeen bit off Dwyer's nose. The maimed Mullen ran screaming toward the Broadway train station as Killeen spat out his nose into the West Broadway gutter and then went back into the Transit Café for a celebratory round.

When Donald Killeen arrived he was told what happened and asked one question: What happened to the nose? When none of his crew seemed to know, he ordered them outside to find it, which they eventually did, covered with dirt and grime in the gutter. When they brought it inside, Donald Killeen asked the bartender to wash it off in the bar sink. Then Killeen filled a cooler with ice, wrapped the nose in s couple of cocktail napkins and tossed it in the cooler. Finally Killeen called a cab and told him to take the cooler to Boston City Hospital, hand it to somebody, and say that "Mickey's nose" was inside.

After the Killeens left the bar, Mullen gang members showed up looking for trouble. They didn't find any Killeens but they proved they would stand up to the neighborhood's established organized crime family. In Southie that meant the Killeens had to respond or risk losing face in the streets. Boston's Irish gang war was about to metastasize like a cancer.

After the nose biting incident, Mullen gang member Buddy Roache arranged a sit down at the Colonial Lounge on West Broadway with the Killeen's most dangerous gunmen Billy O and Whitey Bulger. Billy O was thin with steel blue eyes, he was famous in local barrooms for his wit and charm. "But he was also mean and volatile; he'd shoot you in the eye for a perceived insult," said Pat Nee. Bulger was notorious too – he had spent years incarcerated at the infamous Alcatraz Prison.

Roache informed Billy O and Whitey that Donald Killeen was finished and that if they didn't switch sides they would be too. A heated argument ensued and Billy O pulled out a .22 and shot Roache in the left shoulder. The bullet exited near his spine and Buddy Roache never walked again. The Killeens, probably Billy O and Whitey, claimed another victim when they killed Donnie McGonagle, brother of Mullen gang leader Paulie McGonagle. Donnie

was killed mistakenly by Billy O who mistook him for Paulie. "I'm sure he didn't shed a goddamn tear over his mistake," Nee said.

In March 1971, Billy O was walking toward his home on Savin Hill Avenue in Dorchester after a night of drinks. He staggered slightly and whistled. Meanwhile, Paulie McGonagle had been sitting in the shrubs around Billy O's home dressed entirely in black and wearing a black ski mask. Billy O walked by the shrubs. Paulie McGonagle jumped up and stuck his .45 at the middle of Billy's back. Billy O spun around and gasped, "Oh shit I'm dead."

"You're right," Paulie McGonagle growled and fired four times.

By eliminating Billy O, the Killeens most feared killer, the Mullens took control of the war. Next, they didn't even have to kill Kenny Killeen: a Mullen sniper narrowly missed his head when he bent to pick up his morning newspaper outside his home. Frightened, he didn't come back outside for months afterward.

Whitey monitored all of this and decided to make a move. His old partner, Billy O, had been murdered but he died with an uncollected favor by notorious Boston hit man John Martorano. Six years earlier Martorano killed ex-boxer Tony Veranis on opening night of Billy O's new after hours nightclub. The murder ruined business and meant Martorano owed Billy O a favor. Now, Whitey was in Chandler's, a Columbus Avenue club owned by Martorano and Howie Winter. Martorano saw Bulger approaching and vaguely recognized the 40-year old gangster.

"You may not remember me Johnny. I'm Jimmy Bulger. Billy O told me to come see you if I ever had a problem."

"Any friend of Billy's is a friend of mine," Johnny said and invited him to sit down and have a drink. In Hitman by Howie Carr, Martorano remembered the meeting this way:

"Whitey looked like a gangster-politician in that suit. He says he wants to meet with Howie Winter. He says, I have to get this thing in the Town resolved. That was what they all called Southie – "the Town." He showed respect. He knew how to ask for a favor. You knew he wasn't going to see the Mafia because if Jerry Angiulo intervened he'd want to take over everything. I hadn't really been following what was going on over there in Southie, none of us had. But Whitey must have thought things weren't going well, or he wouldn't have reached out to me, to set up a meeting for him with Howie."

With an introduction from a dead man, Whitey was about to make the first in a string of shrewd moves that would shift control of Boston's underworld toward him for two decades. He and Winter would form the nucleus of the Winter Hill Gang's second generation but first he needed Winter to broker a deal for him with the Mullens. Winter was the Mullens biggest fence and they could be expected to follow his lead if a meeting was arranged.

Howie agreed to arrange the sit down but Whitey wasn't taking any chances. He asked East Boston mobster J.R. (Joe) Russo to go with him to Chandler's Restaurant. Russo spoke for Whitey who was alone at the meeting. Winter spoke for the Mullens, represented by Nee, Jimmy (Weasel) Mantville and Tommy King.

"[Howie] told them, he'd just been through one of these wars, and it made no sense. Everybody'd be better off if it got settled," Martorano said. "At the end of the night I guess they had a deal." Mullen gang member Pat Nee said "everything was split right down the middle. All the horses, dogs, bookmaking, and loan sharking [in Southie] were now going to be under our mutual control."

Whitey had figured out a way to end the war now that he had a deal in place with the Mullens. He would double cross his boss Donald Killeen. May 13, 1972 was a Saturday and Killeen was at his home celebrating his son Greg's fourth birthday. At some point during the celebration, Donald got a call. After hanging up the phone, he told his wife and father-in-law that he needed to run an errand and he would be right back.

A few minutes later, Killeen's five-year-old daughter asked her mother, "Why is daddy shooting off fireworks out by his car?" Donald Killeen's wife and father-in-law rushed out and found him slumped in the front seat of his car, riddled with bullets and bleeding like a sieve. By the time police arrived Donald Killeen was dead at age forty-eight. The next day, at the funeral home, a large bouquet arrived for Donald Killeen from a florist. The card read, "Au Revoir."

One week later, Kenny Killeen was walking in South Boston when a voice called out, "Hey Kenny." Kenny Killeen turned to see the face of Whitey Bulger pop out the passenger side window; he was holding a gun. "It's over," said Whitey. "You're out of business. No future warnings." The car drove off.

With the Killeens virtually wiped out, Boston's gang war was finally over and Bulger's role in it became the stuff of legend. It was the beginning of a period in which the Southie gangster would be linked to just about everything that took place in the city's underworld. By the time the full story of Whitey Bulger's life and times had been recorded, he would hold a special place in Boston's gangland as the city's most revered and vilified mobster of all time.

Corrupt FBI agents backed him all the way.

CHAPTER ELEVEN

THE FBI IN BOSTON: HOOVER, LIES AND MURDER

IN 1960, WHEN Bobby Kennedy launched his historic crackdown on organized crime he had to overcome resistance from the FBI and its director J. Edgar Hoover. For decades, Hoover had vehemently denied the existence of a national network of gangsters.

Privately, he knew that organized crime investigations made for bad statistics – lots of man hours resulting in a relatively small number of arrests. He also knew that mixing wealthy gangsters with underpaid agents – the FBI starting annual salary in the mid-1950s was a pitiful $5,500 – could undermine his FBI's cherished reputation of incorruptibility.

But the Kennedy brothers would not let up. They had pressured Hoover to fight the Italian mob since John F. Kennedy was senator. Now that he was president and named Bobby his attorney general the campaign intensified.

The Kennedy's hated one Mafia don with a particular zeal; Raymond Patriarca had taunted the brothers during congressional hearings, saying, "You two don't have the brains of your retarded sister." Soon after, Bobby Kennedy told a friend that he and Jack were "going after that pig on the hill," referring to the mob boss' Federal Hill stronghold. The brothers increased the pressure on Hoover – even bursting into his office with information requests during his sacred afternoon naps.

Hoover finally acted. He adapted the dirty tricks he used against suspected Communists in the 1950s – illegal wiretapping, bugging, break-ins, and searches - against organized crime. When that proved troublesome Hoover fired off a memo to all regional offices in September 1963, demanding the recruitment of high-level informants from within organized crime. It was called the Top Echelon Informant Program.

The organized criminal enterprise that dominated Boston for decades - and later included James "Whitey" Bulger - was conceived in this Hoover memo. Decades later, as victim's remains were being dug up from shallow graves, the full toll of the FBI's misconduct in Boston's underworld finally came to light. Almost 50 murders would be attributed to the FBI's star informants and four innocent men framed by a killer FBI agent for a murder they did not commit.

In the Boston underworld FBI Agent H. Paul Rico was the bureau's main representative. Born in the Boston suburb of Belmont in the 1920s, he was the son of an Irish mother and Spanish father who worked for New England Telephone. The Mediterranean looks he inherited sometimes led people to believe he was Italian, an assumption he used to his advantage when trying to gain favor with wiseguys. He graduated from Boston College with a history degree in 1950, then joined the FBI. He was first posted in Chicago but was transferred to the Boston office after his father fell terminally ill.

That was when the young agent worked on the Brink's robbery, his first big case and learned the value of "flipping" or "turning" an informant. Rico worked with agent Jack Kehoe – the agent who got Specs O'Keefe to cooperate with authorities and testify against his former co-conspirators. He also worked with future partner Dennis Condon. In time these two agents would manipulate Boston's underworld as if they were the kingpins.

The Flemmi Brothers: 'A Couple of Bad Kids'

Vincent "Jimmy the Bear" Flemmi and his brother Stephen "The Rifleman" Flemmi were introduced to the Boston underworld by notorious kingpin Edward "Wimpy" Bennett. Bennett, who earned his nickname by endlessly munching on White Castle hamburgers, was a treacherous Irish thug who controlled Roxbury and the South End with a cunning attention to underworld politics. Stevie Flemmi, in particular, was said to have learned his devious ways from Wimpy.

"Behind his back everyone called [Wimpy] the fox," infamous Boston hitman John Martorano told journalist Howie Carr. "He always talked with his hand to his mouth, even when he was inside, so that nobody could read his lips. He said he learned it in prison. Then he would hire lip readers to hang around other wiseguys he was lining up, so he'd know what they were talking about. He was continually looking for an edge."

Bennett made sure to maintain good relations with the most powerful gangster in New England. For reasons unknown to anyone else, Bennett always called Patriarca "George." The underworld believed Bennett was "George's" spy in Boston - one reason he was hated by North End gangsters such as Jerry Angiulo.

In the 1950s the Flemmi brothers were valuable killers in Bennett's gang. That didn't mean they were well liked; a Revere wiseguy was quoted in an FBI report describing the Flemmis as "a couple of bad kids."

Born in 1934, Stevie drifted into the underworld after two tours of duty in the Korean War. On his first eight-man combat patrol he earned the nickname the Rifleman when he killed five enemy soldiers. His brother Jimmy the Bear was just as lethal. By the early 1960s, within months after his release from prison he murdered two men. He killed a third man while high on Seconal one night. The man's offense: he bumped into the Bear at a downtown cafeteria.

Accounts of Jimmy the Bear's brutal murders reached Patriarca in Providence. Since the Bear was from Boston, Patriarca told Jerry Angiulo he would have to try to get him under control. Angiulo personally delivered the message to Jimmy that he had to get every murder approved by Patriarca. "The Man says that you don't have common sense when it comes to killing people,"

Angiulo said quietly: "Jimmy, you don't kill somebody just because you have an argument with him."

Meanwhile, FBI Agent H. Paul Rico was plumbing Boston's underworld for informants but The Bear was interfering. In December 1964 Rico recruited George Ash, a forty-one year old ex-con from Somerville. Ash had a long criminal record and knew every wiseguy in the city. Rico thought he had his star informant.

But on the night he was approved by Washington and given his own informant's identification number, Ash ran into the Bear. They ended up in the South End in a Corvair owned by Ash's sister. Suddenly the Bear decided to stab and shoot his old friend Ash. After finishing Ash off, the Bear climbed unsteadily out of the car and wandered away without seeing the two Boston police officers watching him from across the street.

According to Hitman by Carr, the two Boston cops immediately drove to Stevie Flemmi's store, told him what had happened, and demanded $1,000 not to report the murder. Stevie paid them off and then chewed out his careless big brother saying he was lucky the two officers were friends.

Ash's murder was a setback for Rico but within a few months he set his sights on recruiting the Bear himself as an informant. Even as Rico was courting him, he was aware that Jimmy the Bear was plotting another murder. Teddy Deegan, a small time burglar, was in the Bear's crosshairs. At the Ebb Tide Lounge in Revere, the Bear was heard ranting that Deegan was a "treacherous sneak."

On March 10, 1965, Agent Rico even sent a report to his FBI superiors in Washington stating clearly that the Jimmy the Bear Flemmi was about to kill Deegan – "a dry run has already been made and a close associate of Deegan's has agreed to set him up." No one in law enforcement thought to warn Deegan he was about to be murdered.

To lure Deegan to the Ebb Tide, he was told that a finance company in downtown Chelsea was an easy mark for a break in. Deegan immediately declared his interest. On March 12, 1965, Vincent "Jimmy the Bear" Flemmi was officially approved as an FBI informant.

That night the Bear and his friend Joe "the Animal" Barboza met Deegan at the Ebb Tide and drove to Chelsea for the supposed burglary. They got Deegan into an alley and opened fire, killing him. Within an hour, the Bear and Barboza were back at the Ebb Tide celebrating and drinking cheap scotch. The next day, Agent Rico sent a memo to J. Edgar Hoover identifying the killers of Deegan as Flemmi and Barboza. Agent

Rico didn't bother to tell the police investigating the murder.

The Animal Squeals

Jimmy the Bear's old friend, Joe "The Animal" Barboza would one day become the Boston Mafia's Joe Valachi, the inside guy who told all. But the Mafia liked what they saw when it first recruited the young tough guy in the mid-1950s in state prison.

A second generation Portuguese American, Barboza found trouble early in life. At age thirteen, he and his older brother were arrested after a vandalism spree. By 1949, the seventeen-year-old led a gang that broke into homes and small businesses, stealing money, watches, liquor and guns. Sentenced to the Concord Reformatory for five years in 1950, Barboza led a wild break-out in the summer of 1953 that was the largest in the prison's seventy-five-year history. Barboza and six other inmates guzzled whiskey and popped uppers, overpowered four guards and raced away in two cars. They beat people up, cruised the bars in Boston's center of vice at the time, Scollay Square, wandered to Lynn and Revere and were nabbed at a subway station less than twenty-four hours after the escape.

The trip earned Barboza a stay at Walpole, the state's maximum security prison. It was there that the Mafia took an interest in the young convict and it was for the Mafia that Barboza mostly worked after his parole in 1958. Released from prison, he boxed, worked as a dockhand, a clerk in a fruit store, but his only real skill was murder. And during the escalation of Boston's gang wars he had plenty of opportunity to prove himself. Within eight years of his parole, he earned a reputation as one of the state's real killers – allegedly killing at least two dozen men.

By January 1966, Barboza was a big shot in the Boston underworld; in court he was represented by the famous criminal lawyer F. Lee Bailey. He was on shaky ground though, the mob's leadership was growing tired of his reckless behavior. He was on the same probation his pal the Bear was on from Providence: no hits without prior approval.

In October 1966, Boston Police arrested Barboza for illegal gun possession in the city's Combat Zone. When two Barboza pals raised $82,000 for his bail, Mafia thug Larry Zannino had them set up and murdered. In the Charles Street jail, Barboza went wild and vowed revenge.

FBI agents Dennis Condon and H. Paul Rico were monitoring all of this. They had been combing the Boston underworld for the informants Hoover demanded. Barboza, with his troubles, seemed the perfect candidate. They began to visit the Animal in jail, working to recruit him as an informant.

In June 1967, Barboza began naming names. He implicated Patriarca and Angiulo in separate murder conspiracies. In a third case, he covered for his friend and Agent Rico's snitch Jimmy the Bear by implicating four innocent men in the Deegan murder.

The Rifleman is a Rat: The Rise of Stevie Flemmi

As Joe Barboza threatened to bring down the New England Mafia, another Rico informant was rising in the ranks. Rico first met Stevie Flemmi investigating a bank robbery in the city's financial district. He knew Flemmi was tough, smart, vulnerable and connected – just the kind of criminal who fit J. Edgar Hoover's directive for Mafia informants.

Most importantly, Flemmi was scared. In the worst days of the Boston gang wars, connected guys were always looking for sources of information and Rico made it clear to potential informants that he was willing to share information too. In November 1965 Rico sent Hoover a memo saying Flemmi would make a great FBI informant. "This individual… if he survives the gang war would be a very influential individual in the Boston criminal element," wrote Rico. Agent Rico even gave Flemmi and his hit team partner Cadillac Frank Salemme the address of Punchy McLaughlin shortly before they murdered Punchy.

Despite the help from Rico, Flemmi wasn't yet the valuable informant the FBI had hoped he would be. Hoover wanted sources inside the Italian Mafia or at least close to it and Flemmi was part of the Bennett gang who were angling to take on the Mafia and their top hitman Larry Zannino. Wimpy Bennett believed if he could take out Zannino he could rule Boston. The only way Flemmi could be a useful informant for the FBI was if he switched allegiances. He soon did just that, going to his old friend Zannino and pledging to betray the Bennett brothers.

In January 1967, Stevie Flemmi accused the gang's bookkeeper of stealing money from their numbers racket. He pulled a gun and put it to the man's head. The bookkeeper, Peter Poulos, denied stealing the money, and said he'd given it to Wimpy. According to Cadillac Frank Salemme's sworn testimony in 2003, he stepped in and told Stevie that he needed to ask Wimpy directly.

"So we got Wimpy up there that night," said Johnny Martorano. "Peter put it right on him, I gave the money to you, and you did it before. Bennett couldn't even explain himself, and so Flemmi took the pistol out and shot him in the head." They buried Wimpy at a suburban shooting range they'd used for target practice during the recent gang war.

Walter was the next Bennett brother to go. He'd been seen lurking around Larry Zannino's neighborhood in Jamaica Plain and figured out the Mafia angle to his brother's murder. But he still trusted Salemme and Poulos. That was his fatal mistake.

Martorano described the murder: "We lured Walter to the garage to a meeting with me at six o'clock...He drove in and walked up the stairs to the office. Stevie was waiting at the end of the stairs, shot him, and he took him out of the car." They buried him next to Wimpy at the suburban shooting range. Two Bennetts down, one to go.

Agent Rico's memos to Hoover took on a cocky tone. In a memo about the disappearance of Walter Bennett he wrote, "Informant [Flemmi] advised that the FBI should not waste any time looking for Walter Bennett in Florida or any place else because Bennett is not going to be found. Informant was asked what actually happened to Walter. Informant advised that he could not see any point in going into what happened to Walter but that Walter's "going" is all for the best."

On December 22, 1967, after speaking to Flemmi, Rico filed this report: "Stevie Flemmi indicated that they are going to have to do something about Wimpy Bennett's brother...as he has accused them of being responsible for the murder of his brothers and he has indicated that he is going to kill him."

"[Flemmi] advised that Flemmi and Salemme will probably take out [Billy] Bennett because they have much better connections and information on Billy's activities than he has on their activities."

Flemmi and Salemme had reason to be confident. After the murders of his two brothers, Billy trusted almost no one in the underworld, but he remained close to two hoods named Richard Grasso and Hugh "Sonny" Shields, whom he recruited for his mission of revenge. On a snowy December evening, Billy Bennett met up with Grasso and Shields.

Salemme and Flemmi were following behind in another car at a safe distance. They had a plan – and it ended with Billy next to his two brothers in the shallow grave at the shooting range. This way, Flemmi and Salemme joked, the Bennetts could all play cards together.

The plan went awry as Grasso was driving through Mattapan. Bennett spotted Shields pulling a gun out of his coat, and tried to jump out of the car. According to prosecutors, as Bennett opened the door, Shields fired, killing him. Bennett was pushed out of the car and into a snow bank by the bullet's force. A cab was coming from the other direction and Grasso was forced to drive off, leaving Bennett's body in the street. There would be no third Bennett brother for that ghostly card game.

The Animal Testifies

Joe (The Animal) Barboza was about to begin his career as a mob canary in the trials of Jerry Angiulo and Raymond Patriarca. First up to bat was Angiulo. In the January 1968 trial, Barboza testified for four days. He described an elaborate murder scheme engineered by Angiulo. The Barboza testimony was the state's entire case. In less than two hours the jury reached a verdict – not guilty. Angiulo clutched the dock rail and his body shook. He bit his lower lip and swallowed hard. "I don't want to say anything right now," he told reporters. "I want to see my mother."

Next, Barboza was scheduled to testify against Patriarca and a couple of his henchmen. They were charged with conspiracy to murder two brothers who'd been running an unauthorized card game on Federal Hill. Patriarca had contemplated fleeing to Haiti until a deal could be worked out to silence Barboza but he'd been emboldened after Angiulo's acquittal. He'd stay and fight.

At one pretrial hearing as Barboza left the courtroom, Patriarca looked him in the eye and silently mouthed the words, "You rat." Barboza lunged at him, screaming his trademark phrase: "You fuck your dead mother in the mouth!"

During the trial, Barboza taunted the aging Patriarca, staring at each of the three mobsters on trial, smirking at them and then walking away. Patriarca was convicted of conspiracy to commit murder and sentenced to five years in federal prison in Atlanta. "I'm an old man," was the legendary gangster's reaction as he leaned against the courtroom railing and gripped it with such force that his knuckles turned white.

Before the Patriarca trial, the Mafia made an explosive attempt to silence Barboza. On Jan. 30, 1968 Barboza's attorney John Fitzgerald left his office in Everett after another day of coping with The Animal's ongoing legal drama. He walked back to his car and as he always did, Fitzgerald kept the door open and his left leg outside the Olds while he turned the ignition. The explosion came the second he turned the key. Two sticks of dynamite, fifteen inches long and each weighing six pounds, had been inserted next to the fire wall behind the car's engine.

"The windshield began breaking into a thousand pieces," Fitzgerald wrote later, "as if someone had hit it with a sledgehammer. Fragments were coming at me and there was a grinding effect. It felt like my teeth were tearing my jaw apart."

Across the street, windows were blown out. A cop on traffic detail found Fitzgerald lying on his back in a widening pool of blood. The cop bent over to listen to what might have been Fitzgerald's last words. "Call Rico of the FBI," he whispered before passing out.

Rico didn't need a call to learn that Fitzgerald was about to be attacked. His informant Stevie Flemmi had made it clear. "Informant further advised that Attorney John Fitzgerald, who is Joseph Barboza's attorney, is still definitely on the 'hit parade' and will get 'whacked out' if he leaves the slightest door open," Rico wrote in a memo.

What Rico didn't report was that Flemmi and his friend "Cadillac" Frank Salemme had planned the bombing and executed it with another gangster, Robert Daddieco. Flemmi did the bombing with Cadillac Salemme as a favor for the Mafia. Salemme was interested in impressing Larry Zanino but Flemmi may have done it to hide the fact that he had helped to turn Barboza against the Mafia.

John Fitzgerald's habit of leaving the door open saved his life. It allowed the explosion to weaken but it was still enough to blow off his right leg just above the knee. A decade of gang violence had gone by with little public outcry but an attack on a civilian caused an uproar. Newspaper editorials condemned the underworld's "brazen terroristic act…a frontal assault on our system of justice." The legal community and politicians rallied to Fitzgerald's side, putting prosecutors under pressure.

H. Paul Rico and the FBI came to the rescue. The wily Rico announced that he had landed Daddieco as a cooperating witness. Indictments were coming but that didn't mean Rico was about to arrest Flemmi. Flemmi's phone rang at about seven a.m. one morning in the winter of 1969. "You and your friend need to get out of town. The indictment's coming in a week," the voice said. It was Rico.

In late May 1968, Barboza finally took the witness stand in the Deegan murder trial. He falsely claimed that North End gangster Peter Limone hired him to kill Deegan. He then implicated Tameleo when he fabricated a meeting between the two at the Ebb Tide in Revere. He even concocted a quote from Tameleo: "No punk like Deegan is going to push the Office around," he supposedly said. He was on the witness stand for nine days. As defense lawyers challenged him, he was reduced to snarling at a defense attorney: "All I know is I was there and you wasn't."

The trial lasted fifty days. On July 31, the jury brought back guilty verdicts against four innocent men, two of whom were sent to death row. It would be more than 30 years before the communication between Rico and J. Edgar Hoover identifying Jimmy the Bear Flemmi as the true killer would be uncovered.

Cadillac Frank and The Rifleman on the Run

After the Fitzgerald bombing, Flemmi and Salemme hit the road.

They stayed in New York as guests of the five major Mafia families, each of whom hated Barboza, and were greeted as heroes. By early 1970, they were staying in different apartments but each week the two fugitives would get together on a park bench in Central Park to exchange underworld gossip. This went on for two years until Flemmi showed up one day saying things had changed.

Salemme later explained what happened: "One day he shows up in Central Park and tells me he's leaving he doesn't know where he's going but he's leaving…We got in kind of an argument about it…how come so sudden, what did you hear, did you hear anything? It was too spontaneous. It didn't make sense, that two or three days before, nothing, and this day, bing, he's going to leave."

Stevie Flemmi left for Montreal. Soon, FBI fugitive coordinator Dennis Condon – Agent Rico's partner – began receiving detailed reports on where Salemme might be. Condon passed those reports on to a new agent – a South Boston guy named John Connolly who would later be Whitey Bulger's corrupt protector within the FBI.

In December 1972 on a cold bright New York afternoon Agent Connolly arrested Salemme. He claimed he happened to recognize Salemme as they passed by one another in the street but it was Flemmi's cooperation that tipped him off to Salemme's location. Connolly's apprehension of Cadillac Frank Salemme resulted in a transfer back home, an unusually quick return for an agent with only four years under his belt.

Still on the lam in Montreal, Stevie Flemmi rented an apartment in a fashionable part of the city and actually found honest work as a printmaker. He was free from the gang wars and the constant fear of being unmasked as an FBI informant. For the first time in his life he felt free.

Over the next three years, however, he did keep tabs on what was going on back in Boston, calling into Rico under his old code name "Jack from South Boston." For a while there was no reply. Then one day in 1974, as the furor over the Fitzgerald bombing was passing, Rico did call back. J.

Edgar Hoover was dead. His FBI successors said they were focusing on actual crime over domestic spying and dirty tricks. The bureau was ready to open a new assault on the Mafia.

"It's time to come home," Rico said.

The Animal Tries to Survive

Joe Barboza and the FBI quickly weakened the leadership of the New England Mafia. With the convictions, Barboza's legal problems eased. He pleaded guilty to conspiring to murder Teddy Deegan and was given a one year prison term. In March 1969, he was paroled with the provision he leave Massachusetts forever. His cooperation helped to initiate what is today a vast, secret government program.

In July 1970 Barboza contacted prominent Boston attorney F. Lee Bailey to recant his testimony in the Teddy Deegan murder case. Barboza wanted to "set the record straight as to certain perjured testimony he had given in state and federal courts," the famous attorney said in an affidavit he wrote about the incident. Barboza and three other men – Roy French, Ronald Casseso and another man [who was not identified but later records confirmed was Vincent Jimmy the Bear Flemmi] committed the murder. Tameleo, Limone and the other men charged, Henry Greco and Joseph Salvati were innocent.

Barboza said he committed perjury against mobsters Tameleo and Limone because federal agents insisted he implicate "someone of importance." When he was arrested a short time later in his native New Bedford on a gun charge he knew his past as a government witness would put him in danger in the state's maximum security prison, Walpole. It didn't take him long to crack.

Barboza told his lawyer that FBI agents told him if he gave up trying to recant his testimony in the Deegan case, they would get him released on the gun charge. Sure enough, he recanted and was quickly released.

Within a year he was charged with the murder of an unemployed mechanic in California.

Barboza claimed self-defense despite shooting the victim, Clayton

Wilson, twice in the back of the head. Prosecutors expected help from the FBI but instead two FBI agents and a federal prosecutor took the stand for the defense, while refusing to help state prosecutors.

After the agents and a federal prosecutor testified that Barboza was cooperative and truthful, state prosecutors – believing the testimony had bolstered Barboza's credibility – accepted his offer to plead guilty to second degree murder and he was sentenced to five years in prison.

At Folsom State Prison Barboza wrote a series of poems portraying the evils of the Mob and his own fearlessness with titles such as "Boston Gang War," "The Mafia Double Crosses," "A Cat's Lives," and "The Gang War Ends."

Paroled after four years, in October 1975 he moved into a $250-a-month apartment in San Francisco under the name Joe Donati. The mob was waiting. They knew Barboza's location because a wiseguy from Boston named James Chalmas had been living in California, visiting Barboza in prison and befriending him.

Less than three months after he was paroled, on February 11, 1976, Barboza left Chalmas' apartment at midday and walked toward his car. Four shotgun blasts were fired from a white van that pulled up next to Barboza. Barboza was carrying a loaded .38 caliber revolver, but never had a chance. He was killed instantly.

"We clipped Barboza," Larry Zannino would say five years later unaware he was being secretly taped by investigators. He told his soldiers how much he admired the man – J.R. Russo of East Boston – who shot Barboza. "A fucking genius with a carbine." Russo would again blast his way into Boston Mafia notoriety years later but for now he was the mob's Carlton Fisk – owner of the most famous Boston hit in history.

With Barboza dead, the four innocent men convicted of Teddy Deegan's murder would languish behind bars for decades. Tameleo died in 1985 and Greco in 1995 – each still in prison, Joe Salvati was released in 1997, and Peter Limone in 2001.

The FBI agent who aided Barboza's false testimony, H. Paul Rico, was unmoved. During U.S. House Judiciary Committee hearings in October

2003 looking into the Deegan killing, Rico responded to questions about the innocent men imprisoned by saying, "What do you want, tears?"

It was typical arrogance from Rico – an FBI agent corrupted by Boston's gangland. In the years after the Barboza saga, Agent Rico became a kind of mob boss in the city, even killing to maintain his empire.

CHAPTER TWELVE

THE CAMPBELL BROTHERS: GODFATHERS OF BOSTON'S BLACK MOB

NOVEMBER 13, 1968. 370 BLUE HILL AVENUE. OFFICE OF N.E.G.R.O. (NEW ENGLAND GRASS ROOTS ORGANIZATION).

IT WAS 3:45 A.M. but the small Civil Rights office was full, with five men speaking of plans for the future. The next day, the first installment in a two million dollar government contract, was expected to arrive. But Guido St. Laurent, a blind man who led the activist storefront from obscurity to Civil Rights prominence, could feel uncertainty in the voices of the four men in his office.

The tension could have been due to the three men expected to arrive; a crew of infamous gangsters looking for a piece of the $1.9 million grant St. Laurent had been awarded from the federal government. Tonight, the Campbell Brothers, the crime bosses of Roxbury, would try to muscle in on the Civil Rights movement. When it was over three were dead and two wounded. Beyond, it signaled a new era for the black mob in Boston.

Guido St. Laurent and Carnell Eaton: From Armed Robbery to Black Power

Guido St. Laurent was born December 17, 1929 blind in one eye. His first arrest came in 1944 for larceny. He was arrested ten more times by 1956. That year, he and lifelong friend Carnell Eaton robbed an administrative office of a Mission Hill housing project, entering with handkerchiefs covering the lower half of their faces. They tied up six people and

St. Laurent hit one in the back of the head before they emptied a vault of $1,085. St. Laurent was sentenced to 18 to 20 years in prison and Eaton 10 to 12 years.

Official prison reports say St. Laurent was blinded during his prison stay when a barbell slipped from his grip and hit him on the head, irreparably damaging his remaining good eye. Other reports indicated rival inmates may have been involved.

St. Laurent later counted his blinding as a positive event – a turning point. "It wasn't until I was blinded that I began to see," he said, explaining that he would have probably spent the rest of his life in and out of prisons if the blinding had not made him think about ways to use his skills constructively.

At first, however, being blind was a tragedy. He had worked occasionally as a commercial artist and it was months before he decided to use his artistic skills through words and ideas. He thought up acronyms for most of his projects: B.L.A.C.K. (Better Leadership A Community Key) and W.H.I.T.E. [We Have Information Traveling Everywhere].

In 1963 St. Laurent was released from prison. Two years later, he opened the small storefront office on Blue Hill Avenue and named it N.E.G.R.O. for New England Grass Roots Organization. He described it as a public relations office for Boston's black neighborhoods "to let the world know about the people in the black community doing the little things that never get attention from the press because they aren't sensational."

Equipped only with a few telephones, St. Laurent set up contacts with the press and publicized small, positive activities such as a group of teens building their own recreation lounge and mothers campaigning for a stoplight. He held job forums to publicize the "10 mile gap" between employers and Boston's black neighborhoods and the lack of transportation that contributed to urban unemployment. He kept the office open 24 hours a day and quickly built a reputation as a local leader to watch.

The high point of St. Laurent's leadership came in April 1968 when he helped keep Boston streets safe in the wake of Dr. Martin Luther King Jr.'s assassination. After his blinding, St. Laurent operated citizen band radios as a hobby for many years – experience that would come in handy as Boston threatened to burn.

The morning after King's death, Washington Street and Blue Hill Avenue – the black community's two principal thoroughfares – were pocked with smashed windows and burned-out stores. By afternoon, things were heating up again. Several hundred youths began marching down the major shopping streets telling store owners to close up. On the door or window of each shop they pasted a flyer proclaiming, "This store is closed until further notice in honor of Dr. Martin Luther King, the fallen martyr of the black revolution."

The mood in Roxbury that day may not have pleased the apostle of non-violence, however. A leaflet distributed by the Black United Front said flatly, "Non-violence is dead. The Black Community Faces Disaster." As tensions rose, St. Laurent counseled caution.

He set up a radio communications network for a team of volunteers, mostly young black men and women, who had formed their Roxbury Youth Patrol. The volunteers reported fires, kept track of crowd disturbances, transported Roxbury citizens to their homes, carried the injured to hospitals and phoned for legal help for those arrested. They also passed out leaflets that afternoon saying, "Cool it. The riot squad has M-16 rifles-Mace-a machine so high pitched it will make you deaf. They're not playing. Keep off the streets. Defend your home and family. Don't start anything."

They urged young people to stay home that night and watch soul music star James Brown perform live at the Boston Garden on local television. "Don't go downtown brothers," the patrol said. "Stay home. Put on the TV and watch cool James do his thing."

N.E.G.R.O. was the central communications office for all the action. St. Laurent relayed calls from volunteers in the street to the fire and police departments. Partly as a result of his efforts, Boston began to cool off. Within days, peace had been restored with relatively mild damage to the community – 21 injured, 30 arrested, barely $50,000 in damage. This was small compared with what happened in many of the 197 other towns and cities where riots broke out in the aftermath of King's assassination.

Three years earlier St. Laurent was an anonymous, blind prison inmate. Now, on the night of King's assassination, he was credited by the Boston Police Department with preventing serious outbreaks of violence in the city.

However, St. Laurent would always be distrusted; by other Civil Rights figures who questioned his motives; by Boston cops who resented St. Laurent's security patrol that observed police actions in Roxbury; and by the FBI who stepped up their surveillance of him after he stopped the riot.

On Blue Hill Avenue, even St. Laurent's neighbors looked at N.E.G.R.O. with suspicion. The office was located on a strip of the avenue so dotted with community action groups it was known as Agency Row. By the time St. Laurent showed up in mid-1966, many of the agencies had been established in the community for a decade or more. When he was awarded a huge federal grant within two years, "The community was very suspicious about how Guido had hooked up these federal funds and we were all watching to see how this program to train mechanics was going to work out," said Sarah Anne Shaw, an activist on Agency Row.

Shaw, the first black female news reporter in Boston television history, was a veteran anti-poverty and Civil Rights worker when St. Laurent opened NEGRO. "We never knew if Guido was out for the community or just out for Guido. He was very power hungry and could be very cutting in his remarks," she said. "I felt he was a bully."

The FBI was suspicious too. As COINTELPRO, their campaign of dirty tricks against Civil Rights leaders, intensified, the feds were monitoring St. Laurent too. At least five informants were sharing information with the FBI about St. Laurent's daily activities and meetings. Most reports contained jabs at St. Laurent's real motives while questioning how much power he really had in the streets.

"Subject [St. Laurent] described by one source as vicious and has talked in terms of mass destruction where white men are concerned," said a confidential FBI report. On Sept. 26, 1968, an informant told the FBI that St. Laurent was using his CB radio network to spread false rumors that an eight-year-old girl was killed by a police officer who hit her over the head during a riot in Dudley Square. Boston Police investigated but found no evidence to support the claim. Police believed St. Laurent broadcasted the rumor to keep racial tension high in Roxbury.

Tension would remain high throughout Boston. Over the next decade plus the city's working class neighborhoods were engulfed in a particularly vicious brand of racial turmoil: black children targeted by racist white mobs in school desegregation battles; white, working class Boston's violent cry of, "Hell no we won't go;" it all added up to a low point in the city's history.

If white Boston or the police were going to use violence, St. Laurent was prepared. An FBI informant claimed St. Laurent was collecting guns, hand grenades, nitroglycerin and holding classes to make fire bombs. He brought Youth Security Patrol members to shooting ranges in the country. During a nightly patrol, where he and his team monitored Boston Police for brutality, N.E.G.R.O. drove around Roxbury heavily armed.

On June 8, 1968, Boston Police stopped St. Laurent's station wagon with the vanity plate N.E.G.R.O. They found a .38 caliber revolver in the tire wheel, a bayonet under the dashboard and two machetes in the back seat. St. Laurent told police he had written permission from Mayor Kevin White to carry the weapons. The police checked with City Hall and handed the weapons back. St. Laurent went on his way.

St. Laurent's old stick-up partner Carnell Eaton faced his own conflicts. Married with three children, he vowed to stay out of trouble and grew to be a reliable member of Boston's grassroots activism community. In one campaign, Eaton worked with the Boston Action Group to demand that Wonderbread and Hood Milk hire local black drivers. After marches and calls to boycott, Eaton was hired at Hood.

"Carnell was very outspoken," Shaw says. "He said what he wanted to say when he wanted to say it. He was very pro-black, very much for the community." Eaton felt the pull of street life though and he by the end of 1968 he was suspended from his community organizing job after he was indicted in a New York drug dealing case.

Shaw says it was probably Eaton who first brought his old crime partner St. Laurent into the Civil Rights movement. Eaton was trying to bring others from the street life to anti-poverty work too. One of those men, Ronald Hicks, was in the basement Nov. 13 with Eaton and St. Laurent.

Hicks was a reputed drug dealer and pimp - selling heroin and cocaine out of various downtown bars while making $100 a night from each of his four prostitutes. "When I was 15, I was given a five year sentence and I served two and a half years. When I was 20, I got 25 years [for armed robbery] and I served nine and a half years," Hicks said. "And I never had any regret about it." Even as he tried to enter the world of activism, Boston police had reports of "Hicks pushing H & C (heroin and cocaine)."

Although Eaton and St. Laurent had grown from convicted armed robbers to well-known Civil Rights figures in the community, some tension remained. "There was always a rivalry between Carnell and Guido for who would be the one in control," Shaw said. They were unified this morning though; if only as a defense against a more serious threat. The men they were expecting were the notorious Campbell brothers, the crime bosses of Roxbury, and their top enforcer Dennis (Deke) Chandler.

The Campbell Brothers: Boston's Black Godfather's

Alvin and Arnold Campbell were the sons of a West Indian immigrant reported to be a skilled bank robber. Alvin was two years older and taller than Arnold, who was known as shorty. Both were intelligent young men who excelled in school. Alvin was a standout student at Boston

Technical High School and was offered a four-year scholarship to Princeton University. However, he turned it down in favor of the family business of robbery.

"The Campbells had a reputation. They were known to carry guns," Sarah Ann Shaw says. "They were scary guys. If you knew them they could be nice guys; but they were scary guys."

For a while the Campbells fared well and avoided serious prison time. At a later sentencing, a judge angrily read their rap sheets aloud in court describing what he called "fix after fix after fix." "This is a sordid picture," the judge said. "Never in my life have I seen such records."

In 1957, the Campbell's luck ran out. They robbed a branch of the Norfolk County Bank and Trust Company and, dressed in blue suits, stole $32,000 including one woman's $60 cash deposit a moment after she entered the bank. "I'll take the dough," Alvin told her.

The trial made daily headlines in Boston's newspapers. The Campbells were convicted and sentenced to 25-year terms. In the notorious Leavenworth Federal Prison the brothers formed an unlikely bond with infamous gangster and notorious racist Whitey Bulger.

In Howie Carr's *Hitman*, John Martorano relates what Whitey told him about his friendship with the Campbells. "[Whitey] told me later he'd been working out one day in the weight room in Leavenworth, and he heard some guys talking behind him. It was pretty obvious from their accents that they were from Boston, and when Whitey turned around he couldn't believe they were black. It was the Campbells. They used to all walk the track together at Leavenworth, around and around and around, just talking about Boston."

A successful appeal freed the brothers after just four years. They were released to a different world: the new ideas and reforms of the 1960s were in full swing and older brother Arnold got a job as neighborhood assistance director of Action for Boston Community Development. "I came from their ranks," he said of the hardcore unemployed men he worked with, "so I could relate to them."

When the Campbells continued carrying guns and extorting cocaine dealers their sincerity to the movement was questioned. "They were the same gangsters they always had been," says Rodney Draffen, a drug dealer from that time. After Draffen and his brother started a small but lucrative operation they heard the Campbells were coming for a cut.

"They had back up too – that was their whole thing. They'd say, 'If you don't believe me I'll get the mob to come after you and kill your family.' And every time you turned around, someone they messed with was getting shot and killed. They were a real pain in my ass for a time there."

The Campbells must have noticed Roxbury had more federal money coming in than cocaine profits. The problem was St. Laurent and N.E.G.R.O. had already gained control of the $1.9 million grant. Carnell Eaton offered the Campbells jobs, in middle management. When the Campbells heard about a quick trip St. Laurent and Eaton made to New York with Ronald Hicks, Fred Rose and out of town activist Ronald King, they started to think they were missing a big payday.

Now, the Campbells were on their way to 370 Blue Hill Avenue to see St. Laurent, Eaton and the others about how to divvy up the federal money. One party not in the room but integral to the rising confrontation was federal subcontractor Woolman Systems, a mysterious defense firm that fit the term 'poverty pimp' better than St. Laurent or the Campbells did.

Poverty Pimping the Federal Government

The Campbells sudden political awakening was not unusual for gangsters in the 1960s. Gang leaders in major cities across the U.S. were turning street credibility into federal funding during the last, liberal days of the war on poverty. It was the era captured in Tom Wolfe's essay "Mau-Mauing the Flak Catchers" when known gangsters were given preference for government funding based on their criminal convictions.

"Corporations, politicians, well-meaning white liberals were all bending over backwards to show that they were not prejudiced, they weren't racist," says Shaw. "There was white guilt. So a lot of things got funded but they weren't always well thought out."

In stepped Dr. Myron Woolman – an educator looking to profit from the war on poverty and a classic poverty pimp. Woolman boasted a PhD in Learning Psychology but he was also an opportunist looking for a cut of lucrative ghetto grants. The time was right: the government was suddenly pouring millions into urban revitalization projects and profitable corporations such as oil and gas firms were competing for millions.

In May 1966 Dr. Woolman was terminated from Lincoln Jobs Corp Center for charging excessive fees for educational work not being done. Woolman was quickly retained by Northern Natural Gas, also chasing anti-poverty money. With the hiring of Woolman and connections in the Department of Labor and other federal agencies, Northern Gas was poised to implement a program in Roxbury to net them millions. That is, until Guido St. Laurent and NEGRO got in the way.

According to FBI reports, "NEGRO set out to stir up the community against an outsider like Northern coming into Roxbury and called instead for a local group like NEGRO to run the program."

Dr. Woolman saw a solution, however. He left Northern and took his proposal and approached St. Laurent with a deal to operate jointly, FBI documents reveal. Woolman formed Woolman Systems and won a $1.9 million grant from the Department of Labor.

From the beginning, Woolman and St. Laurent plundered it. St. Laurent and Fred Rose formed a for-profit venture that hoped to obtain $147,000 from the grant. On Nov. 12, Woolman hosted St. Laurent, Eaton, Rose, Hicks and King in New York City. They discussed how to divide the money and, in the case of King who was from Cleveland, how to expand their program to other cities.

Woolman had fought for the grant, even betrayed his original partner to team up with St. Laurent. Now, the multimillion dollar reward was near. It was Woolman, with some help from the Department of Labor, who put into motion these events. But he would not be in the Roxbury basement the next morning when it all came to a fatal tipping point.

Murder Scene

On that Nov. 13 morning the only regulators taking a close look at the grant money was the Campbell Brothers gang. According to Fred Rose, who survived the attack, the Campbells and Deke Chandler entered the headquarters and after pushing a gun into the face of Eaton made their way into the back office.

Rose later testified in court: "At one point one of the Campbell brothers, I think it was Arnold, pushed me into a chair. After I was in the chair I saw everyone had a gun in his hand. Carnell was standing in the middle of the floor saying 'What's this? What's this?'

"Alvin then slugged Guido St. Laurent and the gun discharged. Arnold

Campbell was standing over on the other side of the room and he slugged Ron Hicks. I hear Guido saying, 'Don't do that. I have a plate in my head.'

"Next I heard someone say: 'You won't feel it long baby.' Then Guido was shot in the chest."

Unluckiest of all may have been Ronald King, the only one in the basement without a criminal conviction. "Hey what's going on?" he asked the killers as they rushed him. "I just got here from Cleveland."

"Sorry, cuz, you should have stayed in Cleveland," one of the killers replied and shot him in the head.

Fred Rose and Ronald Hicks were shot but managed to survive. St. Laurent, Eaton and King each died. "No one was supposed to be left alive, that's for sure" said a Boston Police detective investigating the incident. "This wasn't a case of an emotional outburst. It was simply cold-blooded killing."

St. Laurent supporters mourned the loss of his leadership. "He was a man in the process of becoming," said one friend. "Tomorrow was his permanent address."

The murders brought scrutiny to the manpower program. Little had been done; five months after the money was released only twelve men were enrolled. Woolman had announced each graduate would receive a job from local companies who pledged their support. In reality, the companies were only compelled to hire 40 of the 500 graduates. The $1.9 million grant to train 500 hardcore unemployed men was cancelled.

The Rise of John Martorano and the Campbells

Initially, surviving victim Ronald Hicks did not speak with police about the triple murder. However, NBC news reporter Walter J. Sheridan convinced Hicks to cooperate with police after interviewing Hicks for a national television special on race relations.

Hicks told Boston Police the Campbell brothers and Deke Chandler were the killers. They were each arrested and charged with first degree murder. They faced the death penalty. Hicks' cooperation with police made him a target for the Campbells.

One night a woman walked into Basin Street, a bar frequented mostly by black Bostonians but owned by white thug Johnny Martorano. The woman was crying and said she needed a favor. She asked for Martorano. "Have you ever heard of the Campbell brothers?" she began, and Johnny's answer was yes he had.

The woman was Roberta Campbell – Bert for short and she was Alvin's wife. She was looking for any help she could get for her husband - currently on trial for the triple murder. Martorano knew Hicks – he was a regular at Basin Street and he dated a waitress there. Martorano began thinking about the Campbells, locked up in the Charles Street jail, awaiting trial and possibly facing the death penalty because of Hicks. Even though he'd never met the Campbells, Martorano made a decision to murder Hicks. He thought it was the right thing to do.

On the evening of March 19, 1969, Martorano went looking for Hicks. He checked out a new spot, the Sugar Shack, where Hicks was a regular. Martorano knew the car his prey was driving: to put it simply, a pimpmobile – a 1967 Cadillac coupe, brown, with a rose-colored top. He spotted Hicks in the Fenway neighborhood and flagged him over into Forsythe Park near the Museum of Fine Arts. Martorano parked and got into Hick's passenger side. As soon as Martorano got in the car, he cut two lines of cocaine on the car seat. Martorano was sitting next to him in the front seat when Hicks leaned over and snorted one of the lines. He still had his head down when he asked Martorano, "You want a line?"

Those were the last words Ronald Hicks ever spoke because at that moment Johnny Martorano shot him in the head. His head snapped back against the horn on the steering wheel and it started blaring.

The district attorney prosecuting the Campbells immediately ordered Fred Rose, the sole surviving witness of the N.E.G.R.O. massacre picked up and placed in protective custody. With only one witness against them, the Campbells and Chandler were acquitted of all charges in the triple slaying. After the verdicts, the Campbells headed to Basin Street to see Martorano.

"We're here to thank you," Alvin Campbell told him.

"I don't know what you're talking about," Martorano told him. "There's nothing to thank me for."

"We're here to thank you anyway," Campbell replied.

Quickly, they got down to business. The Campbells had a plan to take over the drug trade in Boston's black neighborhoods. They would chase away the "outsiders" – not whites but the black gangsters from New York City who'd been moving into the city in recent years and now dominated the Roxbury rackets. Martorano was skeptical of the strategy:

"They were bank robbers, not drug dealers. You don't get rid of people if you don't know how to take over and operate their rackets yourself. It didn't make sense. The Campbells, however, were fully focused on taking over the drug trade now and their new ally, John Martorano, would be of use as they intimidated, attacked and killed holdout drug dealers across Roxbury."

The Campbells Take Over

In September 1969, the FBI sent the following report to the Boston Police Department:

"S/A Matthew Seifer received information that the Campbell Bros. had approached all the cocaine dealers in Boston making it very clear that only their "stuff" would be handled. The terms were that they would protect the dealers, that the dealers would provide their own attorney in the event of an arrest, but that the Campbells would see to it that no one would testify against them as long as it was a state violation. It was further alleged that the Campbells were associated with a white fellow..."

The white fellow was likely Martorano, who forged an unlikely alliance with the Campbells after members of his own crew were killed or turned government informants. "I know what people believe, but I never took any money from the Campbells," Martorano told reporter Howie Carr. "Maybe they gave me a hundred bucks once, but I told them no. They never really made much money anyway."

"What was more valuable to me personally about the Campbells was that if anybody ever tried to make a move on me, they'd have to worry about them. On the street you need somebody behind you like that. The more the better...Every time somebody who doesn't like me sees a black guy walking toward him on the street, he's thinking, Is this one of Johnny's guys?"

Pushback against the Campbells and Martorano was inevitable. One hot summer night, Martorano was drinking at Basin Street with the notorious Vincent (Jimmy the Bear) Flemmi, who was out on a brief parole. Alvin Campbell and Deke Chandler came in and excitedly pulled Martorano aside. They were having some problems with a coke dealer and proprietor of an unlicensed bar on Blue Hill Avenue named Black Sam. Alvin had spotted Black Sam holding court out in front of his bar, entertaining hangers on with jokes and stories. It was a perfect opportunity to take him out.

In *Hitman*, Martorano tells author Howie Carr that he grabbed a handful of dirt and rubbed it on his face to darken it. Then he tore apart a burlap bag and wrapped it around his head. He got into the backseat of Alvin Campbell's car, lay down and picked up the loaded carbine on the floor.

A few minutes later, on Blue Hill Avenue, Alvin slammed the breaks and came to a stop. Martorano popped up from the backseat, drew a bead on Black Sam, and fired. Black Sam fell to the sidewalk, wounded, shot in the shoulder. It would have to do – there were too many onlookers, and not enough time, to get out of the car and finish Black Sam off.

There was another holdout named Nelson Padron. He was an older cocaine dealer who owned a bar and drove a Mercedes convertible. The Campbells told him they were in charge now and it was time to negotiate new terms – in a public place, if Padron was concerned for his safety.

Things got off to a bad start when Padron brought a gun to the sit down. Martorano pulled back Padron's coat, grabbed the revolver out of his belt, and began pistol-whipping him with it. There were too many witnesses to kill him right there but Deke Chandler had an idea. While Martorano beat Padron, Deke ran outside, took out a switchblade, and slashed all four of Padron's tires. When Martorano finally tired of beating Padron and told him, "screw, asshole" Padron bolted for his car and tore off in his Mercedes, throwing off a shower of sparks as he rode the rims. Everyone was laughing and Padron lived – only to be shot by Martorano on another day.

A few years later in February 1973 Padron was about to go away for income tax evasion and he started telling people he was going to settle his old beef with Martorano. One night after hearing this, Martorano found Padron's trademark silver Mercedes on Dartmouth Street. Martorano nodded to Nicky Femia, a member of infamous snitch Joe Barboza's old crew. They got in Johnny's car and followed Padron. Femia at the wheel, Martorano in back with a carbine.

"When Nelson comes back around down Columbus and turns right onto Dartmouth Street, we pull up beside him and I let go with the carbine…Poor Nelson, he was hit pretty bad but somehow he managed to drive all the way to Mass. General, and then he crashed the Mercedes into an abutment… The cops had probable cause to search his car. They found a bag of coke, an unregistered handgun and $2,400 cash in the car. I still remember the headline in the Herald: "He's riddled by bullets, is arrested."

"From then on, whenever I saw Nelson he was on a cane," Martorano said.

A third victim of the Campbell's wasn't so fortunate. A 34-year-old white pimp from Philadelphia named Touch had been getting in the way of the Campbell's plans to take over the local drug trade. He was friendly with one of the last holdouts, a dealer known as Rat, and even stepped in between Rat and Deke Chandler as Chandler tried to strong arm Rat.

One of Touch's prostitutes later told police: "He didn't tell me all the words that were passed between the two of them but it had to do with dope. There were threats…he couldn't come here with any kind of cocaine without the Campbell brothers okay…That is when Deke pulled out his pistol."

Then Touch had the bad luck to run into Martorano at the Sugar Shack. Martorano admits that he stabbed and killed Touch as he left the restaurant with a date. Martorano, however, never heard from the police about the murder. "The thing is," he said, "nobody missed Touch."

The Campbells didn't last long in the cocaine game themselves. Alvin and Deke Chandler were convicted of using lockers in various train stations in Boston to store and sell cocaine. A dealer for the Campbells turned government witness told a jury that Alvin Campbell gave him a key to various train station lockers filled with packages of cocaine that he sold for $20 each. Alvin received a 20-year federal sentence. Chandler was murdered a few years later and Arnold was murdered in the 1980s in a dispute over drug turf.

Darryl Whiting built a $10 million drug empire in Orchard Park Projects in Roxbury.

Joe Kennedy wasn't just the patriarch of America's greatest political dynasty, he was a whisky baron and colleague of mobsters.

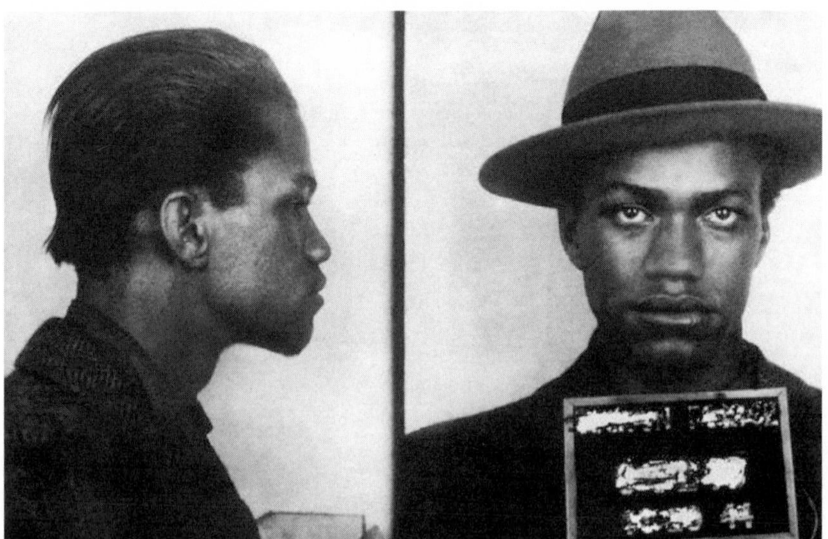

Before he became the pivotal civil rights leader Malcolm X, he was Detroit Red a Roxbury hustler involved in break-ins and drugs.

Joe Lombardo, Boston Mafia don.

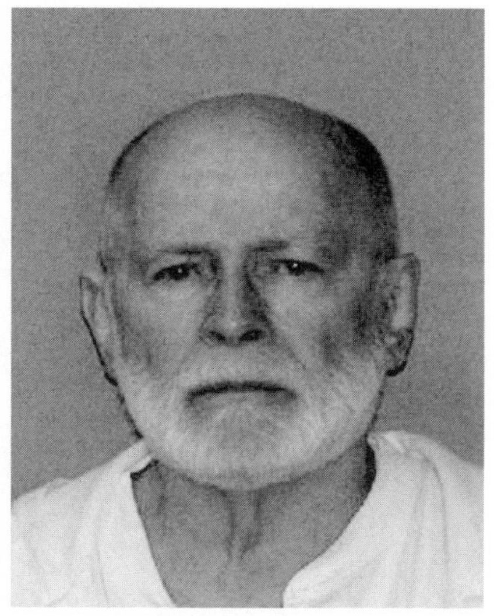

James (Whitey) Bulger after he was captured in 2009 after 16 years on the run.

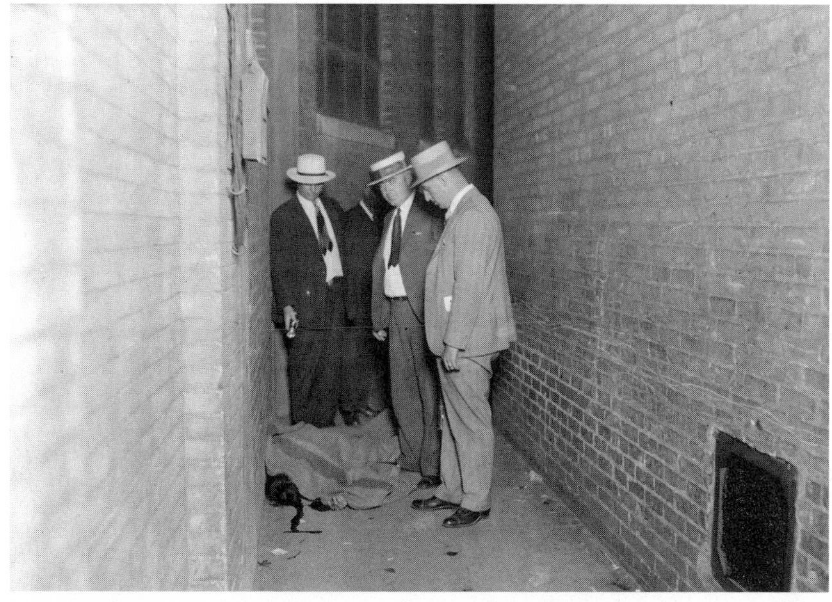

A victim of the tong war in Boston's Chinatown. The male victim was shot nine times in an alleyway. Police speculate the murderer had a silencer. Courtesy of the Boston Public Library, Print Department. Leslie Jones Collection.

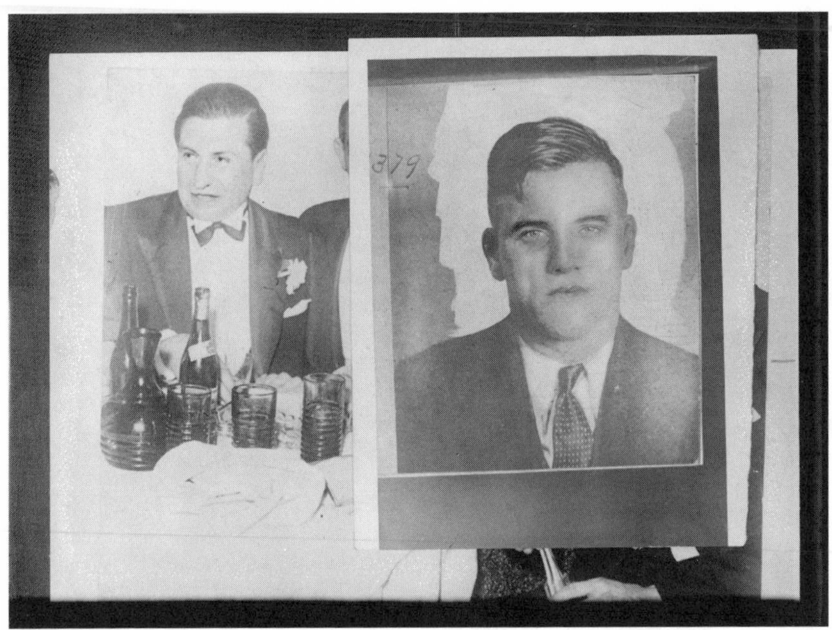

Boston's ruling kingpin during Prohibition was Charles (King) Solomon. Solomon made millions and owned hotels and nightclubs, including the Cocoanut Grove. When he was murdered at the Cotton Club on January 24, 1933, his last words were, "The Dirty Rats Got Me."

Solomon's funeral procession 3,000 spectators. ABoston Globe reporter described the scene as a mixed crowd of cops, reporters, photographers, lawyers, actresses, "small fry racketeers" and "little Caesars of gangland, who kept their right hands in right hand pockets and answered questions with the word "Scram!"

Solomon was buried at the Hand-in-Hand Jewish Cemetery in West Roxbury. The funeral procession included three cars and two hearses filled with floral tributes. More than 500 people followed Solomon's casket through the cemetery to see Boston's gangster "King" laid to rest for good.

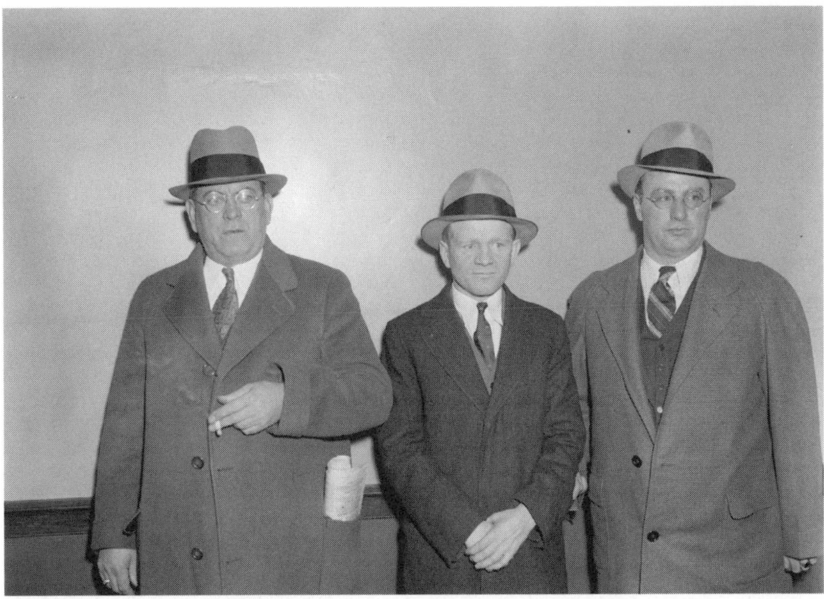

Stevie (Gustin) Wallace was the youngest and wildest member of the Gustin Gang. After being acquitted of a vicious assault on a Boston police officer in December 1933, a new indictment came down. Wallace disappeared until he surrendered to police on October 29, 1934. Capt. Stephen J. Flaherty (left) and Det. William J. Crowley (right) picked up Wallace at Old Harbor Street in South Boston. After Frankie Wallace's murder, most Gustin Gang members descended to alcoholism and street crime.

Wallace met his untimely end at Joseph Lombardo's office at 317 Hanover Street in the North End. When Wallace and two bodyguards walked to the door the bullets started flying. Wallace and bodyguard Bernard (Dodo) Walsh were killed. Here, police investigators survey the damage in 317 Hanover Street. One of the gunmen had thrown a pistol through the glass window. It crashed through the glass and landed on the sidewalk below.

Frankie Wallace, pictured here, was the leader of Boston's most notorious Prohibition-era gang. The Gustin Gang took their name from Gustin Street in South Boston, and most members were Irish. Frankie was the leader of the outlaws. He made national headlines in 1928 when he was accused of taking part in a takeover robbery of the Detroit News offices. He was arrested 25 times before he was murdered by the Mafia on December 22, 1931.

As Prohibition opened, the liquor kept flowing in Boston as seen here with barrels of seized booze being unloaded and destroyed - with plenty more on the way.

A seized shipment of liquor is destroyed during Prohibition.

Oliver Garrett, here seated second from right, was possibly the most corrupt Boston police officer in history. During Prohibition, his Liquor Squad was notoriously corrupt - extorting speakeasy owners and busting those who didn't pay. Garrett's downfall made daily headlines and was Boston's greatest 'dry-era' scandal.

CHAPTER THIRTEEN

WHITEY BULGER AND THE FBI'S DEAL WITH THE DEVIL

IN THE FALL of 1975, FBI agent John Connolly eased his beat-up Plymouth into a parking space along Wollaston Beach. Without any warning, the passenger side door swung open and into the Plymouth slipped the man Connolly had been waiting for, Whitey Bulger. Connolly jumped, surprised he was caught unaware. He, the rising star in the FBI, had left his doors unlocked.

"What the hell did you do, parachute in?" he asked as the gangster settled into the front seat. Connolly had been expecting Bulger to pull up in a car alongside him. Bulger explained that he had parked on one of the side streets and then walked along the beach.

Under the cover of darkness, the two men began to talk, and then Connolly made his offer: "You should think about using your friends in law enforcement."

"Who?" Whitey said at last. "You?"

"Yeah," replied Connolly to the ruthless killer. "Me."

Connolly wasn't in any rush to make his pitch. "I just want you to hear me out," he told Bulger. Connolly carefully played up the threat Bulger and his Winter Hill gang faced from Jerry Angiulo's Mafia.

"I hear Jerry is feeding information to law enforcement to get you pinched," he told Bulger. They talked about how Angiulo definitely called on crooked Boston cops to do him favors. "The Mafia has all the contacts," Connolly said. "I have a proposal: why don't you use us to do what they're doing to you? Fight fire with fire."

The deal was simple: Bulger should use the FBI to eliminate his Mafia rivals while the FBI wouldn't be looking to take Bulger himself down if he were cooperating. In fact, at that moment other FBI agents were making inquiries into Bulger's loan sharking operations. We'll protect you, Connolly promised. Just as corrupt agent H. Paul Rico, a mentor to Connolly, had protected killers such as Stevie (The Rifleman) Flemmi, a Bulger friend, and Joe (The Animal) Barboza.

Bulger was intrigued. "You can't survive without friends in law enforcement," he admitted at night's end. But he left without a decision.

Two weeks later Connolly and Bulger met again in Quincy, this time to cement the deal.

"All right," he informed Connolly, "deal me in. If they want to play checkers, we'll play chess. Fuck them."

So the FBI's sinister deal with the devil began.

Whitey's World

John Connolly was not the first FBI agent to make a run at developing Whitey Bulger as an informant. According to the definitive Whitey Bulger book *Black Mass*, by Dick Lehr and Gerard O'Neill, veteran agent Dennis Condon had previously tried to "flip" Bulger. In May 1971 Condon was able to elicit extensive inside information from Whitey on Southie's gang wars – who was allied with whom, who was targeting whom. It was a thorough account of the underworld landscape. Condon even opened an informant file for Whitey.

But Whitey went cold. In August, Condon reported, Whitey was "still reluctant to furnish info." By September Condon had thrown up his hands. "Contacts with [Bulger] have been unproductive," he wrote in his FBI files on September 10, 1971. "Accordingly, this matter is being closed."

Whitey may have been more comfortable with Connolly given their shared background in South Boston. The two men spoke the same language and shared deep roots in the tribal neighborhood. They both grew up in the first public project in Boston, Old Harbor, a spartan village of thirty-four brick tenement buildings. Boston's Irish were grateful for the housing projects after decades in the waterfront tenements of the North End where three of every ten children died before their first birthday. The Irish presence in the new neighborhood of Southie was so strong that residents moved in by their Irish county of origin – Galway was A and B streets, Cork people settled on D Street, and so on.

Like Ireland itself, Southie was a grand place – as long as you could find a job. During the Great Depression, an unemployment rate of 30 percent badly damaged the Southie worldview that emphasized hard work and keeping your nose clean.

It was to this hard time and place that Whitey's parents James and Jean Bulger arrived in 1938, looking for a third bedroom for their growing family. Whitey was nine, his younger brother Billy four. The Bulgers would raise three boys in one bedroom and three girls in another. Families had to be nearly broke to get into the projects and the Bulgers qualified. As a young man, James Joseph Bulger lost most of his arm when it was caught between two railroad cars. Although he worked occasionally as a clerk at the Charlestown Navy Yard, doing the late shift on holidays as a fill-in, he never held a full time job again.

The first entry on Whitey's police record came in 1943, at age thirteen, for larceny. Soon, he joined a neighborhood youth gang, the Shamrocks. Assault and battery and robbery charges were added to his rap sheet. He became a dangerous delinquent with a Jimmy Cagney flair, known for surviving vicious fights and wild car chases.

His brother Billy Bulger remembered in his memoir: "[Whitey] was in a constant state of revolt against…I'm not sure what. He was as restless as a claustrophobic in a dark closet. "Where's Jim?" my mother was always asking. "I turn my back for a second and he's out the door. He's always out the door. Where does he go?" I couldn't answer. I didn't know. I don't think Jim knew where he was going most of the time – just out."

After an arrest for rape in January 1948, Whitey joined the Air Force. He wasn't cut out for military life though. With his enlistment about to expire he faced a disciplinary hearing and a possible court martial. "You know," his captain told him, you could get a dishonorable discharge, and if that happens, you'll never get a good job on the outside." According to his military records, Whitey had a prophetic response: "I could go back to the work I used to do, no matter what kind of discharge I get."

In August 1952, he received an honorable discharge from the United States Air Force and went back to his old line of work. The Boston office of the FBI started to keep tabs. Agent H. Paul Rico said the office learned of Bulger "because of his suspected implication in tailgate thefts. We knew of his extremely dangerous character, his remarkable agility, his reckless daring in driving vehicles, and his unstable, vicious characteristics."

In early 1955, at the age of twenty-five, Whitey fell in with an older con, a jailhouse lawyer named Carl G. Smith, who was free after he was able to overturn three convictions in Massachusetts Appeals Act on legal technicalities.

Smith, Whitey and several other young hoodlums began organizing a bank robbing gang. Their first score came in May 1955, when they robbed a bank in Pawtucket, Rhode Island, of $42,000. Whitey carried a .22-caliber revolver and ordered two bank employees to the floor. The gang escaped in a stolen car. With $14,000 in his pocket, Whitey was finally a big shot.

In October 1955, still working with Smith, Whitey drove to Indiana to rob another bank. According to an FBI statement, "BULGER, carrying two sidearms, entered the victim bank. BULGER covered the employees and customers in the bank by mounting the counter."

On January 4, 1956 a warrant was issued for Whitey's arrest. In a getaway scenario similar to one he would employ thirty eight years later, he first fled to California, then returned to Boston a couple of weeks later to pick up his girlfriend and head back out of state. He took off across the country. They stopped in Reno, San Francisco, Salt Lake City, New Mexico, and Chicago, before heading back to Boston.

Within two months FBI Agent Rico received a tip that Whitey had been hanging out at a nightclub in Revere. Two nights later Whitey was arrested walking out of the joint. He soon learned a hard underworld lesson: everybody rats. He decided to talk too; not to save himself, as he would years later, but to save his girlfriend.

"Bulger orally admitted who his accomplices were in these bank robberies," FBI Agent Herbert Briick wrote on July 5, 1956.

Bulger persuaded his girlfriend, Jacqui McAuliffe, to do the same, with an FBI promise that she would not be prosecuted, according to the FBI memo. Bulger was arrested; his girlfriend went back to cutting hair.

The next morning at his arraignment, the prosecutor described Whitey as "a vicious person, known to carry guns, and [who] by his own admittance has an intense dislike for police and law enforcement officers." On June 21, 1956, Whitey was sentenced to twenty years in federal prison.

His first stop was a federal penitentiary in Atlanta, where he was involved in a number of scuffles and spent a total of ninety days in the hole. After two years in prison he took part in an experimental drug program for a minor reduction in his sentence. The program was part of a CIA project to find out how people reacted to LSD and Whitey would receive three days off his twenty year sentence for each month he participated.

In handwritten notes he left behind when he fled in Boston in 1994, Whitey painted himself as a victim of a cruel government experiment. "We were recruited by deception," Whitey began. "Once a week we checked into the so-called Nuero [sic] Psychiatric Ward-a large room with bars + steel locked door in the basement of the prison hospital... we were given the LSD in varying dosage – some times light some times massive that would plunge us into the depths of insanity and followed by periods of deep depression suicidal thought and nightmares and interrupted sleep."

In late 1959, Whitey was transferred to Alcatraz. While incarcerated at the infamous "Rock" in San Francisco Bay, Whitey adopted a lifelong habit of studying World War II and military strategy, reading biographies of Rommell and Patton and dissecting battles from all sides. He also became a physical fitness buff. In July 1962, around the time Alcatraz was closed down, Bulger was transferred to a federal prison in Lewisburg, Pennsylvania before being paroled in March 1965, after serving nine years.

He returned to Southie a different person. The young Bulger had been a smart mouthed punk prone to impulsive behavior. The new Bulger was disciplined and serious. He was ready to exploit every advantage he had to survive. It was a skill he shared with his younger brother, the Senator.

Billy Bulger: Mom's Good Boy

Whitey's brother Bill attended court the day Whitey was sentenced to two decades in prison. Billy, younger by five years, was in his second year at Boston College at the time. Four years later, in 1960, Billy Bulger ran for public office because he needed a job as he neared graduation from law school. John Connolly was one of his campaign workers and Will McDonough, the Boston Globe sportswriter, was his campaign manager.

Billy's father told him his opponents would use Whitey against him. In one incident, a man snarled at him, "You belong in prison with your brother." Despite the crowded field of candidates, including two future felons, Billy's team outworked everyone on election day and won. Billy moved up to the Senate in 1970 and went on to be the longest serving president in Massachusetts history.

Some of his neighbors in Southie believed that Bill Bulger's drive to achieve great things in legitimate society in spite of his brother's gangster reputation was a gift to his aged mother. Billy presented himself to the public as nearly puritanical: a devout churchgoer, scholar, teetotaler, devoted husband, and father of nine children. With his groomed blond hair, cherubic face and piercing blue eyes, the senator was the kind of classic "good boy" who could make a mother proud.

As he progressed through the legislature, Billy came to epitomize South Boston, with his jutting jaw and conservative agenda. When federal judge Arthur Garrity ordered the integration of the city's segregated schools through forced busing, the racial violence that followed received national and even international press.

In the midst of the crisis, Billy showed his tough side. When anti-busing protestors were arrested outside a neighborhood school, Bulger was on the scene and denounced police for overreacting. He went nose to nose with the city's police commissioner, Robert diGrazia, jabbing his finger at him about his "Gestapo" troopers and angrily walking away. DiGrazia yelled a response about politicians lacking "the balls" to deal with desegregation earlier. Bulger spun around for more, storming up to the much taller diGrazia. "Go fuck yourself," the senator hissed into the chief's face.

As busing turned Southie on its ear, Billy wasn't the only Bulger involved in the drama. Whitey played a significant behind the scenes role in Southie's federal disobedience. He harbored teenage kids chased by cops for throwing rocks at buses carrying black schoolchildren into Southie. He was also believed to be the muscle behind the South Boston Marshals, an armed vigilante group whose slogan "Hell No, We Won't Go!" became the rallying cry of the antibusing resistance.

In the wake of the busing crisis, the myth of Whitey Bulger took hold of Southie – the battered, impoverished neighborhood was in need. The gangster filled the void. Author Michael Patrick MacDonald, whose memoir *All Souls* is a beautiful, heartbreaking account of life in Southie during and after the busing years, says:

"Whitey stepped up as our protector. They said he protected us from being overrun with the drugs and gangs we'd heard about in the black neighborhoods…He was our king, and everybody made like they were connected to him in some way…Everyone bragged about how his uncle was tight with him, or his brother had been bailed out of jail by him, or how he'd gotten them a new pair of sneakers, or his mother a modern kitchen set. All the neighbors said they went to see Whitey when they were in trouble, whether they'd been sent eviction notices from the Boston Housing Authority or the cops were harassing their kid. Whitey was more accessible than the welfare office, the BHA, the courts or the cops. If your life had been threatened, your mother could always visit Whitey and get him to squash a beef."

After a long criminal career, Whitey had skillfully manipulated the Irish gang wars and the busing crisis to become the ultimate neighborhood godfather. Now, sitting in Connolly's car, he sensed an opening to bring the FBI under his deadly rule.

As a project kid from Southie, Agent Connolly got to know both Bulger brothers. He became good friends with Billy, tagging along after him on the way home from mass at St. Monica's. It was Whitey who would save him though. At eight years old, Connolly was in a ball game that turned ugly. An older boy fired a ball into the middle of the boy's back. When Connolly instinctively picked up the ball and fired a high hard one into the kid's nose, the older boy was all over Connolly, pounding away at the smaller boy. Then, from the margins of the playground, Whitey swooped in to break up the one sided fight. Bloodied, Connolly staggered to his feet, forever grateful. In some ways, Connolly would always look up to the macho mystique of Whitey Bulger.

In America's most Irish city, these three pieces of the Irish mob – Whitey the gangster, Connolly the lawman and Billy the politician – would form a holy trinity of corruption and power that devastated all competitors and, above all, their own neighborhood.

Jai Alai Gangsters

Brian Halloran was the kind of everyday schmuck typical of the Boston underworld in the 1970s and 80s. A veteran criminal from the heyday of the Winter Hill Gang, Halloran was doing his best to stay on the good side of Whitey Bulger now that much of the original Winter Hill crew was dead or in jail.

In early 1981, Halloran was an average Boston palooka looking to make a score. On this night, he backed his ratty Cadillac into a space in front of a busy North End restaurant and bounded upstairs to the loft apartment of his drinking buddy John Callahan.

They were an odd pair that got along. Halloran, the thug, and Callahan, an accountant and consultant to Boston banks. They first met in the wiseguy hangout Chandler's, a South End bar owned by Howie Winter. Callahan talked to bankers by day and socialized with mobsters by night. The wiseguys saw him as a big spender who knew how to launder money.

After Halloran was buzzed into Callahan's apartment overlooking Boston Harbor, he was surprised to see Whitey Bulger and Stevie Flemmi sitting in the living room. Callahan gave him an effusive greeting. Stevie said hello. Whitey said nothing. There was some strained small talk and then, nervously, Callahan got to it. He said a serious problem had come up at the World Jai Alai company he, Bulger and Flemmi were stealing from. The problem was a new owner from Tulsa named Roger Wheeler.

Callahan had been president of World Jai Alai until 1977 when his associations with Winter Hill gangsters got him stripped of his state license to run a betting pool – without which he couldn't run a Jai Alai game the heavy betting that comes with it. Wheeler, a native Bostonian who had made a fortune in high tech, stepped in and paid $50 million for the company. The bank that loaned him the money was mobbed up too though and they insisted Wheeler keep Callahan and corrupt ex-FBI agent H. Paul Rico on the payroll.

Quickly, however, the CEO from Oklahoma discovered something was not right. Wheeler learned someone was skimming one million dollars a year. Now the owner planned to fire the company's top financial officers and replace them with his own people. This Wheeler was a danger, Callahan told Halloran that night, and Callahan feared he'd end up in jail because of an internal audit.

But then John Callahan also pitched a solution. Brian Halloran, he proposed, could "take Wheeler out of the box" a way of saying shoot him in the head. Halloran knew it was not idle talk. He had helped Bulger murder Louis Litif, one of Whitey's bookmakers, who killed two men without clearing it with the boss first. But all Halloran had done was deliver Litif to Whitey. This time he was being asked to pull the trigger. Sitting in Callahan's apartment listening to the casual discussion of murder, he got darty-eyed, cleared his throat, and asked if there was any alternative to "hitting the guy." This brought him one of Bulger's patented cold glares. The hour long meeting broke up without a definitive plan but Halloran left Callahan's apartment believing Roger Wheeler would soon be a dead man.

So he was surprised a few weeks later when Callahan handed him a bag with $20,000 in cash and told him they decided to take care of Wheeler without him. Slapping him on the shoulder, Callahan said the group "should not have involved you to begin with." Always strapped for cash, he took the money and headed for the door.

With Halloran on the sidelines the Winter Hill hit squad of Johnny Martorano and Joe MacDonald arrived in Tulsa three months later. MacDonald joined in the murder plot as a favor to ex-FBI Agent Rico. Rico had set up Ronnie Dermody for Winter Hill Gang boss Buddy McLean in 1964 during the gang wars and MacDonald felt he owed the agent.

Rico sent them a piece of paper with all of Wheeler's addresses, usual haunts and even parking spaces. "At the bottom there was a description of what Wheeler looks like," said Johnny Martorano. "Rico said he had a 'ruddy complexion.' A ruddy complexion – when I read that I knew a cop had written it, an FBI guy. John Callahan or anybody else would have said, 'a red face.' Ruddy complexion is how an FBI guy talks when he's trying to impress somebody."

Shortly after arriving in Oklahoma City, they picked up a package at the bus station – handguns, a carbine, a grease gun, silencers, bulletproof vests, ski masks, a shimmy, and a dent puller for stealing cars. It was the standard Winter Hill hit kit sent along with a bit of underworld humor – the package was addressed to Joe Russo, the Boston Mafia's top hitman.

Rico gave the killers a tee-time for Wheeler at his country club, two o'clock Saturday at the Southern Hills Country Club. Martorano and MacDonald drove to the golf course and spotted Wheeler's Cadillac. "But remember, I've still never seen this guy," Martorano told journalist Howie Carr. "So we park a few rows closer to the club. I'm in full disguise…full beard, sunglasses, a baseball cap.

"Finally I see a guy coming down the hill from the club to the parking lot, might be Wheeler. I let him walk past our car, then I fall in behind him. If he gets in the Caddy, I clip him. If he goes to another car, I just keep walking. But it's him, he's getting in the car. He doesn't hear me, he's about to close the door but I grab it to keep it open. He jumps back in the seat, startled, and I let him have it, one shot between the eyes, .38 snub nose. But when I fired the gun exploded. The chamber flew open, the bullets fell out – I'd wiped them down as I was loading the gun, so there were no prints. I just left the bullets there on the pavement. I closed the door to Wheeler's car; I walked back to our car, got in, and Joe drove off."

They returned to their hotel, where Joe MacDonald chopped up the .38 with a special saw that had been sent down from Boston. Johnny Martorano meanwhile was cutting up the false beard with some scissors, then flushing the pieces down the toilet. They'd driven by a marsh one day, and now they returned to throw pieces of the gun into the water. Next, they went to the airport where they flew to Florida.

Back in Tulsa, the investigation into Wheeler's murder went nowhere. The trail quickly led back to Boston, but the FBI office there seemed determined to stymie the Oklahoma cops. The feds in Boston finally agreed to send down mug shots of Whitey and Stevie – but when the photos arrived Tulsa detectives were shocked that the two gangsters were wearing suits and ties, as if the feds were trying to make them look as little like criminals as possible.

Tulsa police detective Mike Huff flew to World jai Alai headquarters in Miami to interview H. Paul Rico. Rico was a hostile interview, refusing to answer even the simplest questions. "I walked out of Rico's office in a state of disbelief," Huff said. "I'd been expecting to talk to another cop, and instead I ran into the Godfather."

Through the underworld grapevine, Halloran learned that the Oklahoma hit went off without him. He knew that, as the only person with knowledge of the murder who wasn't directly involved, he was a marked man.

The small-time hood became frazzled and paranoid. With a wife and a young child, he couldn't pack up and leave town. He tried to raise some money by selling cocaine but he started using it heavily instead. His unraveling continued a few weeks later, this time by his own hand. He shot and killed a Mafia connected cocaine dealer in a Chinatown restaurant.

After hiding out for a month, Halloran turned himself in to the authorities. He was charged with first degree murder and released on $50,000 bail. Back on the streets, Halloran was a frazzled cocaine addict with both Whitey Bulger and the Mafia after him. In a no-man's land at the end of the line he decided to strike a deal with the FBI. In exchange for a reduced sentence in the Chinatown murder, he would provide information on the Wheeler murder.

He signed a statement that read in part: "I was offered $20,000 by John Callahan to kill Roger Wheeler. Bulger and Flemmi were present at Callahan's apartment when the offer was made. Callahan said the owner, Wheeler, discovered someone was ripping off one million dollars a year from the Jai Alai operations and was planning to fire the executives, conduct an audit, and bring in state officials to investigate."

Halloran was dealing with Agent Robert Fitzpatrick, assigned to the FBI's labor racketeering squad. Halloran had known enough to avoid Bulger's allies in the Organized Crime task force where at least two agents had become so corrupted they might as well have been part of the gang.

Connolly was already in the bag for his star informant Bulger, who didn't provide the agent with much more than underworld gossip. Connolly's supervisor Agent John Morris had been compromised by Bulger with a small cash payoff of $7,000 and a few expensive bottles of wine.

Thinking he was safe dealing with Agent Fitzpatrick, Halloran talked nonstop from January 3 to February 19, 1982. He moved between three safe houses as agents pressed him for corroboration. They had him wear a wire but the wiseguys sensed Halloran's desperation when he came around. Agents demanded a polygraph but Halloran refused. The Halloran debriefing became a stalemate with agents demanding more hard proof than Halloran could provide.

The decision to formally protect Brian Halloran as a federal witness was up to Assistant U.S. Attorney Jeremiah O'Sullivan. O'Sullivan knew all about Whitey Bulger's role as an informant; O'Sullivan was the one who had severed Bulger and Flemmi from a 1978 horse race-fixing case, which had resulted in convictions for every high ranking member of the Winter Hill Gang except Bulger and Flemmi.

This time, O'Sullivan was being asked to choose between Brian Halloran and Whitey Bulger. Agents Connolly and Morris were telling him Halloran was a drunk and a wannabe who knew nothing about Bulger. Agent Fitzpatrick was telling him that Halloran's life was in imminent danger. For the second time, O'Sullivan chose to protect Whitey Bulger. Halloran was denied protective custody.

Toward the end of his debriefings Halloran learned that Whitey Bulger was an FBI informant. He didn't know that Connolly had tipped Bulger to his cooperation but he knew he was in trouble. Panicking, Halloran suddenly felt he had nowhere to turn – he was in danger on the street and in FBI offices. In May 1982, the small time thug's role as an informant was terminated and he was cut loose. The FBI had chewed him up, set him up to be killed and spit him back out on the street. He couldn't live at home with his wife who was pregnant with their second child for fear that one of Whitey's gunmen would burst in and shoot them all. Moving from safe house to safe house, he trusted no one and slept with a gun under his pillow.

On the afternoon of May 11, less than a week after being dumped by the FBI, Halloran was drinking at a waterfront bar when he was spotted by an old-time hoodlum. The old hoodlum told Whitey and Whitey immediately enlisted his flunky Kevin Weeks to help him take out Halloran.

Whitey arrived wearing a light brown wig and a floppy mustache. "He looked just like Jimmy Flynn," Weeks said. Flynn, an old-time Winter Hill Gang associate, had shot at Halloran in two separate incidents but Halloran had escaped unharmed.

Whitey was driving the Tow Truck – a souped up blue 1975 Malibu. With the push of a button, the vehicle would emit a billowing cloud of blue exhaust. Another button opened a specially built tank, allowing Whitey to dump gallons of oil onto the street, causing any pursuing vehicle to spin out.

Halloran was given the code name "Balloonhead" and Weeks set up outside the restaurant in another car to serve as lookout. He looked over to the Tow Truck where Whitey was sitting with a second man in the back seat. The second man, his face hidden behind a dark blue ski mask, raised himself up and waved at Weeks.

Ten minutes later, Halloran and Michael Donahue, a man he'd been drinking with, walked out of the restaurant. "The balloon is in the air," Weeks told Whitey over a scanner, referring to Halloran who earned the name for his big head. "The balloon is in the air," Weeks repeated. Whitey whipped the Tow Truck next to Halloran and yelled through gritted teeth, "Brian!" Halloran turned his head and the shooting began. Whitey was firing a .30-caliber carbine and the masked shooter in the back seat popped up with a fully automatic Mac-10.

It was a beautiful Tuesday night in May and people walking along the waterfront were screaming and ducking for cover as Whitey blasted away. A few stood paralyzed with fear and didn't move as the bullets flew by their heads. Donohue, the innocent man who offered Halloran a ride, was killed. Halloran stumbled out of the car, straight into the path of the shots coming at him. He staggered a few more feet and finally went down. When a Boston police officer arrived on the scene, Halloran was slipping in and out of consciousness. The cops asked who had shot him.

"Jimmy Flynn," he said and died.

There was still one more person to kill.

Killing Callahan

About a month after Halloran's murder Stevie Flemmi called Johnny Martorano – who was hiding out as a fugitive in Florida – and said he and Whitey needed to meet him in New York, face to face. When he arrived at a hotel near LaGuardia airport, there was only one agenda on the item: John Callahan, the accountant who liked to play with wiseguys and set in motion the chain of events that ended in Wheeler and Halloran's deaths.

"Whitey did all the talking. He was in his politician mode, making the case, point by point," Martorano said. "He said, 'We killed Halloran for you; he was telling the FBI that you killed Wheeler. Zip [Whitey's codename for Agent Connolly] told us."

Whitey left out a few key points: Halloran had also named Bulger and

Flemmi in his statements to the feds; they had been the ones to offer the contract to Halloran before involving Martorano; Halloran was a witness to Bulger's murder of Louis Litif which Martorano had nothing to do with.

But Whitey was putting the pressure on Martorano now. "Zip says the feds want to talk to Callahan, Whitey said. "I'm asking you, Johnny, can you guarantee he'll stand up? If he cracks, Zip says we're all going to jail for the rest of our lives."

Martorano was convinced. In July 1982, he and his partner Joe MacDonald shot their friend John Callahan in the back of the head in a Miami parking garage. The wannabe was finally the real thing – he died like a genuine wiseguy.

It had all started with Callahan's pitch to Halloran, in the presence of Whitey and Flemmi, that they kill Roger Wheeler. Now, for Callahan, it was all over. But the murders by the FBI's star informants, Whitey Bulger and Stevie Flemmi kept coming.

Next was Arthur (Bucky) Barrett, an expert safecracker who had pulled off a $1.5 million heist at the Depositors Bank Trust in Medford. Shortly after the robbery FBI agents Morris and Connolly approached the safecracker with an off-the-books double mission: they wanted to soften him up for Bulger with a friendly "warning" that Whitey would be looking for a cut from the bank job. And then they offered him the perilous haven of the FBI informant program if he would become a snitch. It was a mission of staggering corruption. Here were two seasoned FBI agents acting as Whitey Bulger's emissaries on the street – shakedown artists with FBI badges.

Barrett rejected the FBI offer and made what turned out to be a fatal mistake. He reached out to Stevie Flemmi's old partner Cadillac Frank Salemme, giving him $100,000 to keep Bulger and Flemmi away from the rest of his money. That didn't sit well with Whitey.

Barrett was lured to an abandoned home on South Boston's East Third Street by an associate promising to sell him stolen diamonds. When he stepped through the door of the small two-story home, however, Whitey stepped out from behind the refrigerator, holding a Mac-11 nine-millimeter machine gun with a silencer and yelled, "Bucky Barrett, freeze."

Flemmi handcuffed Barrett, put chains around his legs and waist and sat him in a chair. Negotiations began and Barrett offered to pay Whitey and Flemmi $40,000 a month to let him live. Whitey rejected the offer and had Barrett call his wife to tell her he was bringing some friends over and she had to leave. Whitey and Flemmi returned from the house with $47,000 in cash from a hiding spot Barrett told them about. Next, Barrett had a partner give Whitey another $10,000.

Finally, as Barrett muttered prayers under his breath, Bulger suggested he go down to the basement "and lay down." Barrett turned his head and looked at Whitey and said in a compliant way, "Yeah, lay down."

Still shackled, he started to walk down the stairs, very slowly, one step at a time, with Whitey following behind. A few steps from the bottom, Whitey put the gun to the back of Barrett's head and pulled the trigger, but nothing happened. Whitey stopped, took his glasses out of his shirt pocket, and, realizing the safety was still on, flipped it off. Barrett was still walking slowly down the last two stairs. Whitey put the gun to the back of his head and pulled the trigger a second time, this time killing Barrett instantly, splattering blood, brains and skull over the floor.

As Flemmi and Bulger flunky Kevin Weeks cleaned up the mess and buried the body in the basement, Whitey went upstairs to take a nap. "I noticed that [Whitey] seemed to calm down after a murder, almost as if he'd just taken a Valium," Weeks said. "I noticed this after other murders, too. Nothing seemed to relax him or make him feel quite so good as a murder."

The abandoned home on East Third Street would be a final resting place for other victims of the Bulger gang. Less than a year later, John McIntyre was killed and buried there. He was a young boatsman who ran afoul of Bulger after taking part in an IRA gun smuggling operation led by Southie gangster Pat Nee. When McIntyre started singing to federal authorities, Agent John Connolly tipped off Whitey. McIntyre disappeared, buried in the basement on East Third Street next to Barrett.

A third victim would meet the same grisly fate. Stevie Flemmi had been molesting his stepdaughter, Deborah Hussey, since she was thirteen. As she grew older, Deb Hussey had become a drug addict and a prostitute. She even revealed Flemmi's abuse of her to her mother.

Offering to buy her a new coat, Stevie lured Deb to the same house. When she walked in, Whitey jumped her with a rope, breaking five of her ribs as he strangled her. After his stepdaughter was dead, Stevie performed his usual routine of removing her teeth. Flemmi's post-murder operations were so intricate, Whitey once joked to Weeks, "I told you Dr. Mengele was crazy."

Weeks helped bury Deb Hussey but mostly took commands from Flemmi. "He was all business, going about the task of cleaning up and pulling teeth," Weeks said of Flemmi. "Stevie was actually enjoying it, the way he always enjoyed a good murder. Like a stockbroker going to work, he was just doing his job. Cold and relaxed, with no emotion or change in his demeanor, he was performing a night's work."

Deb Hussey was not the first Flemmi girlfriend killed by the gang; three years earlier Whitey and Flemmi strangled Debbie Davis after she learned of their relationship with the FBI. However, Hussey would be the last victim buried in the two story structure on East Third Street. Six months after Hussey's murder, the house was sold. On Halloween night in 1985, the gang exhumed their victims and relocated them to a wooded spot overlooking the highway.

Cocaine in Southie and the Whitey Myth

One of the cornerstones of the Whitey Bulger myth was that he kept drugs out of South Boston. During the busing crisis one of Southie's confrontational chants had been that Roxbury was plagued with drugs. Whitey, they said, kept that "fucking shit" out of grand old Southie.

It was all a lie. Bulger had an iron grip on the drugs moving through his neighborhood. He made dealers pay rent on every gram of "Santa Claus" a Southie code name for cocaine. He extorted a share of everything from nickel bags to kilos, loose joints to bales of marijuana. Apartments in the Old Colony projects had visitors tapping at the door at all hours of the day and night. Young men, and even some mothers, were selling drugs out of their homes – angel dust, mescalin, valium, speed, coke, and heroin – and nothing moved without Whitey's okay. Whitey's drug lieutenant, Paul (Polecat) Moore kept a place in Old Colony. Southie's drug business smoked hotter in the neighborhood's housing projects than it did in the more middle class section of City Point. It got to where "P-dope," a heroin mixture, cost only four dollars a hit – cheaper than a six-pack.

The neighborhood suffered in Whitey's hands. Southie's teenagers became addicted, overdosed and committed suicide at alarming rates, but it would be another decade before the code of silence surrounding drug abuse in the neighborhood broke. In the 1980s everyday people still clung to the notion that Whitey was their protector. Drugs and prostitution might be "a way of life in other sections of the city, but they will not be tolerated in South Boston," the South Boston Information Center declared in one of its newsletters, even as crime statistics showed that the neighborhood was like any other in the city – awash in drugs. Yearly drug arrests were tripling in Southie between 1980 and 1990. Narcotics cases doubled in South Boston District Court from 1985 to 1990, and one Boston police detective said he thought there was more cocaine in Southie per capita than anywhere else in Boston.

Just as Southie was in denial the FBI in Boston did not want to know the true story about drugs and Bulger. In fact, agent John Connolly was doing his best to protect his star informant. When the DEA opened an investigation into Bulger's drug activity and tapped telephones used for drug transactions, Agent Connolly tipped them off. Instead of agents capturing criminal conversations, they overheard Flemmi talking in nonsense. Bulger never touched the phone.

Next, the agents bugged Bulger's black Chevy. Three days later, what they overheard signaled the end of their investigation.

"He's right – they did put a bug in the car."

The agents jumped out of their van and raced in to retrieve their electronic surveillance equipment. They found Bulger tearing open the door panel and Kevin Weeks standing nearby holding a radio frequency detector that located bugs just like the bug the DEA had used. Facing down the agents, Bulger put on his take-charge attitude that characterized his interactions with cops. He said he was surprised they'd been able to install a bug. "I got a pretty good alarm system," he said as agents pulled out the microphone

"Hey," the crime boss announced, "We're all good guys."

How so?

"You're the good good guys. We're the bad good guys."

DEA agents immediately believed the FBI had tipped off Bulger but no governmental inquiry was ever undertaken to examine this belief. Whitey had won again.

Agent John Connolly was far from Whitey Bulger's only ally in the Boston office of the FBI. Former agent Robert Fitzpatrick said he could name at least six agents who worked in the Boston office in the 1980s who were corrupt. That corruption reached the top of the FBI office. Organized Crime Squad supervisor John Morris was supposed to be Connolly's superior overseeing his handling of the dangerous informants Bulger and Flemmi. Instead, he accepted gifts and bribes as Whitey and Flemmi murdered eight people during their time as top echelon informants.

It was as if the FBI had been absorbed into the Winter Hill Gang. Bulger even had his own colorful nicknames for the F.B.I. agents he wined and dined and used: Zip, Agent Orange, The Pipe, Doc and Vino.

Morris, whose nickname Vino referred to the expensive wines he favored, was essentially in Whitey's backpocket. He had solicited and taken $1,000 from the gangster in 1982 to fly his girlfriend to Georgia, where he was attending an FBI seminar. In early 1984, as the DEA was starting its doomed drug investigation, Agent Morris took a second bite from apple Bulger held out for him.

"Connolly called me and said, 'I have something for you from these guys. Why don't you come on over and pick it up?' I went over; I picked it up. It was a case of wine. On the way out he said, 'Be careful with it, there's something in the bottom for you.' So I took the case of wine, and then when I opened the case I found that there was an envelope on the bottom that contained $1,000 in it." The conspiracy between Agents Morris and Connolly and killers Bulger and Flemmi paused for a year when Morris was specially assigned to Miami to investigate, ironically, a corrupt FBI agent.

When Morris returned in the spring of 1985, the rest of the gang was happy to see him. The supervisor who replaced Morris was Jim Ring - a tough mark even for Connolly and Bulger. "Connolly, Flemmi, and Bulger had arrived together," Morris recalled. It was Morris who hustled from living room to kitchen, the dutiful host and cook. They poured wine and got down to business.

John Connolly, Flemmi said later, provided updated accounts on who the two crime bosses should avoid. He disclosed the identities of several police informants. It was as if, as the tenth anniversary of Whitey and the FBI's secret deal approached, they all renewed their vows.

It was good timing too. Whitey's brother Bill, the senator from Southie, was about to have his own need for a friendly FBI. A corrupt scheme he hatched three years earlier was threatening to knock him from his powerful position on top of state government (through shrewd negotiating and power broking he had eclipsed Gov. Michael Dukakis).

The scandal became known as 75 State Street and it showed Bill Bulger may not have been his mother's good boy after all. The complex twisted tale involved Bulger and his law partner, Thomas Finnerty, essentially shaking down the state's biggest landlord for $500,000 – which they split between themselves in exchange for using their power to secure the undervalued, available piece of downtown property at the State Street address.

As the story broke and became a local sensation, Bulger claimed he paid the money back but the truth was found in a circle of financial transactions in which he and Finnerty funneled the money between accounts controlled by one another.

Despite the public clamor, the matter was already closed within the bureau. John Connolly took his compromised supervisor, Agent John Morris, aside and pressed him on whether the senate president should agree to be interviewed. Morris told him that Bulger should do it because the landlord's uncorroborated accusations made for a soft case. When the FBI reopened the case it was to make Bill Bulger look good rather than conduct a real investigation.

Connolly and Whitey's alliance had been kept secret through multiple murders. But the FBI agent always made it known that he was good friends with the Senate President, Bill Bulger. Bill, after all, had been Connolly's real hero in their Southie childhoods – with Connolly tagging along after the older Billy on the way home from Mass at St. Monica's. He worked on Bulger's campaigns from the beginning and when another Southie pol, Ray Flynn, was elected mayor, Bill lobbied hard for Connolly to be appointed the city's new chief of police.

Years later, Bulger claimed unconvincingly that he had no idea about Connolly and Whitey's "special relationship," but he did admit to telling the agent, "I expect you to take care of my brother." The implied understanding was that Connolly would be Whitey's protector inside law enforcement. In return, Bulger would exert his considerable influence for a steady stream of FBI agents whom Connolly brought by his senate office by providing reference letters and finding government jobs. No way was Connolly going to allow a hostile FBI interview of Billy. The reopened investigation consisted solely of a two-hour speech from Billy to FBI agents in his lawyer's office.

Even U.S. Attorney Jeremiah O'Sullivan got involved in one final cover-up for the Bulger brothers. Years earlier, O'Sullivan had looked the other way on Whitey's involvement with the Winter Hill Gang's horse race fixing. He was also the one who banished a doomed Brian Halloran from the witness protection program. Now the prosecutor proclaimed the Bill Bulger case dead on arrival.

The scandal showed Whitey and Billy might not be so different. One year after Bill Bulger and his law partner split up $500,000 from the state's largest landlord, Whitey told a small South Boston realtor he'd be blown away by a shotgun unless he came up with $50,000. The realtor eventually complained to the FBI. Instead of launching an investigation, John Connolly tipped Whitey and told him to back off.

The Last Hurrah

John Connolly retired from the FBI in December 1990. Whitey Bulger did not attend his retirement party, but Senator Bulger did. In fact, Billy Bulger reprised his role as Master of Ceremonies, as he had at so many FBI retirement parties. A few months later, the former agent Connolly landed a high-paying position as head of corporate security at Boston Edison, an ally of Senate President Bulger's. Five other agents landed jobs at the public utility company thanks to references from Bill Bulger.

Not long after his retirement, Connolly moved into a condominium in Southie that had an adjoining unit that belonged to Whitey Bulger. They were now next door neighbors and had every reason to believe they would grow old together, telling stories of how they outlasted the Mafia and lived like kings during the Age of Bulger.

Whitey was working on his own retirement plans. In July 1991, he "won" the Massachusetts State Lottery. A winning ticket sold at Bulger's Rotary Variety Store hit and the ticket's owner claimed he'd agreed to split it with Bulger months earlier. However he arranged it, Whitey ended up with a share of the $14.3 million jackpocket - $89,000 tax free every year for the next 20 years.

Around this time, Bulger began a series of international forays. He opened bank accounts and safe deposit boxes in the Carribbean, Ireland, and London. He acquired driver's licenses under assumed names from multiple states, including New York. With his FBI benefactor in retirement, Whitey must have known federal authorities would be coming after him.

That year, just a few months after Connolly's retirement, a major narcotics investigation involving the DEA and Massachusetts State Police netted 51 Southie drug dealers, most associated with the Bulger organization. The indictments rocked the neighborhood, where Whitey apologists had always maintained the lie that he would never sell drugs in his own backyard. But even with the indictments nobody "flipped" and offered to testify against Whitey, demonstrating the fear that the kingpin still inspired.

The feds were no longer afraid of him though, and in 1992 a sprawling investigation into Boston bookies turned up a bookie who did not want to go to jail for decades. The bookie began to sing and it soon became clear that all of the bookies rounded up had one thing in common: In order to operate, they paid tribute to Whitey Bulger.

As the case grew, the FBI got involved. Connolly was retired but he was still in the loop. He monitored the grand jury investigation of Bulger and his partner in crime Stevie Flemmi and shortly after New Year's Day, 1995, Connolly learned the indictment would be handed down on January 9 or 10. Connolly had long ago promised Bulger that he would give Whitey a "head start" in the event of an indictment. Now, he called Bulger and told him everything he knew.

Whitey was already on the road with his longtime girlfriend Theresa Stanley. They had been crisscrossing the country as Whitey squirreled cash away in safe deposit boxes in Memphis, New Orleans and California. The only problem was that Theresa Stanley, his girlfriend, did not want to go on the lam and say goodbye to her family forever.

He was driving her back toward Boston when it was announced over the car radio that Stevie "The Rifleman" Flemmi had been arrested. Whitey turned his car around and headed toward safe house in New York, where he dropped off his girlfriend. Soon, he was being accompanied by another longtime girlfriend, Catherine Greig. The couple arrived in Grand Isle, Louisiana in late January 1995.

By the fall, they were back in Long Island. Whitey was still communicating with his old flunky Kevin Weeks, who had funneled at least $90,000 in cash to his old boss. H. Paul Rico, the FBI agent who "flipped" Joe (The Animal) Barboza and helped the Winter Hill Gang kill Roger Wheeler, had been arrested for murder. When informed of his arrest he said, "You're shitting me." He died of a heart attack shortly after. Whitey, though, had successfully disappeared and no one heard from him.

Except John Morris. One afternoon in October 1995 his secretary told him that an insistent "Mister White" was calling. The brazen Bulger, on the lam for ten months, was calling from a pay phone on the road.

He had a short message for Morris: "I'm taking you with me you fuck," Bulger said.

"I hear you," said Morris. That night John Morris suffered a major heart attack. Whitey almost killed him with a phone call. Whitey was gone. The next time he was seen by the public would be 16 years later, long after the Age of Bulger had passed in Boston.

CHAPTER FOURTEEN

ARMED ROBBERY CAPITAL: CHARLESTOWN'S CRIMINAL SUBCULTURE REVEALED

IN OCTOBER 2010, Ben Affleck's *The Town* debuted as the number one movie in America. For most audiences it was their first look at Charlestown's culture of robbery and violence.

But Charlestown's criminal tradition stretches back beyond the days of bootlegging. Decades before *The Town*, the criminal ethic that would one day become known as the Code of Silence came of age along the waterfront docks and in the shadows of the old state prison.

Some in Charlestown say the Code of Silence began with dock workers keeping their mouths shut when a fellow worker picked up a dozen canned hams or a case of whiskey from a broken crate. But if the docks gave birth to the code, prison reared it. According to legend, the ancestry of some Townies traces back to the old Charlestown State Prison. History has it that around the turn of the century, some families set down their roots in the community to be closer to loved ones who were "away," as some referred to doing time.

The community's proud stony silence became twisted as drugs flowed into the neighborhood and solid jobs began to dry up. In April 1973, President Richard Nixon closed the Charlestown Navy Yard after 174 years of service. At the time it was seen as direct retribution from Nixon against Massachusetts – the only state he lost to McGovern in 1972. For thousands, it was a direct loss of livelihood; it also took a heavy toll on the bars, restaurants, variety stores and newsstands that served Yard employees and sailors temporarily stationed there.

By that time, Charlestown was struggling. After swelling to 41,000 residents in 1910, by the 1970s it was down to 13,000 – and one in three residents living in public housing. That year sixty-eight percent of children in the neighborhood's sprawling public housing complex lived in households with no father. One of the country's first housing projects, Bunker Hill went up in 1940 as part of Roosevelt's New Deal. The development's 45 buildings hold 1,106 units and about 2,500 residents. In *Liberty's Chosen Home*, author Alan Lupo described the Bunker Hill project "as close to Belfast or Derry as anything in America."

Court-ordered busing came to Charlestown in 1975 and there were helicopters over the neighborhood when Metropolitan Police, State Police, deputy US marshals and Boston's Tactical Patrol Force lined the streets to guarantee the safety of black students. On the same streets the antibusing mothers of Charlestown knelt in front of police lines and said Hail Marys while network TV cameras rolled. The images were lasting.

The Charlestown criminals of the 1990s were the children of men who fought in the Irish Gang Wars a generation earlier. But they were also the children of busing who left school for street corners. The result: a generation of disaffected youth who raised the stakes on the neighborhood's criminal traditions with more violence, more drugs and bigger heists. The neighborhood's unique sub culture even had its own overriding ethic – the Code of Silence.

The Code of Silence

For victims, the Code of Silence meant fear and death. Between 1975 and 1992, 33 of Charlestown's 49 murders went unsolved, a no-arrest rate double other Boston neighborhoods. In one stretch from 1990 to 1994, police made no arrests in seven different murders in the Bunker Hill neighborhood. It was true: in this Town, you could get away with murder.

Daily, mothers of murder victims crossed paths with their son's killers. Families of victims tried their best to avoid walking past the stretches of sidewalks where sons and husbands were left for dead. "What you have," said the neighborhood priest, "is children growing up in a community where murder is acceptable. People might feel badly but they're not shocked anymore. It happens, and then it seems you just go on with your life."

In 1992 the Boston Globe published a front page article detailing the effects on the neighborhood. "I really get the feeling over there that you're raised from birth not to speak to police," a cold case homicide detective told Globe reporter Dick Lehr. "In Charlestown, the code of silence is at its zenith. Nowhere else in the city is it as strong, as pervasive or as much an obstacle, and it's nothing to be proud about."

Over the next week, the Globe offices were flooded with calls and letters from Charlestown residents addressing the code – anonymously. A young Charlestown man in his early twenties said the Globe coverage didn't emphasize enough the fear of retaliation. "See, the real way it is, 'You open your mouth and you will be next.' Not keep your mouth shut so he or she don't get in trouble."

For years, city homicide detectives could offer little protection for witnesses. "The local authorities didn't have the resources," said former Assistant U.S. Attorney Paul Kelly. "They'd put people up on a house in Castle Island, some fleabag apartment. Then within a week or two the person goes back on the streets of Charlestown and ends up in a morgue."

One man who never informed to authorities, even after he was shot in three separate incidents in a year, became a local folk hero.

The Ballad of Butchy Doe

Arthur (Butchy) Doe Jr. is few people's idea of a hero – a convicted bank robber suspected in three unsolved murders, Doe owned one of the most fearsome reputations in the whole city. That reputation was not enough to protect him though, as he feuded with old friends about control of drug territory.

In May 1989 Doe was the intended target of a deadly attack in the Bunker Hill housing project. At 3 a.m., two masked men burst into the apartment of his girlfriend Maurine Szymielewicz, a 28-year-old mother, and shot her in the stomach, killing her. The dead woman's two daughters – ages 1 and 2 - watched the shooting. The assailants then turned their guns on their intended targets, Doe and his friend Joseph (JoJo) Burhoe, another bank robber.

Doe was shot in the head but the .22 caliber bullet hit his forehead at an angle and literally bounced off. "A couple of inches, either way, and he's gone," said one detective. A bullet that entered his neck narrowly missed an artery. Burhoe, who a few months before survived a knife attack only because he was so drunk he passed out and slowed his bleeding, was shot in the torso but survived. Sticking to Charlestown's underworld code, Doe and Burhoe refused to implicate anyone in the shooting even as police focused on suspects.

As surgeons worked successfully to repair Doe that night, someone called Boston City Hospital. "Don't bother stitching him up," the male voice told the hospital operator, "because when he gets out we're going to shoot him again."

Three months later, the would-be assassins kept their word, ambushing Doe as he walked into a neighborhood deli. They shot him in the side. When paramedics arrived to treat Doe they recognized him. "A regular customer," as one put it.

Doe was even said to have repeated the famous boast of another shot-after man – 1930s New York mobster Jack (Legs) Diamond – and declared, "The bullet hasn't been made that can kill me." Five days later, his brother Ronald Doe was shot. Ronnie Doe might have had worse luck than his brother Butchy; he'd been a hard luck case from birth. He was named for his uncle Ronald (Pebbles) Doe, who was killed in the Irish Gang Wars of the 1960s.

"It ain't easy being a Doe in Charlestown," Ronnie said.

This time it was five months before anyone tried to kill Butchy Doe. He survived of course – despite a spray of shotgun pellets. When he again refused to cooperate with police he became something like a folk hero for some in Charlestown – a twisted perspective of a man who refused to help police after his girlfriend was gunned down.

For all of Doe's notoriety, he was a single, wild gun. The dominant criminal organization in Charlestown was far more dangerous – to witnesses, civilians and rivals.

The Rise and Fall of Michael Fitzgerald and the Code of Silence Gang

Michael Fitzgerald would one day become the most feared man in Charlestown. Even as he served a life sentence behind bars, Fitzgerald used a generous prison furlough program to oversee a violent drug empire.

Born in 1954, by age 20 Fitzgerald was convicted of second degree murder for killing two men in an Everett barroom; one of the men called him a punk. In prison, Fitzgerald became a pivotal figure among white inmates, controlling gambling activities. In the prison yard he often stood at the center of a crowd of inmates from Charlestown. In the early 1980s Fitzgerald met a new generation of townies – particularly Joseph Nardone, Billy Herd and James Boyden Jr. Nardone and Herd would go on to be Fitzgerald's most trusted assassins and Boyden Jr. would be hard pressed to avoid their wrath.

Despite serving a life sentence, Fitzgerald returned to Charlestown each day to work a shift at Kerrigan's Flower Shop on Main Street. While Fitzgerald was filling orders at the shop he was also maintaining a local drug empire. Next door to the flower shop, Fitzgerald's wife Jennirose Lynch sold teenths, bags of 1/16 of an ounce of cocaine, from her job at a beauty salon. Supplied by Florida dealers, Fitzgerald's crew earned as much as $10,000 a day selling cocaine in Charlestown's housing projects.

"Fitzgerald was the brains behind the enterprise," says former US Attorney Paul Kelly. "He was older, he was smarter. He was feared. He was legendary in the community for showing he was just a psychopathic violent type," says former assistant United States Attorney Paul Kelly.

If Fitzgerald ruled by fear, the drug gang's other head, John Houlihan, could have been mistaken for an average Townie – coaching pop warner football, little league baseball and boxing. "Houlihan was not cut from the same cloth as Fitzgerald," says DEA agent Joe Desmond. "Fitzgerald was a hardened, institutionalized individual. Houlihan was the Pop Warner football coach who went to the Warren Tavern on Friday nights to drink and sing."

Inside his home, however, there were slight clues to his profession. He had one set of law books in which the only marked pages concerned racketeering and drug violations. Another note headlined "Steve Lillis Rats" listed cooperating witnesses in convicted kingpin Lillis' federal PCP case out of neighboring Somerville.

"Houlihan wasn't a career criminal," Kelly says. "And that's not uncommon in places like Charlestown. He grew up in the neighborhood, he's well known. He's somebody who neighbors and community leaders think has done some good for the community. At some point he crossed the line."

In time, the little league coach would go on to prove he was just as vicious as the convicted double murderer Fitzgerald.

*****

James Boyden Jr. was one of the younger Townies Fitzgerald met as they cycled through the state prison system. In 1986 Boyden Jr. robbed an armored car shooting the driver several times. His partner in that crime was Billy Herd – an infamous thief and killer who robbed 15 banks and 15 supermarkets in less than five years. In the prison yard, Boyden Jr. stayed in the same circle of about two dozen men, most from Charlestown, as Fitzgerald and Herd.

On the street a couple of years later, however, the men clashed. Boyden Jr, was selling cocaine in territory run by Fitzgerald's girlfriend Jennirose Lynch. Lynch warned Boyden Jr. not to sell cocaine in the area but Boyden Jr. was bold. He went to Kerrigan's Flower Shop and taunted Fitzgerald calling him a piece of shit. In response, Fitzgerald beat Boyden Jr. up until his own hands were covered in blood. The next day, Fitzgerald told a drug runner, "I'll just have to kill him."

Boyden Jr. was not getting the message – he continued to sell cocaine around Monument Street. To trap him, Fitzgerald needed to use a friendly face – so one day Boyden Jr.'s old stick up partner Billy Herd picked Boyden Jr. up for a drive around the neighborhood.

In the car someone lit a joint of PCP and passed it to Boyden Jr. Herd placed a loaded .38 revolver at the base of Boyden Jr.'s skull as Boyden took a drag. In the next moment Herd pulled the trigger and Boyden Jr. was dead.

Haugh and Herd drove to an abandoned parking lot in Charlestown, removed Boyden Jr.'s sneakers, laid them next to his body and covered the body with a board of plywood. The public undressing was deliberate; the body didn't disappear - it was left in a public playground where it would inevitably be discovered. And the shoes were taken off, a message that Boyden Jr. would never walk on Fitzgerald's territory again.

Boyden Jr.'s killer, Billy Herd, had been raised in the neighborhood of Brighton but had met Fitzgerald and the Charlestown crew in state prison. Tall and skinny, weighing no more than 150 pounds, Herd didn't look like much of a threat. But his criminal resume included murder and violent robberies.

"Billy Herd was a frail looking guy, he was kind of slight. He had an eerie look about him. He was just one of these guys who had no problem putting a bullet in somebody's head for little or no reason," Kelly said.

Boyden Jr.'s father had previously tried to speak with Fitzgerald about the ongoing feud. Now with his son dead he had a good idea of who was responsible. He began speaking with police, passing on what he knew and what he heard from neighborhood sources. Fitzgerald and Houlihan finally had enough of Boyden Sr. - they approached hit man Joseph Nardone and offered him $5,000 in cash to kill the father.

Nardone was a cold blooded killer whose history of violence went back to Charlestown's days of racial turmoil. In 1979, Nardone was one of three teenagers on a project roof top shooting guns when one of the bullets struck and paralyzed black teenager Darryl Williams – a high school football star playing across the street.

Now, more than a decade later, Nardone was a hired gunman stalking Boyden Sr. On May 12, 1992, two months after Boyden Jr. was killed, Boyden Sr. was returning to his home in Charlestown. He pulled to the curb, opened the door of his car and just as he was about to step out, Nardone, dressed in dark clothes, stepped out of the darkness and fired several shots killing Boyden Sr. The shooting took place directly underneath Boyden Sr.'s window where his seven year old daughter was sitting and looking out at her father. The next day Nardone went to Kerrigan's

Flower Shop and picked up $5,000 in cash in a shoe box.

Next, Nardone murdered another wayward dealer, George Sargent, who had begun cooperating with authorities. On June 28, 1992 Nardone spotted Sargent leaving his apartment on Bunker Hill Street. Nardone jumped out of his car, ran up behind Sargent and shot him twice in the back, dropping him in the crosswalk in the middle of a busy street.

Bud Sweeney was the next target. At 65 years old, Sweeney was selling drugs for Fitzgerald and Houlihan – making about seventy sales a day of $100 bags. But when he started to drink again, he became careless. He eventually claimed to have lost a $30,000 package of cocaine he received from Fitzgerald.

Nardone couldn't kill him though. Sweeney survived three separate shootings including one in which Nardone shot him repeatedly in the neck. That shooting, however, left him paralyzed. Sweeney joined the Witness Protection Program and provided the key testimony in convicting Fitzgerald and Houlihan. After a dramatic trial in which witnesses' cars and homes were hit with homemade bombs, Fitzgerald and Houlihan were convicted and sentenced to life in prison.

After the conviction Fitzgerald lived up to the Code of Silence tag, prosecutor Kelly says. "Fitzgerald never cooperated with the police, never talked to the authorities at all. He was just one of those guys that lived by that code. Some guys try to ease their situation by supplying information in return for some kind of concession on sentencing. But Fitzgerald was one of those guys he had no interest in talking even after all the convictions were in. It was just a way of life for him," Kelly says.

Fitzgerald and Houlihan were off to federal prisons for life. The scars of the Code of Silence, however, was not about to fade in Charlestown.

Code of Silence: Final Act

Patrick Nee Jr. was caught in the web of Charlestown's conflicting street codes. The son of notorious Boston criminal Patrick Nee Sr. and Veronica Boyden – code of silence witness and James Boyden's wife, - Nee lost his brother, Boyden Jr., and stepfather to the Code of Silence wars. When Veronica Boyden agreed to testify against Houlihan and Fitzgerald, Pat Nee Jr. became a target for retaliation.

James "Jimma" Houlihan was the nephew of John Houlihan. After his uncle was convicted, Jimma Houlihan harassed Nee Jr. almost daily with taunts. "My uncle had your father and brother killed. You'll see, Pat. You're dead next." Nee Jr., six foot four with a minor criminal record but a serious PCP habit – never asked for protection from the authorities.

But he did tell a family friend, "Jimma Houlihan is going to kill me." In December 1995 they met on a Charlestown street at for the last time. Houlihan, with an oversized knife in hand, cut Nee Jr.'s throat from ear to ear. He chased Nee Jr. out into the street, pointing the knife and yelling, "You didn't get enough boy!"

A neighborhood woman stopped her car and tried to help Nee Jr. who was shouting, "He got me in the neck…I'm getting tired." The woman asked Nee Jr., "Who did this to you?" He uttered, "Jimma." Houlihan eventually pled guilty and was sentenced to 14 years in federal prison on the strength of Nee Jr.'s dying declaration – the last, deadly gasp from the Code of Silence's evil empire.

Welcome to Charlestown, Armored Car Robbery Capital of the U.S.

It may seem hard to believe that a movie such as *The Town*, based on one aspect of the neighborhood's criminal subculture, would fascinate movie goers across the country, but then again, it is hard to believe the scope of Charlestown's obsession with stick ups. Charlestown bank robber Ronald Doe put it this way: "With the kids I hung around with, robbing banks wasn't a bad thing. It was like playing hockey."

There are certain peculiarities about the Charlestown hoodlum that even criminals from other once-predominantly white slums can't match. The Townie criminal alone retained an affinity for angel dust, a hallucinogenic that induces psychosis, chased by Budweiser. And while many young Boston criminals aspire to the easy money afforded by selling drugs, among Townie hoods the stickup man remains an icon.

In the 1990's, when Boston easily led the nation in armored car robberies, it was gangs from Charlestown that drove the spike. In fact, federal law enforcement authorities have said Charlestown produced more armored car robbers than any other square mile in the world.

"For years it appeared to be a rite of passage [in Charlestown] to pull an armored car robbery," said FBI agent Richard S. Swensen, who led the bureau's Boston office. "I've had agents tell me they arrested a father for a robbery and 10 years later they arrested the son," said another G-Man.

Between 1990 and 1996, the Boston area averaged 16 armored car robberies a year, three times more than statewide averages across the country. Underworld figures and the FBI both knew: the overwhelming number of armored car robbers came from Charlestown, a neighborhood where the stick-up man, not the drug kingpin or mob boss, captured the criminal imagination.

In the mid-90s, one in five armored car heists in the country happened in Boston and entire states such as California, New York and Florida experienced just half the robberies of this single city. But numbers don't capture the craze: Charlestown crews robbed "cans" in those states too. Townies were even printing and selling souvenir t-shirts of masked leprechauns robbing an armored car under the words "Boston Bandits."

"Robbing armored cars just seemed natural, it seemed normal," Anthony Shea, a Townie doing life in federal prison for 11 armored car heists, said. "We thought it was the cool thing to do. Everyone was doing scores. When you're young, you're impressionable. You see people make a lot of money, they had a skill, they were wise at what they did. Your uncles or cousins were doing it and they passed on the experience as they got older, it was almost passed down from generation to generation. The older guys told the younger guys in the neighborhood how to do it, you share the tricks of the trade. If our uncles were dentists, we'd all be pulling teeth."

One of Charlestown's most infamous robbers was Susan DeAngelo – the most accomplished female bank robber of her time. DeAngelo rose to the top of a dangerous game dominated by men, becoming a leading player at a time in the early 2000s when bank robberies were surging.

The 37-year-old with dirty blonde hair and a ruddy face was linked by police to more than a dozen bank robberies and earned the nickname "Charlestown's Bonnie." Cool, calm, sometimes armed and always brazen – that was her signature style.

Hooked on heroin, DeAngelo started out by robbing pharmacies but soon moved onto banks – bypassing the crimes female drug users usually turn to – shoplifting and prostitution. Women – usually as a driver – participate in between 5 and 10 percent of all bank robberies.

DeAngelo was an exception – a bold robber who was always armed. She was no mastermind though and said little planning went into her robberies. "Most of it is split second decision," she said. "It's all drug induced. The fear of being sick. Nothing is really planned." DeAngelo was eventually nabbed after being suspected in over a dozen heists.

To put it in underworld Boston-terms, Anthony Shea is not just a notorious bank robber, he is one of the last "stand up guys" – exalted status in Boston for tough guys who refuse to cooperate with authorities. The first man charged under the federal three strikes law in both Massachusetts and New Hampshire ("His N.H. charges make 6 strikes" was the headline in the Boston Globe), Shea is now serving a life sentence in federal prison for his role in Charlestown's most infamous robbery crew. After two escapes from federal prisons, Shea spent three and a half years in solitary confinement inside the country's most secure prison, the supermax, Florence ADX.

Shea was raised in Charlestown's Bunker Hill housing projects by a father who survived the 1960s Irish gang wars in Boston. And he quickly learned the neighborhood's culture.

"Charlestown's a spirit," Shea says. "Whether you're a citizen or a criminal there's a spirit of honor, pride, character. If you left and went to prison, you came back everybody knew who you were, they never forgot you. It's a tight community. There were large families and people grew up with different parts of people's families."

Soon Shea learned the neighborhood's criminal culture too. He committed his first bank robbery at 14 and quickly picked up tips from seasoned crooks. "In the 70s in Charlestown you could go down to the corner with a robbery all worked out in your mind and find a kid like me to help you pull it off," Shea said. "Then you drop me off at the same corner and we don't see each other again. Charlestown's been like that since I was a little kid.

"It wasn't that we admired [the older criminals], we wanted a better life, we wanted nice things. Every decade had one big crew. You see people they got nice houses, nice cars and you say how do we get that? Oh he robbed a bank. And you say damn I want that."

Shea's career was interrupted in 1982, when he was convicted of bank robbery and sent to federal prison at age 18. "Back then it was just bank robbers, organized crime, Indians and guys from D.C." in the federal system, he said.

In 1990, the authorities say Shea helped form a crew of Townies who went on to commit more than 100 planned, carefully executed armed robberies, stealing several million dollars in four states over five years. (Also in the crew, according to the feds, were: Mike O'Halloran, Matt McDonald, Pat McGonagle and Stephen Burke.)

They treated robbery as a profession. Hours of research and surveillance went into following armored trucks and learning their routines. Getaway cars were torched to stymie the forensics. And after each job, the crew huddled to divide the money and clinically critique their performance. If a guy committed a serious mistake, he had to pay a fine. "Hey," Shea says, "good waiters get good tips. You do your homework, prepare, watch. Then, bang! You make your move."

On August, 25, 1994, four masked men were lying in wait on the floor of a Chevy Lumina minivan in the parking lot of a Hudson, N.H. bank. When an armored car pulled in, the gang spilled out with weapons drawn. Guard Ronald Normandeau opened the door of his truck, and the gang members picked him up and threw him against the side of the Lumina, shot him in his side and hauled him into the minivan.

A robber leaped into the back of the armored car and grappled with the other guard, Laurence Johnson, who struggled and pulled off the mask worn by the gang member, who slammed a .45-caliber weapon into Johnson's mouth and pulled the trigger.

With their robbery plans turned bloody, and both guards dead, the gang drove the armored car and the minivan to a remote field where a third vehicle awaited their escape. They made off with at least $600,000.

Normandeau was 52 and Johnson 57. Both were described by friends as good neighbors and fathers. On the run from the feds, Shea fled to Palm Beach, Florida where he and Burke allegedly robbed three more armored cars for six-figure scores.

The Feds watched as Charlestown's criminal subculture exploded and beginning in 1991, the FBI and DEA targeted the community. "We decided this is something that's got to be stopped whatever it takes, and we're going to stop it," said Swensen, the Boston FBI boss.

After the crew was arrested, Shea's trial featured the biggest breakdown in Townie loyalty yet: brother versus brother. John Burke flipped mid-trial and snitched on his codefendants, including younger brother Stephen Burke, to avoid a long jail term.

"Look at your family there," Stephen Burke yelled to John Burke sitting on the witness stand. "I hope you are proud of yourself!"

"How do you feel about yourself now?" Shea said, taunting the rat.

John Burke provided damning testimony against Shea and his co-defendants. He described months of painstaking "research and planning" before each "case" and spoke like a military briefing officer, referring to the robbery car as "the primary assault vehicle" and his task in one robbery as supervisor of the "neutralization of the guards."

On Charlestown streets, the next day, one Townie called John Burke "the lowest form of rat. All he has to do is take up child molesting for a hat trick. He could be a junkie, rat and diddler."

The crew was convicted on RICO charges and sentenced to life in prison.

The New York Times called Charlestown "legendary" in law enforcement circles nationwide for its "hoodlums, thieves and drug dealers" and intricately planned heists. But in a direct attack on the Code of Silence, authorities spent millions to provide many of those thieves and drug dealers immunity and new identities with the witness protection program.

Younger Townies, devastated by Oxycontin and heroin addiction, turned away from armored cars and started robbing pharmacies. By 1997, armored car robberies in Massachusetts dropped to just two. An FBI agent in Boston told reporters, "I think this is the end of an era."

CHAPTER FIFTEEN

FALL FROM GRACE: THE DECLINE OF THE NEW ENGLAND MAFIA

FOR ALL THE upheaval in Boston's underworld, Gennaro Angiulo had managed to remain on top for almost two decades going into the 1980s. He successfully fought off conspiracy charges in state court in the 1960s and the little man had come to view himself as shrewd beyond his merit. That turned out to be a mistake.

In 1981, the FBI successfully bugged the Prince Street office that served as Angiulo's headquarters. The feds received a detailed description of the office by none other than Angiulo's hated rivals Stevie Flemmi and Whitey Bulger. In the recordings, Angiulo, his brothers and top enforcer Larry Zannino, spoke freely about murder, extortion and life in the Mafia.

The most talkative member of the crew was the notorious killer Zannino. On the very first day of the FBI's secret bugging, agents listened to the capo lecture Jerry Angiulo on the art of killing. "If you're clipping people, I always say, make sure if you clip people, you clip the people around him first. But get them together, cause everybody's got a friend, Jerry. He could be the dirtiest motherfucker in the world, but someone, someone likes that guy, that's the guy that sneaks you, you don't even know it."

They listened as Zannino, the loyal mob man, harshly instructed his soldiers on the ways of Mafia life. "Who the fuck are you to make a decision?" Zannino once accused a soldier in a diatribe on the chain of command. "You'll make no fuckin decisions. You know when you make a decision? When they put fucking stripes on you."

Other times, Zannino would simply profess his love for mob life.

"That's the one thing we got going for us. No one can hide. But we can. In other words, no one can hide from us, but we can hide from everybody. You understand?"

"This thing comes first," he once reminded another soldier, John Cincotti. "Johnny, This Thing we got here is beautiful. You understand? This Thing is so beautiful that if someone slapped Debbie in the mouth tonight, your girl, we would kill…don't underrate it."

Inside the drab room, Angiulo had more pressing concerns. He worried out loud about the ease with which a case under the new Racketeering Influence Corrupt Organizations (RICO) law could be made against his long-running criminal organization. FBI bugs captured a frustrated Angiulo shouting, "They can stick RICO."

He lectured his brothers about the danger posed by federal prosecutors only having to prove the Angiulos committed two of thirty-two federal and state crimes over a ten-year period to establish a pattern of racketeering. He lamented that "if you break one of those crimes this year and within the next ten years you break the other one, they will take your fuckin' head off."

Angiulo, however, took delusional refuge in a mistaken belief that RICO applied only to those infiltrating legitimate business. Oblivious to the finer points of the law, he railed on, with hidden microphones picking up every word. Then, in a fateful misstep that sealed his fate, Angiulo unwittingly outlined the racketeering case against himself in an exchange with Zannino.

"Our argument is we're illegitimate business," he said to Zannino.

"We're shylocks," answered Zannino.

"We're shylocks," echoed Angiulo, warming to the idea.

"Yeah," said Zannino.

"We're fuckin' bookmakers," Angiulo added.

"Bookmakers," confirmed Zannino

"We're selling marijuana," said Angiulo.

"We're not infiltrating," replied Zannino.

"We're, we're, we're illegal here, illegal there. Arsonists. We're every fuckin' thing," said Angiulo, warming to his own argument.

"Pimps, prostitutes," added Zannino.

"The law does not cover us," Angiulo declared. And then: "Is that right?"

Zannino again brought the discussion back to reality. "That's the argument," he said glumly. The truth was, the argument was a big time loser. Later that same night a talked-out Angiulo confronted the cruel reality. "The law was written for people like us," he said wearily.

Two years later in September 1983, Angiulo was dining at a North End restaurant with two of his brothers when FBI agents interrupted his meal with arrest warrants. As agents led the handcuffed mobsters toward the door, the always defiant Angiulo tried to get the last word, vowing angrily to anyone within earshot, "I'll be back for my pork chops before they're cold."

It was a promise Angiulo would not keep. He was sentenced to forty-five years in prison [Angiulo died in 2009, two years after being released from prison after serving 24 years.]

Zannino was sentenced to thirty years in federal prison. While being taken out of the courtroom a reporter asked what he thought of the verdict. "I hope they all die in their beds," he said referring to the jury.

The next year, in 1983 legendary boss Raymond Patriarca died of a heart attack. In a business where violent death is often inevitable, Patriarca died peacefully at seventy-six years old. He had risen from small-time bootlegger to take the New England Mafia to places it had never been before –access to the highest levels of political corruption and millions invested in legitimate businesses.

Without Patriarca's ruthless but practical leadership, the New England Mafia would be thrown into chaos that returned the family to the irrelevant position it held before the days of Prohibition and the Gustin Gang war. (Deadly Alliance by Ralph Ranalli offers a thorough account of the New England Mafioa's sharp decline).

Junior Mafia

Three of the major figures to fight for control in the new mob landscape were Raymond Patriarca Jr., J.R. Russo and "Cadillac" Francis Salemme. After his powerful father's death, Patriarca Jr. received the New York Commission's approval to become boss of the New England family. But like so many other Mafia "Juniors" he was a weak copy of the original; hesitant where his father was decisive, timid where the old man was bold. Contrasted with his father's intimidating, narrow-eyed appearance, Patriarca's doughy face didn't help him much either. Wiseguys called him "Rubberlips" behind his back.

"Junior did not have the brains or the power to lead the family. Had his father not come before him, he wouldn't have got the job. He couldn't lead a Brownie troop," a Rhode Island State Police organized crime expert said. It was true, by the late 1980s, he was leading the different factions of the New England Mafia right into war.

First he snubbed Boston by naming Billy Grasso, a close ally and tough guy from the Hartford faction, as his underboss. The move made Boston third fiddle in New England and insulted the local Mafia's tough-as-nails new leader, J.R. Russo.

Russo rose from the East Boston waterfront to mafia stardom by killing Joe (The Animal) Barboza in 1975. A sharp dresser and suave talker, he dropped out of sight after the Barboza murder. He returned to Boston in the summer of 1986 when he was promoted to capo regime. He made his first local appearance as a boss at a North End street festival – a move authorities said was "a show of force."

With his eyes set on ruling not just Boston but all of New England, Russo would have to face off against another mob legend who made his bones in the Barboza years. Patriarca Jr. pushed a confrontation with Boston forward by sponsoring Cadillac Frank Salemme to be a made member of the Mafia.

Salemme and Russo both earned their stripes in the Barboza years, with Salemme spending 15 years in state prison for bombing the car of Barboza's lawyer. But that didn't make them friends. In fact when Russo and Boston heard Salemme had been made they were outraged. The Boston faction was badly depleted after the Angiulo case and Russo desperately wanted to make new soldiers to fortify the ranks. Raymond Jr., however, had said "the books were closed" meaning no new members were to be made. Russo started to believe that Salemme was lining up a takeover of Boston and made an unsuccessful plea to Gambino boss John Gotti to mediate the dispute.

The situation was inflamed when corrupt FBI agent John Connolly leaked a story to the Boston Herald that claimed Salemme had the support to overthrow Russo. A few days after the story, FBI informant Sonny Mercurio, part of the Russo faction, called Salemme and suggested that the two men meet at an International House of Pancakes restaurant on busy Route 1 in Saugus, a town north of Boston.

When Mercurio was late, Salemme went out front, thinking there had been a mix up. A car was coming toward him and he waved, thinking it was Mercurio. The windows rolled down and a .45 caliber pistol and an M-16 rifle popped out firing. Salemme was hit once in the chest before he ducked inside an International House of Pancakes and hit the floor.

The men kept firing and Salemme saw a chunk of plaster explode from the wall from gunshots directly above where a little girl was sitting with her parents. Afraid children would be hit by stray gunfire, Salemme got up and ran out the door toward the gun car. Apparently startled, the gunmen stopped firing for a moment but opened up again and hit Salemme in the leg. This time Salemme ducked into a Papa Gino's pizza shop and grabbed a knife from the counter, crouching low behind the door and waiting for the shooters to follow.

The shooting suddenly stopped and the failed assassins were gone leaving behind the sounds of squealing tires. Salemme fell into a booth and pressed a pile of napkins against the bloody wound in his chest. "Call 911," he said to the gape mouthed girl behind the counter.

Later that afternoon, as Salemme was under heavy guard in a North Shore hospital, two fishermen found the dead body of new underboss Billy Grasso on the banks of the Connecticut River in Weathersfield just outside Hartford. He had been shot in the back of the head and left on the western side of the bank – an indication that he should have stayed in his territory.

After Salemme survived the attack ordered by Russo and the Boston faction, their plans to kill the other Junior Patriarca supporters on the hit list – eight people in all – were abandoned. Still, J.R. Russo had made his point - Grasso was dead and Salemme was in hiding.

Junior Patriarca was badly shaken by the loss of two of his toughest soldiers. Conceding the loss, he made a peace offer to Russo; Russo would be promoted to consigliere, or chief advisor, and the books would be opened to let the Boston faction "make" some new soldiers before expected indictments against Russo and the leadership came down. The Mafia ceremony was meant to broker peace but it would turn out to be an iconic blunder in United States Mafia history.

"Only the Ghost Knows"

Talk of an impending ceremony began reaching the FBI from several sources. One source was Sonny Mercurio. The Mafia soldier who had tried to set up Salemme was leading a double life as an FBI informant. Mercurio told the feds the New England Mafia planned to "make" three Boston soldiers, Vinnie Federico, Richie Floramo and Carmen Tortora and one Providence wiseguy. Mercurio's chief job would be as chauffeur, transporting members from Wellington Circle, a busy shopping center in the suburb of Medford, to the actual location, which was still a secret.

One hitch was that one of the prospective members to be made that day, Vinny Federico, was in prison serving time for attempted murder. Fortunately, Massachusetts had a generous furlough program in place that allowed inmates out of prison to see family and friends. Surprisingly, Federico put the correct address of the induction ceremony on his application, describing the occasion as "family business."

An FBI agent picked up a copy of Federico's furlough application and saw an address on Guild Street in Medford that was suspiciously close to Wellington Circle, where Mercurio said he was meeting some of the guests.

When two FBI agents visited the neighborhood they realized the

Guild Street home Federico listed was two doors down from another FBI agent's home. Soon, they spotted Russo and other made men at 34 Guild Street making last minute preparations. They realized they had located the induction ceremony site. Shockingly, it was only two doors down from an FBI agent's home.

Sometime in the middle of the night Saturday and early Sunday morning a tech team of FBI agents installed a hidden microphone inside 34 Guild Street. By the time Sonny Mercurio began ferrying wiseguys to the house Sunday morning, the feds were listening.

By mid-morning the New England Mafia was assembled in the small house. The largest group was from Greater Boston including the three associates who were being sponsored for membership – Vincent Federico, Richard Floramo and Carmen Tortora. From Providence there was boss Raymond Patriarca Jr., capo Matty Guglielmetti, soldier Pasquale Galea, and inductee Robert DeLuca. Two other soldiers from Hartford, Domick Marangelli and Louis Failla were also there. There were a few notable absences, including Frank Salemme, who had tried in vain to persuade Patriarca not to attend.

The inductees took their seats in front of a table laid out with a knife, four holy cards and a lit candle. The rest of the men sat in strict hierarchical order, Russo and Patriarca and the capos up front, the soldiers behind them. Biagio DiGiacomo, the mobster with best command of Italian, presided over the ceremony.

"In onore della Famiglia, la Famiglia e abbraccio," he intoned. (In honor of the Family, the Family is open.)

J.R. Russo, in English, took over.

"Do you have any brothers, Carmen?" Russo asked inductee Carmen Tortora.

"One," the fierce looking enforcer replied.

"If I told you your brother was wrong, he's a rat, he's gonna do one of us harm, you'd have to kill him. Would you do that for me, Carmen?"

"Yes."

Would you do that? This kind of favor, would you do that?" Russo pressed.

"Yes."

"You know that. So you know the severity of this thing of ours."

"Yes."

"You want it that badly, that desperately? Your mother's dying in bed and you have to leave her because we called you, it's an emergency. You have to leave. Would you do that Carmen?"

"Yes."

"All right, this is what you want. We're the best people and I'm gonna make you part of this thing. Biag," Russo said, turning to Biagio DiGiacomo, "give him the oath."

All four men eventually repeated the same oath in Sicilian that Tortora did.

"Io, Carmen, voglio entrare in questa organizzazione pre proteggere la mia famiglia, e per proteggere tutti I miei amici. Io lo guiro di non svelare questo segreto e di ubbidire di amore ed omerta."

(I, Carmen, want to enter into this organization to protect my family and to protect all my friends. I swear not to divulge this secret and to obey with love and silence.)

Omerta is the Sicilian word for silence, and a vow never to betray the Mafia, on the penalty of death.

The four initiates each pricked the index finger on their gun hand and smeared the blood on a card bearing the picture of a saint. The card was then burned over the candle.

"As burns this saint, so will burn my soul. I enter alive into this organization and leave it dead," they each repeated in Sicilian.

After the ceremony, the new members were told to always remember the hierarchy of the crime family. "We have one family in New England. One family. Remember that. One family. New York has five families," Russo said.

As the FBI bug captured the end of the meeting, Russo and capo Vincent M. Ferrara were preparing to leave the house. "Only the…ghost knows what really took place over here today, by God," Ferrara said. Make that God and the FBI. Two doors down FBI agents had caught the first Mafia induction ceremony ever on a law enforcement bug.

The taping of the Boston Mafia's induction ceremony was a huge blunder from a bush league faction of a once powerful organization. The recorded ceremony marked the beginning of the local Mafia's rapid underworld fall.

Chronicles of the Cheese Man

The plummeting stock of the once profitable New England Mafia is evident in the story of the Boston mob's Cheese Man. Carmen "The Cheese Man" DiNunzio, a made man since the 1990s, became the underboss of the New England mafia and the top mobster in Boston in 2004, according to the FBI. He served as underboss for New England Mafia head Luigi "Baby Shanks" Manocchio of Providence.

When DiNunzio took the reins the Boston Mafia had fallen on hard times. Some of his underlings earned money by shoplifting; one aging soldier was spotted peddling electric toothbrushes in the North End. The Mafia, which traditionally denounced drugs, now tolerated addicts in its ranks. More experienced members turned down promotions in fear of inevitable FBI raids.

In 2008, a State Police detective said the local Mafia had about 30 made members, half of what it was in the 1980s. They lost their grip on pornography and prostitution rackets. Maybe that was why Carmen (Cheese Man) DiNunzio personally delivered a $10,000 bribe to a near stranger, a man who turned out to be an undercover FBI agent.

The 400-pound DiNunzio, who earned his nickname as owner of the Fresh Cheese Shop on Endicott Street in the North End, passed the bribe to secure a $6 million contract for the city's infamously tardy and expensive Big Dig highway project.

"I'm the Cheese Man," DiNunzio said in an apparent boast to the undercover agent, who was worried the deal could fall through. "We straighten out a lot of beefs, a lot of things."

DiNunzio's bribery attempt earned him six years in federal prison, leaving a big – very big in fact – void in the Boston Mafia.

Back on the Streets: Elderly Gangsters

What is left of the Boston family is a strange mix of geriatric old timers home from prison and young members from middle class suburban homes. Unlike the old guard, who grew up in poor, ethnic neighborhoods such as East Boston and the North End where they were groomed by elders, the new generation is less street smart and attracted by the glitz and glamour of shows such as HBO's The Sopranos. "The guys now want to appear to be like Tony Soprano," said a State Police detective in the organized crime unit. "They're flashy." Experts say the family's weakness is a lack of midlevel managers.

One aging mobster fresh out of prison is Peter Limone. The one-time muscle behind Gennaro Angiulo who spent 33 years in prison after being framed by Joe (The Animal) Barboza and the FBI was finally free after 33 years in prison on a wrongful conviction.

In 1967, Limone was sentenced to death after a jury convicted him for the murder of Teddy Deegan on the strength of lying star snitch Barboza. He walked out of Middlesex Superior Court a free man on Jan. 5, 2001, one arm cradling a bouquet of yellow roses, the other wrapped around his tearful wife. Six years later, he and three other men falsely accused in the Deegan murder – including the families of two men who died in jail - were awarded a $101.7 million lawsuit against the FBI for deliberately withholding evidence in the 1965 killing.

However, authorities said Limone continued in organized crime activity from almost the moment he stepped out of prison. Within a few months he was running a tightly controlled illegal gambling operation that brought in hundreds of thousands of dollars. Although he claimed to work at a wholesale fruit distributor, prosecutors said Limone spent most of his time hosting organized crime figures at a North End meat market and coffee shop.

Limone engaged in loan sharking and extortion and made four illegal gambling parlors pay him tens of thousands of dollars in rent or face violence. Underlings referred to him as "Chief Crazy Horse" and "The Camera Guy" in secretly recorded conversations. The racket collected bets on football, baseball, basketball and horse racing.

The gambling ring had an office in Boynton Beach, Florida that kept records of customers identified by code names. The bets were called into the Florida office. Limone had final approval over any loans and he insulated himself by delegating underlings to make the actual transactions.

Interest rates rose two percent per week and when gamblers fell behind Limone showed little sympathy. "Tell him I want to see him and I want the fucking money," he said in a phone conversation taped by the State Police. He was talking to an associate about a bookmaker who had been unable to make payments.

Prosecutors called Limone the Chief Operating Officer of the business. Profits were healthy if not staggering: in seven years Limone deposited $178,000 in cash into his bank accounts. But he was done in by cooperating witnesses and wiretaps. Prosecutors wanted him behind bars again, saying, "He alone made the choice to assume the role of an organized crime kingpin."

Judge Leila Kern, citing Limone's age and potential for rehabilitation, decided against prison time. He was ordered to serve five years of probation, with conditions that he stay away from known mob figures and wear an electronic monitoring bracelet. The judge said she did not factor in Limone's wrongful conviction when she made her decision. "It is not a get-out-of-jail-free card," she said. According to the agreement, if Limone can stay away from his old Mafia pals, he will not have to go back to jail.

Consigliere or Snitch?

Mark Rossetti appeared to be one of the last true-blue gangsters in what remained of the Patriarca Crime Family. He'd robbed an armored vehicle, been caught with guns and chose to serve jail time rather than testify about organized crime murders in a thirty year career. By 2011, he was acting consigliere of the family. But when Rossetti was busted for heroin dealing that year it soon became clear he had betrayed his own crew.

Rossetti had been an FBI informant for twenty years. Just as they protected Whitey Bulger, FBI agents protected Rossetti – even as he gained a reputation as a violent thug suspected of six murders.

In 1991, ATF agents went looking for Mark Rossetti to lock him up. The Bureau of Alcohol, Tobacco, Firearms, and Explosives agents had a warrant for Rossetti on a gun charge, but every time they came close to arresting him, he somehow caught wind and eluded them. After the ATF men finally caught Rossetti, they complained that an FBI agent named Mike Buckley was too cozy with Rossetti and didn't want them to lock him up.

The ATF was on to something. Rossetti had been working for the FBI and Agent Buckley as an informant. Agent Buckley was one of the agents involved in the Bulger scandal. He had been part of the organized crime squad that took down Gennaro Angiulo while protecting Whitey Bulger and Stevie Flemmi. Flemmi testified that the Bulger crew gave money and gifts to a half-dozen FBI agents, including Buckley. Buckley, who retired in 2003, denied that under oath, and was never charged.

The FBI, however, did not close out Rossetti as an informant even as Massachusetts State Police were building a case against his violent loan sharking and drug dealing ring. In fact they were telling him to keep snitching – and they would continue to protect him. According to taped conversations contained in the court documents, Rossetti's FBI handler told him not to worry, that "my job is to keep you anonymous and keep you safe."

"You don't have anything to worry about if things down the road happen, but if that happens, we'll have to deal with it as it comes," the handler told Rossetti when Rossetti was worrying about the state investigation. "I will have to start working it out."

Rossetti was still worried though. "This has got to be forever," he told his handler. "I don't want you guys turning on me and putting me in the headlines that I'm doing something with you." He was arrested and exposed as a snitch later that month.

***

When authorities busted Rossetti's organization, they were surprised to see black and Latino gangsters working at top levels in an Italian organization. But the face of organized crime had been changing for decades in Boston and as the city's demographics shifted so too did its hoodlums, syndicates and gang wars.

The gangs might have looked different but they had a lot in common with their predecessors. Asian crime families such as the Ping On were as sophisticated as Italian groups, importing criminal societies rooted in centuries of outlaw tradition, and a Cape Verdean gang war matched the old Irish one when it came to senseless self-annihilation.

CHAPTER SIXTEEN

CHINATOWN TONGS AND CAPE VERDEAN GANG WARS

THE STORY OF Harry Mook is the story of the two sides of Boston's Chinatown - a 46-acre patch hemmed in by the New England Medical Center, the Combat Zone, the Massachusetts Turnpike, and the Southeast Expressway. For decades, Mook controlled gambling and money laundering in the neighborhood but he was also a respected businessman with political clout.

Mook was born into neighborhood aristocracy as the son of George Mook, known in Boston as the "King of the Chinese." His father was influential enough that Governor James Michael Curley attended young Harry's christening. The boy was seven when his father started to lose his eyesight but blindness only added to the old man's mystique.

George Mook had come to Chinatown as a boy before the turn of the century and served 10 terms as national president of On Leong (Peaceful Virtue). The descendants of underground movements in China, tongs such as On Leong kept peace yet sometimes feuded bloodily with one another in Chinatowns across the United States. They supported charities and social events yet operated prostitution rings and gambling parlors.

Taught by decades of discrimination to be wary of US authorities, Chinese-American residents in Boston, as in other cities, rarely aired complaints about tongs to the police -- who were usually content to leave Chinatown alone. "The police would say, `Just keep it in Chinatown,' " one resident recalled." `Just don't let it reach Newbury Street.' "

Boston's first tong war began with the October 2, 1903 murder of Wong Yak Chong, a thirty-year-old Laundromat owner and member of the Hip Sing Tong. Chong's death on Harrison Avenue was the first murder in the city's Chinatown neighborhood in over twenty years. Two Chinese men, one described as wearing a shirt of steel and carrying a hatchet, were arrested shortly after the shooting.

Ten days after the murder, an army of police and immigration officials, operating without warrants, began raiding restaurants and laundries, arresting every Asian male who could not produce the registration papers required of Chinese immigrants since 1892. In all, more than three hundred men were detained. The incident further isolated Chinatown and On Leong continued to grow as white authorities proved to be arbitrary and racist.

During George Mook's heyday leading On Leong to power, his Chinese Consolidated Business Association was the important authority in neighborhood disputes. The association presided over an isolated, tightly knit Chinatown, where most residents traced their origins to Tuoi-san province, in southern China, and their political loyalties to Chiang Kai-shek, even after the Communists drove his Nationalists out of mainland China to Taiwan, in 1949.

By the time of his death in 1960, George Mook presided over one of the nation's largest tongs. Reflecting his status as the last holder of the honorary title "Mayor of Chinatown," two thousand mourners from around the United States and other countries attended his funeral. A one and a half-mile procession, including 95 limousines, followed his hearse and 10 flower cars through Chinatown's narrow streets.

Brash and insecure, young Harry Mook desperately wanted to emulate his father. After graduating from Boston University, he realized that Chinatown needed many services -- and tried to provide all of them. He became a real estate and insurance broker, notary public, and justice of the peace.

The enterprising Mook even challenged his father's old tong, On Leong, on their gambling stranglehold. Boston police believed that Mook became the Mafia's numbers contact in Chinatown, allegedly funneling receipts from the numbers racket to the North End.

For Mook, his place in legitimate society revolved around his restaurant, the Four Seas. In its heyday, the Four Seas had Boston's most eclectic clientele. "When midnight struck, the night people flocked to Chinatown," Mook wrote in a 1975 tribute to Chinatown restaurants. "Cab drivers, actors and musicians made it their `after-hours' rendezvous. . . . Chorus girls made their dates take them there and the food was authentic, tasty and, of course, inexpensive."

Night people who flocked to Mook's place ranged from cops to crooks, suburban teen-agers on prom dates to Combat Zone topless dancers, Larry Bird to Andre the Giant, Irish politicians to Italian gangsters. Sammy Davis Jr. rented the Four Seas one night in 1964 to await reviews of his performance in Golden Boy, playing at the nearby Shubert Theatre.

Next door to the Four Seas was the other half of Mook's neighborhood power base. The Chinese Freemasons Society were so notorious in Mook's heyday that one Boston police officer observed, "Not every Freemason in Chinatown is a criminal, but every criminal is a Freemason."

With no charter to operate as a Masonic lodge the Chinese Freemasons Society is a pseudonym for China's oldest secret society, Hung Mun. By the 1970s, Hung Mun ceased to be a significant factor in most Chinatowns. Only in Boston's Chinatown and under Harry Mook's guidance did Hung Mun rise again. Mook also took advantage of some luck too: Stephen Tse, an ambitious young gang leader, had been ejected from On Leong. Together, Mook and Tse would move to take over Chinatown.

A soft-spoken but ambitious Hong Kong native with the street name Sky Dragon, Stephen Tse arrived in Boston from New York City in the mid-1970s and soon organized Ping On. Ping On was composed of young, unskilled immigrants who felt snubbed by American-born Chinese. The gang started by extorting protection money from prostitutes on Chinatown street corners, but Tse had bigger plans.

Tse was able to recruit young men with criminal records in Hong Kong who were more ruthless than the youth gang members or other Chinese gangs like the Ghost Shadows. He also employed Vietnamese youth who cemented their reputations as fearless gunmen during the fall of South Vietnam – a tenuous alliance that would not last.

In 1979, Tse and the Ping On filled a power void when Boston's Ghost Shadows were called to New York to take part in a gang war. When the Ghost Shadows returned, the Ping On gang had surfaced, leaving no room for the old gang. Following the pattern in New York, where upstart gangs such as the Flying Dragons and Ghost Shadows were sponsored by centuries-old tongs, Tse and Ping On belonged to On Leong.

On Leong's elders forced Tse to resign, however, when Ping On kidnapped a restaurateur's children for ransom. Tse responded by joining Mook's tong, Hung Mun – the Chinese Freemasons Society – and brought in a new Chinatown dynasty. The merger was mutually beneficial: Tse acquired a patron to lend him legitimacy, while Mook gained the soldiers to oust On Leong from supremacy. Most importantly for Harry Mook, he would inherit his father's mantle as king of Chinatown.

Tse had arrived as a gangster too. In 1983, authorities say he attended a five day summit in Hong Kong in an effort to centralize Chinese organized crime in North America – a meeting compared to the 1957 Apalachin meeting of Italian Mafia members. Soon after that summit, Tse joined other Chinese traffickers in smuggling heroin from the Golden Triangle in Southeast Asia to fill the void left after the French Connection operated by the Mafia was busted.

According to the 1988 US Justice Department report, Tse "experimented with innovative methods of smuggling heroin, such as placing it inside frozen fish and saturating imported rugs." He traveled at least twice to the People's Republic of China to arrange to buy heroin. Tse also ran a promotion company that held a monopoly on the booking of Chinese entertainers in Boston. His contacts in New York helped him build an alliance with the Italian Mafia, including the Patriarca crime family that ruled New England.

But the foundation of Mook and Tse's empire was gambling. Far from being considered a crime, high-stakes gambling was an accepted pastime in Chinatown, with game schedules often posted on lampposts and walls. Ping On members were paid to guard gambling dens and escort winners home.

For a cut of the profits, Mook handled the police. In one 1986 transaction recorded by authorities, Mook paid off three Boston police officers including a lieutenant. "Since, you know, the beginning of time . . . whoever's down here we take care {of}," Mook told them. "They go somewhere else, somebody else take care of them. They come back here, we take care of them."

'They've created a Frankenstein'

Mook and Tse had police and court officials on the payroll and rival tongs under control but demographic changes in Chinatown and a band of wild teenagers were about to end their reign. Since he first took power, Tse had used Vietnamese youths as enforcers. In 1986, when he was jailed for 18 months after refusing to answer questions at a president's commission on organized crime, the tenuous alliance began to fall apart.

"The PO's [Ping On] fell into disarray when Steve Tse went away, and Stephen's mistake was he did not designate lieutenants to act in his stead," a police investigator told the Boston Globe. "Tse supposedly gave the Vietnamese part of the action, but he wanted them only to have the Vietnamese community. By letting them join, the Vietnamese found how the gambling was run, they knew where all the joints were."

"They've created a Frankenstein," said a police officer.

Young Vietnamese gangsters poised to take over Chinatown were far more ruthless and violent than Ping On's two dozen hard core members. "The Vietnamese kids are not gangs in the traditional sense," said a Boston police detective. "Their traditional family structure is gone. Some of them are foster kids. These kids consider each other family, brothers and sisters. And they will do whatever they have to do to protect family members. That includes threatening to kill anyone who will testify against their brothers or sisters."

Initially, the renegade Vietnamese gangs extorted and terrorized only South Asian merchants and left Chinese business owners alone. They expanded their ambition though when they robbed more than a dozen Chinese gambling dens the next year. "They figure, 'Why work for an hourly rate when we can run the operation ourselves?'" said a police officer.

A loosely organized national network emerged in which Boston youths traveled through cities such as New York, Philadelphia, and Arlington and Falls Church, Virginia, to commit crime. The Boston Vietnamese group was mentored by a "Godfather" figure who police described as a Vietnamese man in his 40s holding menial jobs in Chinatown restaurants. The man, a former South Vietnamese army officer, met with the teens once a week to groom young gang members.

The leader of the gang appeared to be Trung Chi Troung, a man known on Chinatown streets as The Pimp. His intense anger was his trademark, with its roots in his childhood in Saigon in the early 1960s. Truong was surrounded by the Vietnam War's destruction until his late teen years. He fled in 1978, and, after a four day ride on a rickety boat, Truong and his brother landed in a desolate refugee camp in Malaysia, where they lived for 11 months.

They moved to Texas and then to Boston in 1980. It was in Boston where Truong first began doing the dirty work of the leaders in Chinatown gangs, collecting extortion money from store fronts and building an alliance with Stephen Tse.

Truong gained a reputation for planning audacious heists, including two of the same jewelry store in Lowell. Even when he was convicted for the second robbery, he managed to escape state prison after thirteen days. For the next four years he was on the run in Canada, employing desperate Asian immigrants who pulled off criminal schemes in exchange for shelter.

In 1990, Truong choreographed a $500,000 bank heist in Calgary using a cell phone half a continent away in Montreal. In 1991 he was arrested in Toronto after his underlings committed a triple murder over a glance at a woman in a nightclub. But he was never convicted.

One investigator said Truong was "the most dangerous Vietnamese gangbanger in North America. You just mention his name and everybody runs." At its height, authorities say, Truong's extortion empire brought in close to $1 million from Boston, Montreal and Toronto.

His run ended in 1995, however, after he executed a rival gang boss.

In the end Truong was brought down like many mobsters: his closest confidantes quickly pointed a finger at him when they were picked up for murder.

Chinatown's other Godfathers, Mook and Tse, were soon off the street too. Mook was sentenced to four years in prison for racketeering and Tse fifteen years in federal prison for ordering the failed execution of rival gangsters. Although getting the three gangsters off the streets was seen as victory by law enforcement it created a vacuum of power in the Asian underworld. The resulting gang war led to the worst massacre Boston had seen in almost two decades.

Massacre in Chinatown

On January 18, 1991, five men playing cards at an after-hours Chinatown social club were shot to death and a sixth was critically wounded in an attack by Vietnamese gunmen. Killed were Chung Wah Son, 58; Van Tran, 31, Man Cheung, 55; David Quang Lam, 32; and Cuong Khanh Luu, 26.

"It looks like a war scene," Mayor Ray Flynn told reporters after emerging from the blood-spattered basement club. "It's a real ugly scene down there." Flynn, who had arrived at the scene with a patrolman within minutes, told officers, "We have to chase the guys responsible for this, even if we have to go to the ends of the earth."

They did. Two of the gunmen, Siny Van Tran, also known as "Toothless Wah,", and Nam The Tham, also known as "Johnny Cheung", were arrested in China for drug possession in 1998. But China did not have an extradition treaty with the United States, and it was unclear whether they would be returned to Boston. District Attorney Ralph Martin said negotiations "at the stratospheric level" led to the return of the two suspects in 2001 ten years after the murder.

The main witness in the case against the gunmen, who both immigrated to the United States from Vietnam, was the sixth victim that deadly night. Pak Wing Lee, also known as "Bruce Lee," was shot in the head and lost consciousness in the massacre but came to a few minutes later, after the shooters left, and crawled to the club's back door, calling for help.

Lee entered the federal witness protection program immediately but returned to Boston as the star witness. The third gunman, Hung Sook, was not apprehended.

In his testimony, Lee gave chilling details of the massacre. Pressing an index finger to the back of his head, Lee said Pham put a pistol to his skull and fired as he was forced to squat on the floor. He said that he had implored the gunman to spare his life. "I said to Hung Sook, `Don't fire the gun, don't!'" Lee testified in Cantonese through an interpreter. "He did not listen to me. He fired."

Lee's dramatic testimony was pivotal in convicting the gunmen. When he was sentenced to life in prison, Toothless Wah smiled and laughed. The grisly murders actually proved to be a turning point for the neighborhood, a place where the tongs have all but disappeared.

"It's like a different world now," said a Chinatown resident in 2002. "Some of those old guys [gang members] are still here, but they don't act like they used to. They don't start trouble."

In recent years, free and frequent bus runs from Chinatown to the big Foxwoods and Mohegan Sun casinos took a huge bite out of the local gambling that once funded the gangs. Police crackdowns throughout the '90s pressured the remaining few parlors to shut their doors.

Today, with what are believed to be only one or two illegal gambling rooms left in Chinatown - down from nearly 30 in the 1990s - gang activity appears to have dried up or been driven underground.

"There is no organized gang activity that we know of in Chinatown," said Boston police Captain Bernard O'Rourke, commander of the police district that covers the area. "There are sometimes small groups of kids around, but that's about as far as it goes now."

Alan Yen, now a business owner there, lived near the massacre site and recalled the fear that enveloped the community in the days after the killings. "It's now better," he said, expressing relief at the verdict. "They killed people. They have to be punished."

Though the killings have become part of Chinatown lore, Yen said many locals are still reluctant to talk about it. "They are afraid," he said. "There were gangsters there. With gangsters, you never know where they are."

Gang War Redux, Cape Verdean Style

In early September 1978, Isaura Mendes left her home in Dorchester, turned right and walked a few houses down to the corner, to a three-decker on Hillsboro Street, to welcome home Celeste Lopes, a distant cousin who had just given birth to a son. They named the boy Arnaldo, and soon everyone in the neighborhood knew him by his nickname: Nardo.

When the Lopeses first moved to Boston in the early 1970s, they lived at a home of Isaura's relatives, mainstays of Boston's tight knit Cape Verdean community. "Cape Verdeans are beautiful people," Isaura says. "We look after each other, take care of each other."

In Boston, they also killed each other at an alarming rate. There are about 500,000 people of Cape Verdean ancestry in the United States, the majority of them in New England. Massachusetts has the largest, and oldest, Cape Verdean population in the nation, tracing its origins to the early 1800s, when islanders were attracted to work in the whaling industry.

There are about 30,000 Cape Verdeans in the Boston area, according to the U.S. census. Some of the children of these hardworking immigrants became enamored with guns and drug dealing. Isaura Mendes calls the generational shift "the disease." For members of the older generation, who grew up in a country where one makes the sign of the cross even before slaughtering a chicken, the violence was a dramatic signal that their children lived in a new world of gangs, guns and drugs.

Nardo Lopes had that disease. By the time he was 16 he was known to ATF agents investigating a Boston man who attended college at Mississippi's Jackson State University. The man bought weapons at gun shows throughout the South and sold them at a profit on Boston streets. Nardo learned that the man had stashed a suitcase stuffed with 25 handguns under a porch in the neighborhood and set out to steal them.

Nardo was a skinny 16-year-old but had a criminal daring that belied his age and unimposing physique. Witnesses told police they saw him struggling to lug a suitcase through a backyard. "It was so heavy that Nardo needed a buddy of his to help him lift it over the fence," an officer said.

Soon it was all over the street that Nardo had stolen the guns, and when police spotted him and gave chase, Nardo discarded a handgun. He was arrested but escaped from a youth facility while awaiting trial. He was still on the run when he got into a fight with a man he believed had ratted him out. Nardo was chasing the man when Isaura Mendes' son, Bobby Mendes, stepped in. Nardo stabbed him in the chest, ending his life and beginning a gang war that would be the city's deadliest since Irish gangsters clashed in the 1960s. And the whole time, Nardo would remain a phantom, protected by friends and family who saw him not as the aggressor, but as a victim of circumstance.

Before the Bobby Mendes killing, police had little reason to investigate the small criminal element within the Cape Verdean community and were just getting to know the players as the war gained intensity. That gave Nardo and his allies the upper hand. They were more aggressive and they had a charismatic, ruthless leader at the top: Nardo's big brother Gus Lopes – a thug involved in three murders and more than 20 shootings. Gus would psych up his crew of killers by telling them, "Let's go do dirt." For Gus, it was kill or be killed.

The Mendes faction, called Wendover, was much weaker. "They just stayed up on Wendover Street, a captive audience," a Boston Police detective said. "Nardo was able to stay on the run, while the people left behind got rid of the witnesses."

Larry Andrade was the first to go. He was shot dead on May 18, 1996, as he stood outside the Fundonzinho Lounge, a notorious bar in Roxbury. Two years later Luis Carvalho, another Mendes cousin, was ambushed on a Dorchester street; he was shot but survived. Gus Lopes was determined that Big Head Lou, as Carvalho was known, would not escape the next time. Lopes and an accomplice punctured Carvalho's car tires and cornered him in a repair shop where they shot him dead.

Even as Bobby's mother, Isaura Mendes, became one of the city's most prominent antiviolence activists, the Wendover crew was still trying to avenge Bobby's death. In 2000, a week after police raided a home in Brockton, looking for Nardo, a 21-year-old man living there was gunned down.

Between 1999 and 2004 one in eight of Boston's gang related homicides were attributed to the feud centered in the Upham's Corner and Bowdoin Street neighborhoods of Dorchester. In all, more than twenty murders and sixty non-fatal shootings were attributed to the feud. In Boston and as far away as Providence, indiscriminate gunfire – from car sunroofs, from back windows, at a sweet sixteen party – sprayed the innocent and the not so innocent.

As police raced from shooting to shooting, they became convinced that Nardo's fugitive status was contributing to the lawlessness. Young gangbangers would taunt them, invoking Nardo's name. "I hate to call him a legend but to some people he was," said one cop. Gus Lopes, epitomized this brazen new attitude. One of his many tattoos captured his philosophy: "Let them hate as long as they fear." In prison, with Nardo still free, Gus added another tattoo: "Only God can judge Nardo."

Nardo was an expert at staying on the run and he became the city's most infamous fugitive not named Whitey. An arrest anywhere in the nation would have alerted police to his whereabouts but he stayed out of trouble. Then police got a tip that Nardo Lopes was living in suburban Maryland.

At first the tip seemed odd: why, police asked, would Nardo go to Maryland? He had no associates there, no friends, no family. There was no Cape Verdean community there. They'd answered their own question: what a perfect place for Nardo to disappear. Through public records searches, police learned Nardo was living as Mike, a Puerto Rican from New York. He shared a condominium townhouse with a girlfriend who didn't know about his past and he was frequently seen walking his dog around the quiet, well-kept neighborhood.

Soon Boston, Maryland and federal law enforcement were waiting on Nardo at a Baltimore airport as he returned from a vacation in Jamaica. Moments later, Nardo Lopes stepped into view. "Hey," Boston Police

Detective Bob Fratalia said, flashing his gold detective's badge, "Remember me?" Lopes said nothing. There was no resistance as the detective steered him into a waiting police car.

It was a quiet climax to a bloody saga that cut a swath of pain and suffering through Uphams Corner, the heart of the city's Cape Verdean community. Isaura Mendes lost two sons and two of her sisters also lost sons to the war. The murders inspired her, however, to build a network of support for survivors of Boston gang violence. Annually, she leads over 500 people in her Parents and Children Walk for Peace; her "Christmas with Bobby" parties provide gifts and rewards for good grades for neighborhood children; and she has registered so many voters and driven so many to the polls that a State Representative credited her with doubling the turnout in her precinct.

On the day of Nardo Lopes' arrest for the murder of her son, Isaura Mendes had gone on a long drive and when she came home, there were so many cars parked on Groom Street that she had to park a block away. Some kids ran up and told her that a bunch of cops and the mayor were at her house.

She rushed home. As she looked at the faces in her living room, she assumed police made an arrest in the murder of her 24-year-old son Matthew, who was killed in 2006 on Wendover Street.

"Isaura," a police officer said gently, "we got Nardo."

Isaura Mendes slumped to the floor, as the mayor and police commissioner rushed to her side. After she assured them she was alright, Boston Police Superintendent Paul Joyce stepped out onto the front porch. He looked right and could see Hillsboro Street, and the three decker where Nardo grew up. He looked left and saw kids, running from corner to corner, spreading the news of Nardo's arrest, just as they had spread word of Bobby Mendes' death 12 years before.

"That's what struck me," Joyce said. "The small confines of all this. The news, the word of mouth, the kids running and shouting. Everything had changed, and some things had not changed at all."

***

Throughout the 1970s, 80s and into the new century, Boston's increasing diversity was changing the organized crime landscape. Nowhere was that more obvious than in Roxbury's Orchard Park projects where a new school black gangster known as God reigned supreme.

Darryl (God) Whiting was a New York thug who relocated to Boston on the eve of the crack epidemic. In a city where organized crime had been dominated by Irish, Italian and Jewish gangs, Whiting was a new force on the streets. The organization he built grossed millions and his generosity and charity were legendary. Only when he believed his stature in the streets made him untouchable could a heroic undercover agent get the chance to bust the man known as God.

CHAPTER SEVENTEEN

GOD AND THE CRACK ERA: THE RISE AND FALL OF DARRYL WHITING

IN 1974 FEDERAL Judge Arthur Garrity ordered the integration of Boston public schools, setting off years of racial upheaval. The crisis, known as "busing", and the racial violence that followed was captured memorably in the Pulitzer Prize winning photo The Soiling of Old Glory in which a white teenager attempted to spear a black man with a flag pole with the American flag waving at the end. Seen around the world in the year of America's bicentennial, Boston became a symbol for the nation's most entrenched racism.

Following the worst years of busing, the 1983 mayoral race – between candidates too easily adopted as symbols of the warring factions – could have pushed racial hostility over the edge. Ray Flynn, a populist from South Boston, the center of anti-busing sentiment and working class anger, faced Mel King, the charismatic African American progressive from the South End.

Rather than playing dirty, Flynn and King waged a respectful, issues-oriented campaign. They met an astounding 76 times for debates and forums in the months leading up to the election and 70 percent of voters showed up to the polls on Election Day (the most since 1949), making the race a high water mark in Boston political history.

In the primary election, King finished second – ahead of a high profile field of candidates – and less than 300 votes behind Flynn going into the general election. When he received only twenty percent of the white vote in the general election, Flynn won an easy victory, taking sixty percent of the total vote.

Still, Mel King's run for mayor was one of the most public examples of the advances African Americans were making as the 1980s began. "In the eighties we were feeling good about ourselves," says George (Chip) Greenridge of Boston's Greatest Minds Initiative. "We had the Cosby Show, something called the black buppie was coming out, we started getting new jobs in government, but something came out of nowhere like a Hiroshima hood bomb and said pow!"

The "bomb" was crack cocaine and, just like a bomb, it was sudden, explosive and deadly. Crack made its earliest appearance in Boston in 1985 and drug counselors immediately warned police and the public about this potent new drug and its horrific effects on users. Soon after, the city's first crack house opened in the 100 block of Columbia Road in Dorchester.

Boston police did little to stem the growing trouble. By their own accounts, they were slow to grasp the enormity of the epidemic and the lucrative business it spawned. Youth gangs and career criminals appreciated the changes happening though. One ex-con known as God built a crack dealing crew that became the most infamous in the city. Before God and crack, however, Boston's black mob was already organized and dangerous.

The Dope Game

Boston's African American neighborhoods had seen sophisticated drug operations before crack cocaine. Two heroin organizations in the early 1980s competed for millions in profits and territory as federal investigators doubted that black criminals could build and monitor a complex criminal enterprise.

The Capsule Boys were South Carolina gang members who relocated to Boston and built a $50,000 a day heroin empire. Known as the Cap Boys, they used armed rooftop guards and children as lookouts equipping them with walkie-talkies, binoculars and automatic weapons to keep one step ahead of the police. The Cap Boys dominated the inner city drug trade throughout the early 1980s based on their connections to the Country Boys gang led by the brothers of Harlem dealer Frank Lucas.

When DEA agents dismantled the Cap Boys with a series of arrests, a rival crew led by a flashy drug dealer named Foots stepped up to fill the void. Anthony (Foots) Simon led an organization of two dozen drug dealers who sold $10,000 to $15,000 of heroin a day in Dorchester and Roxbury. Simon earned his nickname with his trademark pricey shoes bought from designer stores at Copley Place.

The ring had the trappings of a legitimate business. Some employees went on strike over wages and working conditions. The group stamped its heroin packages with the impression of a tiger paw and labeled it with brand names such as "Masters of the Universe" or "Souper Duper" to distinguish it from competitors.

In 1983, Simon made more than $2 million in heroin sales, according to the federal government. Authorities said he dealt directly with Mafia figures in New York City. His ring allegedly obtained large quantities of high purity heroin in New York and brought it to Boston where they diluted it and sold it for $60 a gram.

Foots Simon shared management of the ring with his brother Charles. When the brothers were arrested on Christmas Eve 1986, authorities found a pound of heroin in a home used by Foots. One federal investigator said authorities were reluctant to investigate Simon because of skepticism that black neighborhoods could produce an organized crime powerhouse.

"I wouldn't say it was racism, but there was a certain reluctance to believe that black people could organize and run a conspiracy bringing in millions of dollars every year," the anonymous investigator told the Boston Globe. "You can believe if drugs were being sold like this in [wealthy suburbs] Wellesley and Newton there would have been a lot more attention."

From Stickup Kid to Kingpin

Boston's crack era began in earnest in late 1986, when Darryl Whiting stepped into Roxbury's Orchard Park projects for the first time. The jewels he wore, rumored to be made from a huge diamond he brought back from Africa, seemed to blind the whole city to what was coming.

They already called him God. The nickname came from his religion; he'd joined the Nation of Gods and Earths when he was 12 years old.

Whiting was an early member of the group known as Five Percenters and experienced his conversion in New York City's infamous juvenile detention facility Spofford Youth House. The religion's founder, Clarence (13X) Smith, sponsored Whiting upon his release from jail.

When he was 16 and still in high school, he climbed into a car with a friend. The car happened to be stolen. The friend got probation. Whiting got 36 months at Rikers Island Reformatory. "They tricked me into taking a youthful offender," he said years later. "They took three years of my life."

After he was out for about half a year, he robbed a little store while carrying a gun. "I was a stick up kid," he says. "From there I just started robbing everything, banks, supermarkets, drug dealers." He did six years of a 12-year stretch. In prison he took up engineering and mechanical drawing and got his high school equivalency.

After his release, he attended La Guardia Community College in Queens and studied business but he never graduated. "I didn't have time to study hard, to participate in class between trying to survive, so I would go over there and gather what I could to help me along in life," he said.

He and a partner started a small contracting firm. Sheetrocking, masonry and painting. After a series of arrests – including one for the attempted murder of a police officer – Whiting and a group of friends moved to Boston, a city he had once visited on a ski trip. "New York had it out for me," he told a reporter. He moved there in 1986 "to venture on, try out new ideas, because New York definitely was not letting me get at it."

Whiting relocated to Boston on the eve of a boom in the cocaine trade. But it was not until he built his $11 million empire that the full force of the crack epidemic hit Boston. By the time he was done, the poorly maintained street around Orchard Park projects known as Bump Road was a 24-hour cocaine depot that grossed as much as $100,000 a day.

'Classic Big-Time Drug Dealer'

Mann Terror, an Orchard Park native and member of the Boston rap group Wiseguys, was 12 when Whiting and a small group of New York gangsters first entered Orchard Park.

Whiting eventually introduced almost one hundred young men from his old Queens neighborhood to Orchard Park over a four year period. The young dealers usually arrived in Boston in groups of two and three. They came for different reasons; Kenneth (Shyan) Bartlett wore out his welcome in New York after years of wild behavior that included shootings and drug robberies. Others wanted to get out of Queens after the murder of Edward Byrne, a rookie New York City cop shot as he sat in his patrol car outside a witness's home in the South Jamaica neighborhood of the borough. The murder, ordered by an imprisoned kingpin, became a flash point in the history of the War on Drugs but more immediately it sent a stream of dealers to Boston. "After those dumb motherfuckers killed a cop, I put a note on G's windshield and said, 'Bring me to Boston,'" said an ex-dealer. When they got to Boston, Orchard Park residents called them the New York Boys.

On arrival, Whiting's MO for establishing a beachhead was simple: he found a series of vulnerable women — usually single mothers — and convinced them, through bribes or threats, to let him stay with them and run drugs out of their apartments. The first was a woman known as Miss Carol.

"Miss Carol was the older OG lady in the projects," said Mann Terror. "Everybody would go through her house, smoke a little weed. When [Whiting] came in through her it wasn't like they took the project over. They just started a little operation."

Women would eventually suffer the worst scars of the crack epidemic. In contrast to heroin, where addicts were three fourths men, females gained a perverse equality in the 1980s when they made up half of crack addicts.

Gregory Davis, a substance abuse counselor with the Boston Housing Authority, said the drug's effects on women meant black families paid the price. "The anchor, the person who held the family together was the woman. All the pressures she had on her, all of a sudden she checked out this thing called crack and she never was able to get back," Davis said. "Crack was the final straw that destroyed the black family."

In Orchard Park, Mann Terror says he saw an immediate change. "I saw the project go from an ok place to live to fucked up real fast after crack." Addicted women were supplied with a continuous stream of crack in exchange for around-the-clock sexual services to dealers.

Amidst the misery, Whiting was building a myth that he was an all-powerful figure, according to former federal prosecutor Paul Kelly. "Darryl was a big, physical, athletic-looking guy," Kelly recalls, "over six foot two, sharp dresser, deep voice, rode around in a Mercedes Benz, always wore dark glasses and a leather coat. Very quickly if you saw him, you'd think: classic big-time drug dealer. And he seemed to like that."

To young project residents, Whiting's gangster pedigree was awe-inspiring. "He was that dude," says Mann Terror. "He brought that energy. When God walked through the projects it was like everything just kind of stopped."

To Boston's growing gang culture, though, the New York Boys were outsiders in Nike sneakers who had overstepped their bounds into a territory where Boston gangbangers wore Adidas. One New York drug dealer was shot when he wandered into an area controlled by the Intervale Street Posse, and two more were severely beaten when they tried to sell drugs in Columbia Point projects. But when local Grove Hall drug dealers tried to retake some of the ground lost to the New York Boys, a New York enforcer named Chill Will arrived to deliver a fatal message — shooting one of two cousins to death, and wounding the other.

In a recent phone interview from federal prison, Whiting painted himself less as an instigator of the city's crack wars than a negotiator. "I took on somewhat of a mediator role for conflicts between New York and Boston dudes," Whiting said. "Before I introduced the New York dudes to Boston there were certain things that they had to agree to. Because dudes in Boston, they weren't having it — they'd run them right out of town, bag 'em up, and the whole nine. So we set an agreement. When [New Yorkers] come [to Boston], don't try and take over the whole town, just sell coke up there and let them sell the heroin and the reefer. Also, don't travel out of the Orchard Park area. Don't go to other projects trying to sell shit, because those gangs will run you right out. Finally, don't get involved with those guys' girls. That was the agreement."

But Whiting was more likely to surround himself with triggermen than peacekeepers. Enforcers like Steven (Mohammad) Wadlington, William (Cuda) Bowie, and Kenneth (Shyan) Bartlett still inspire fear in Orchard Park twenty years later; residents and police recall grisly murders, including one in which the victim was tortured and dismembered by New York Boys high on PCP.

Bartlett, in particular, cut an imposing presence, with his bodybuilder's physique and far-away stares. "Shyan, he was the scariest motherfucker in the world," says Mann Terror. "When he came around everyone held their breath, scared."

"Anyone who encountered Kenny Bartlett on the streets of Roxbury would have been terrified," says Kelly, the former federal prosecutor.

Whiting held these killers out as threats but publicly insisted he had nothing to do with murder. "I'm a religious man, right," he told a reporter. "And I try to abide by the 10 Commandments as much as possible. And one of the strongest Commandments is 'Yo, thou shall not kill.' As the Commandments say is how I abide. As much as I possibly and physically can."

"I Guess I'm Just a Humanitarian"

By 1989, Whiting had largely won the turf wars. The New York Boys were selling more than a kilo of cocaine a day in $40 and $60 bags; Whiting was getting a steady supply of high quality cocaine from a New York dealer allegedly supplied by a major Colombian cartel. Eight women were used as couriers, making multiple trips to New York City each week and carrying between 125 and 1,000 grams of cocaine back to Boston, according to federal investigators. Whiting said the New York Boys were paying $12,000 for a kilo and grossing $60,000.

Security measures were elaborate. Pitbulls roamed off-leash in project hallways used for dealing. Crew members had binoculars, walkie-talkies and headphones; one project apartment was used solely to store an arsenal of weapons, ranging from riot pump shotguns to Uzi's. In particular, Stephen (Mohammad) Wadlington was known for nightly armed patrols of the projects in which he scaled roof tops to get the best view of the projects. "Mohammad was quiet. The only time you saw him, he would just pop up and you would be like 'damn where'd he come from?" Terror said.

On the outskirts of the New York Boys security patrol was 10-year-old Jose (Glacy) Medina. After school each day, where he was an honor roll student, Glacy allegedly went to Orchard Park to work as lookout for the New York Boys. Instead of yelling "Five-O" at the sight of the police, Glacy used Five Percenter numerology and language to yell "power – cipher" (which represents five - zero) as a warning to the New York Boys. Records of multiple $700 payments to Glacy were found and the grade-schooler dressed in expensive leather jackets and sneakers. "In [federal surveillance] pictures you could see how small he looked in comparison to his surroundings," Kelly said.

The Boston police were caught off-guard, unable to respond to the rising violence and sophisticated drug trades throughout the city. "There was a little bit of denial [in response to crack cocaine], we weren't ready for it and almost from the start we were playing catch up," said Boston Police Deputy Superintendent Paul Joyce.

As the cocaine epidemic worsened in Boston, Whiting was organizing charitable events and investing in high profile business ventures. Shortly before Memorial Day 1989, posters hyping a Whiting excursion started appearing around the projects. They read:

SECOND EXODUS PRODUCTION PROUDLY PRESENT ITS FIRST ANNUAL BUS RIDE TO RIVERSIDE AMUSEMENT PARK ON SUN MAY 28, 1989.THREE BUSES WILL BE LEAVING AT 7:30 A.M...COME ONE COME ALL. ALL WELCOME. FREE RIDES FREE LUNCHES. A $5 RAFFLE DRAWING WILL BE HELD AT APPROXIMATELY 8:30 PM...IN THE ORCHARD PARK HOUSING DEVELOPMENT. 1ST PRIZE WINNER WILL HAVE A CHOICE OF MICROWAVE, VCR, BICYCLE, 13" TV. 2ND PRIZE. 3RD PRIZE.

On the trip, Whiting fed everybody, paid their admission, and handed out spending money. The day was so successful that other gatherings were planned: barbecues, dances, prizes for honor roll students; a Christmas bash where Whiting played Santa and distributed 250 toys free; a basketball rim for kids at Orchard Park with nothing to do. Despite the increasing violence and drug activity, Whiting's generosity was a public relations coup.

"No one had ever thought to put up a basketball rim in the projects for us," said Mann Terror. "When God came around, the day turned great. He might buy out the ice cream man and make him serve the whole projects."

In July 1989 Whiting opened Crown Video in Roxbury on Warren Street near Martin Luther King Boulevard. In December the second piece of his Corona Enterprises Portfolio, Crown Barber Shop, debuted next door. Crown Sneaker on the same block soon followed. Second Exodus Productions, according to Whiting, was "designed to provide food and clothing for the homeless...and sponsor certain recreational and charitable events for the handicapped, elderly and disabled." In January 1990 Whiting described Corona this way: "A minority owned and operated business that seeks to provide quality goods and services to the community at affordable prices with 10% to 15% discounts and up to 25% discounts for public servants."

In August 1989 Whiting and two associates purchased 48 Geneva Avenue for $285,000 - $100,000 down in cash - and converted the 10,000 square foot space to the Crown Social Hall. Crown Social Hall opened each day at 6 am and was used by dozens of families as a day care center, complete with a professional staff of counselors and instructors. It also featured a non-profit organization offering drug counseling, health care resources and job training.

"I [opened the center] to set an example for all black guys getting drug money to give back to the community in some way," Whiting said recently. In 1990 he explained his motivations to a reporter, "I guess I'm just a humanitarian."

Crown Social Hall also hosted some of the era's biggest rap stars during the music's golden age. Whiting hired Queen Latifah, Poor Righteous Teachers, EPMD and more to perform in Boston at a time when few venues in the city supported hip hop. When he brought Kool G. Rap to Boston, the seminal east coast gangsta rapper stayed in the city almost a week enjoying the lifestyle of Whiting and the New York Boys. "He didn't really want to leave, he enjoyed himself so much," Whiting says.

In Too Deep

US Attorney Wayne Budd first realized the extent of Whiting's empire after reporter Ric Kahn's devastating profile of the dealer, a 1990 cover story in the Boston Phoenix. "He threw down the gauntlet, in a way when he had the audacity to appear in the newspaper," Budd said. Budd prioritized the prosecution of Whiting over a case against New England mafia boss Raymond Patriarca after he learned Orchard Park kids viewed Whiting as a role model.

"In an interesting way Darryl Whiting was a new and different kind of organized crime figure than Raymond Patriarca," Budd said. "He was the perfect negative role model for inner city kids. He induced them with gifts and trips to amusement parks to get them into the organization and sell drugs. He did not hesitate to kill or maim folks who got out of line. He was just the kind of guy I thought was deserving of the full weight of the federal government's resources."

However, Whiting was more insulated than a triple goose down jacket. He rarely got directly involved in the daily operations of the New York Boys and had layers of managers monitoring the business. To reach him would require an exceptional undercover agent.

On April 4, 1990, a flamboyant Rhode Island drug dealer named Jay Reed walked into Crown Video, a store owned by Whiting, and met Whiting's employee Raymond (L.A.) Ward. A month later he bought a shotgun from Ward for $250. Ward told Reed he could roll in Orchard Park and that Ward would get him all the drug customers he could handle.

Jay Reed was actually Jeff Coy, an undercover Boston Housing cop working with the DEA. A veteran of more than 20 undercover missions in two years, Coy once estimated he made over 400 undercover drug buys. Kelly says Coy was a "street-smart African-American guy, who had the look, had the game" to infiltrate the most closed-off crack organizations.

For the next six months, Coy walked and talked like a gangster, carried Uzis around OP, and snorted cocaine chased by Valium, as he would later testify in court. He also testified that he shot two local stick-up men in an Orchard Park hallway who mistook him for an average drug customer, and was involved in a near drive-by shooting in the Lenox Street housing development.

Coy's tactics were effective. He bought a total of 16 ounces of cocaine in six weeks from the New York Boys. In one transaction, he purchased two ounces from Whiting's top lieutenant David (Divine) Waight as Whiting himself looked on. Coy scored another major victory for the DEA investigation when he walked into Whiting's barber shop wearing a recording device and made a deal to sell Whiting eight guns.

However, by this time, Coy was cracking up, becoming the character he created. A DEA psychologist diagnosed him with post-traumatic stress disorder and depersonalization, the loss of identity. He was hospitalized a month after his supervisors pulled him off the case. He returned successfully, however, to provide the pivotal testimony in the trial against Whiting and the New York Boys.

The trial's star witness may have been Whiting himself. On the stand, he implicated three of his co-defendants. When a prosecutor asked Whiting, why he put three drug deals on his friends Whiting's lawyer objected.

"Overruled," Whiting yelled out over his own lawyer. "I only put two drug deals on them."

"Whiting paralleled [Nino Brown, the fictional drug kingpin played by] Wesley Snipes in the film New Jack City, in that he got on the stand and pointed his finger at his codefendants," Budd said. "I was in court the day he testified, and he pointed his finger at his associates and away from himself. It was a pitiful thing. Just pitiful."

One of the only members of the crew to follow the gangster's code of silence was 13 years old. Glacy, the 10 year old lookout, took the stand three years after joining the crew but he wasn't saying much. "Glacy was too small for the podium," says an ex-New York Boy. "All you could see was his eyes and hear him saying, 'Nah, I don't know nothing.'" Prosecutors presented pictures of the child in Orchard Park with the New York Boys. "Nah, that's not me man. I had a job cutting grass that summer," Glacy told a US attorney Kelly. "You should leave me alone."

"Glacy," an ex-New York Boy known as Budda says, "was one of the only guys to stand up." Until he was murdered, Glacy would stick to his code. In 1993, he survived a shooting and refused to speak with police. Instead, he shot two men a month later. He survived a stabbing in February 1995 and again refused to help investigators. Three months later he was dead after getting shot near Orchard Park.

"After [working for the New York Boys] Glacy was hardened to the life. He let the streets take control of him. He knew how to get money but he was caught up in the gangbang life," says Mann Terror.

Glacy's refusal to incriminate Whiting did little to help the accused kingpin. Guilty verdicts for Whiting and his co-defendants sealed his fate he faced a mandatory life term in federal prison. Judge Walter Jay Skinner called the term "extremely harsh" and "severe," and pointed out that he had no discretion in imposing it. "As I read it, there's only one sentence possible, and that's a life sentence."

Budd says that Whiting became visibly upset as federal marshals took him away to prison. "One of the marshals told me that Darryl Whiting, this self-styled God, broke down and cried and pleaded, 'I don't want to go jail, I don't want to go jail.' He was crying and carrying on so much he needed a handkerchief to clean himself up. I always thought that was the perfect postscript to the story of Darryl Whiting."

Jeff Coy sat in the back of the courtroom smiling and watched as Whiting and the New York Boys were marched off to prison. Three years later, he would hang himself in his apartment. "He was undercover too deep for too long," said George Festa, the region's DEA Special Agent in Charge during the Whiting investigation. "He was a decent man and committed to doing the right thing."

(Coy and Whiting inspired the 1999 film In Too Deep, with LL Cool J as the drug lord nicknamed "God," and Omar Epps as "Jeff Cole," the cop sucked into the underworld. For reasons unknown, the director moved the action to Ohio.)

Boston After Crack

Today, the Orchard Park projects look a lot different than the days of the New York Boys. The dirt path of Bumpy Roads has been paved over. The bricks have been covered with brighter exteriors. Officially speaking, Orchard Park is gone; it is now called Orchard Gardens. In many ways, though, the devastation of crack remains.

The effects of the crack epidemic fell disproportionately on women, according to substance abuse experts. "Out of all the females I treated they came in from crack. All women who haven't been able to sustain long term sobriety was because of what the crack had done to them mentally and emotionally," said Gregory Davis a substance abuse counselor with the Boston Housing Authority and Metro Alive. "It took their whole self-esteem because once crack came into women's lives they did things to get crack that they would never ever think of doing in their life. It's a struggle to be able to free yourself from that bond. It was worse on the female than it was on the male."

For men and women battling addiction, support is at an all-time low. "We don't have a voice any longer for substance abuse and treatment in this state," says Davis. "Treatment on demand is out the door. I used to keep them in detox for thirty days and my boss would say, 'They're not supposed to be here more than fifteen days.' Today, three days – five if you're good and if you don't get it then, too bad. That's where we're at twenty five years later."

Whiting's conviction is widely credited with beginning the momentum for Boston's late-1990s dramatic crime decrease known as the Boston Miracle. But the demise of the New York Boys was not the end of drugs in Orchard Park. The housing project saw three major drug sweeps by DEA agents in the next seven years, mostly targeting members of the Trailblazers gang who modeled their operations after the New York Boys. "Everything [the Trailblazers] learned," says Mann Terror, "we learned from God."

The most devastating legacy of the crack epidemic is even more direct. "Between 1988 and 1997 there were 300 unsolved homicides of young men involved with gangs in Roxbury, Dorchester and Mattapan. The children of those 300 young men are our teenagers today," Police Superintendent Paul Joyce says. "The sons are being told by people in the neighborhood about who may have committed the homicide of their father; they are being put in very difficult positions."

Today, Darryl Whiting is locked up in a federal prison in Florida, about 50 miles outside of Orlando. Barring a successful appeal, Whiting will remain in prison for the rest of his life. Over the last few years, with nothing but time on his hands, Whiting completed a fictionalized memoir. In the book, called Taking It To Another Level, he is released from prison after a successful appeal. "I open up a trendy neighborhood barber shop and immediately begin killing my eight co-defendants who testified against me," he said.

Whiting says he will forever be sorry for introducing the New York Boys to Boston while insisting he was a legitimate businessman in the wrong place at the wrong time: "I'm sticking to my innocence." When asked how he maintained hope in the face of a life sentence, he said, "I don't deal in hope."

CHAPTER EIGHTEEN

STREET GANGS IN BOSTON: 25 YEARS OF DEADLY RIVALRY

FRIDAY, AUGUST 19, 1988.

THE 911 CALL came in to Boston police at 9:22 p.m. "There's a little girl shot on Humboldt Ave!" Screams and shrieks swirled in the background as the woman caller continued: "Oh God! Oh, the little girl on the ground, shot!"

It was a hot summer night in the Grove Hall section of Roxbury. The girl on the ground was Darlene Tiffany Moore, a 12- year-old who moments before was perched on a mailbox, talking with friends. Blood poured from three bullet wounds.

An unintended victim of street gang vengeance, Tiffany Moore became an instant symbol of the drug-fueled lawlessness rocking the city. Police launched a massive search for the Halloween-masked killers. Officials sought to calm a public crying out for an arrest - some in the community called for the deployment of the National Guard.

Two tense weeks later justice was apparently in hand. Shawn Drumgold, 22, and a second man were charged with killing the girl. In their trial 14 months later, only Drumgold was convicted. Guilty of first-degree murder, he was sentenced to life without parole, an outcome confirmed on appeal by the state's highest court eight years later.

From the beginning Drumgold always maintained his innocence. An explosive 2003 Boston Globe story by Dick Lehr backed that claim up and maintained "the conviction was built on sand." Prosecution witnesses recanted, admitted to perjury and detailed pressure from investigators to lie. [Drumgold was freed on appeal that year and eventually won a $14 million judgment against the city of Boston.] A key point in Drumgold's case for innocence concerned gang politics in Boston.

Before Tiffany Moore was killed she was seated near Humboldt gang leader Swervin Mervin Reese. Reese got his nickname due to his ability to dodge bullets – just recently, rivals had missed him but killed his stepfather, 43-year-old Inacio Mendes. Tonight, masked men from the Castlegate gang ran toward them across the small grassy lot. When the shooting started, kids scattered and fled, except Tiffany Moore. She lay dead.

Police, according to court records, concluded almost immediately that the shooting was part of an ongoing feud between the Castlegate and Humboldt street gangs - revenge for the wounding of a Castlegate member two weeks earlier. That should have ruled out Drumgold. He was living on Humboldt Avenue with his girlfriend and daughter that summer and he was selling drugs, but he had no involvement with the local street gangs, according to authorities.

"Shawn was dealing in peace, not bothering either gang," said a police investigator who worked in Roxbury at the time.

Police kept books listing street gang members and anyone who might be loosely associated with a gang. Drumgold and Taylor were not listed in the Castlegate book or in any gang listing, according to police records and later trial testimony.

Even more puzzling was the notion that Drumgold, who lived on Humboldt Avenue, would be an agent of the Castlegates. "He was living on Humboldt. Why would he shoot at [Humboldt]?" one investigator asked. Drumgold and Taylor would have been hunted down and killed by the Humboldt gang, he said.

A misunderstanding of Boston's complex gang culture caused authorities to bungle the murder of Tiffany Moore. Boston police further eroded their trust with Boston's black community the next year when they fell for a racial hoax from a killer con man.

The Charles Stuart Hoax: Race, Lies and Murder

On October 23, 1989, Charles and Carol Stuart were shot in the Mission Hill section of Roxbury. Carol was pregnant with the couple's first child and she and her unborn child died within days. Charles Stuart suffered a less serious wound and told police at the scene that the couple, on their way home from a Lamaze class at Brigham and Women's Hospital, was accosted by a black gunman in an Adidas jogging suit while waiting for a stoplight.

Stuart said the attacker forced them to drive several blocks away, robbed them of $100 cash and their watches. Stuart told police at the scene that the gunman said, "I think you're 5-0" when he saw a phone in the car. Believing they were police, the black man allegedly shot the couple, Stuart said.

Investigators told reporters they were convinced that the gunman either lives in or routinely commits crime around the Mission Hill housing project. The day after the shooting Republicans in Massachusetts House of Representatives moved to reinstate the death penalty.

Stuart's claims triggered a massive manhunt in Boston's black community that activists called a "South Africa-style attack" by hundreds of police officers. Police planted evidence on black teens in Mission Hill in order to secure testimony and, for three weeks, threatened and harassed residents of the neighborhood's housing project.

Nineteen days after the shooting, a paroled convict, William Bennett, 39, was arrested on a motor vehicle violation, and named as a top suspect in the murder. Bennett, a Mission Hill resident, had been convicted in 1973 of shooting a Boston police officer in the leg and threatening another policeman with a shotgun in 1981. Prosecutors were preparing to ask a grand jury to indict him for murder.

It seemed to be the embodiment of the yuppie nightmare: a white expectant mother from the suburbs shot point blank in the head and her husband gravely wounded by a crazed black mugger. In fact, it was all a fantasy created by Charles Stuart who had plotted his wife's murder for weeks in an attempt to collect $82,000 in life insurance money.

In his plot, he played on white Boston's paranoia, racism and insecurity to overlook key holes in his story: why did the gunman jump into the car? Why did he shoot a woman passenger first before taking aim at the man? For five weeks, professional skeptics - news media and police - skipped those questions.

Charles' 23-year-old brother Matthew went to investigators after reading in the newspapers that his brother was about to allow Bennett, an innocent man, to be indicted on murder charges. The next day police were ordered to arrest Charles Stuart but he had found out they were looking for him. He was seen driving home about 4 p.m., staying just five minutes and then speeding off again. He spent the night at a motel in a suburb north of Boston and checked out early Thursday morning.

A few minutes before 7 a.m., Charles Stuart drove his new Nissan Maxima north on Route 1 and parked on the lower deck of the bridge. On the passenger seat, he left his driver's license and a suicide note that said in part "the allegations have taken all my strength." Then he jumped.

The Stuart story had already taken so many twists and turns that police believed it was possible Stuart could have faked his own death. Officers were deployed to Logan International Airport to make sure he was not on his way out of the country.

It was not until State Police divers pulled his body from the frigid Mystic River that the authorities felt they could say with certainty that Charles Stuart, like his wife and unborn child that he killed, was now dead too.

The black killer in the Adidas jogging suit turned out to be a figment of Charles Stuart and white Boston's imagination. Boston's gang culture, however, was very real.

Boston's Original Gangsters: The Johnson Brothers

In the 1950s and 1960s black street gangs such as the Marseilles Dukes, the Emperors, the Park Boys, the Pythons, the Band of Angels and others roamed streets and fought hand to hand in pitched battles. The gangs were old school; they each had a hierarchy of leaders and wore distinctive sweaters. By the 1970s, as racial consciousness took hold, gang activity dropped out of sight. In the 1980s, though, gang culture reemerged in Boston and the results were deadly.

The first of the new generation of gangs was the Corbet Street Crew – founded by the Johnson Brothers in the early 1980s. Boston hip hop pioneer, activist and fashion designer Marco Antonio Ennis (E Devious) remembers the day the Johnson family moved to his Dorchester neighborhood from down South. "We called them the Hillbillies because there were so many of them. One day there was this huge family around the corner and they're making themselves right at home," he said. "They would be in the streets playing ball, riding dirt bikes. The Johnsons."

Early on, Corbet was the biggest gang, with over 100 members not including the junior and female divisions. They hung out at the end of Corbet Street – a street that connected the Dorchester and Mattapan neighborhoods – openly dealing drugs and sporting expensive clothes and jewelry, driving slowly around town in sleek Cadillacs. Younger members fascinated with the power and the lifestyle were initiated by stealing a triple goose down coat.

"That's where it all started," one longtime resident told a reporter at the gang's peak, pointing at a yellow house on Corbet Street. "That's where the leaders lived before they went to jail. They used to hang out there. That's where they organized themselves." Eventually, gang members came from all over Dorchester and Mattapan, but they continued to use the name, the longtime residents said. "They're not Corbet Street boys," said a woman. "They come from all over. But they kept the name because it has status. It carries weight and people are afraid when they hear, 'the Corbet Street Gang.'

If the Johnsons provided a foundation, crack cocaine financed the first generation of Boston gangs. Boston rapper and ex-gang member Tangg the Juice says, "When crack first hit, there was no drug unit, there was no gang unit. The police weren't prepared for it. It was so lucrative. It was just a good time to be a drug dealer," Tangg says.

In 1988, "Colors" a Dennis Hopper film, provided a final, devastating inspiration for Boston's street crews. For the first time, "Colors" put Los Angeles's gang culture of Bloods and Crips on the big screen and broadcast it to the world.

"Colors was the sparkplug," says Ennis. "Colors gave everything a visual. Cats in Boston didn't know how dudes in Los Angeles were living. We didn't know they were walking around with AK-47's in their neighborhoods. Now street after street in Boston is a different gang and they're wearing hats to represent it."

"Colors made gangs seem larger than life," says Boston rapper Raymond (Benzino) Scott. "And everyone wants to be larger than life."

Rapidly, teens in sections of Roxbury, Mattapan and Dorchester adopted names and symbols to represent their new allegiances and feuds. The Franklin Hill Giants, Magnolia Street Steelers, Orchard Park Trailblazers, Castlegate Raiders, Vamp Hill Kings and others used Starter hats and jackets to represent their sets.

"In the Spring of 1988, the Boston Police Department started to see the formation of gangs in the city," says Boston Police Superintendent Paul Joyce.

"[At the time there was] roughly 15 gangs, less than 500 kids involved. [From police there was] a little bit of denial, we weren't ready for it and almost from the start we were playing catch up. We focused on ways to get out of this quickly.

"Over next two years, we probably went through the most difficult time in the history of this police department," Joyce said. "We saw Tiffany Moore killed in August 1988 sitting on her mailbox on Humboldt Avenue, caught in the crossfire of two rival gangs. We went through Charles Stuart. We went through [controversial "search on sight" police procedure] stop and frisk. In all of these areas [the Boston Police Department] failed."

In 1990 the murder rate reached a record high - 152 homicides. In one forty day period there were 100 shootings. "That was an incredibly difficult time for this city and I think all our responses as a community, as police, and as a city fell short and we paid a big price," Joyce said.

The tragic effects of crack and gangs would play out in Boston for the next twenty-five years.

Intervale Street Posse and Adidas Park

Intervale Street travels a narrow path along a quarter mile from Columbia Road to Warren Street. Brownstones, single family houses and low-rise apartment complexes dot its landscape. To many, it is the most dangerous street in the city. To the city's most tightly organized street gang, it was home.

Compared to other street gangs, authorities said the Intervale Street Posse was a sophisticated criminal enterprise with strict internal codes and initiation rituals. As a greeting, Intervale members hugged and kissed one another on the cheeks, mob style. "It's like the mob," a member declared, describing the gang's attitude. "Any means necessary. You find a way to make money. There's no more black and white colors. The color is green."

"The Intervale Posse was originally a stick up crew," says ex-leader Derrick Tyler. In 1987 when Tyler returned from a prison sentence he says he shifted the crew's focus from robbery to crack dealing. On New Year's Eve that year, Intervale leaders gathered a dozen teen agers into a huddle. On their feet, they each wore Adidas sneakers. "We're the Intervale Street gang," a leader declared. "We're all down together."

"We didn't allow anybody to hang on the block except the dudes that were [with Intervale]," Tyler says. "We had codes and guidelines that had to be followed if you were with us. If a member got locked up, everyone on the team had to chip in with bail money. Violators of the rules were dealt with very harshly and without sympathy."

Intervale earned their street reputation through loyalty and violence. "What put the team on the map was when drama came we came heavy, we brought the full team to the beef," Tyler says. In one fatal incident, Intervale Posse members had repeatedly warned a non-affiliated dealer to stay off their turf but word was not heeded. A gang member was heard to tell the man, "Surprise, surprise" moments before he was shot dead in front of his home.

The harshness even extended to those in violation of Boston's street fashion codes. Intervale like most Boston crews of that time preferred Adidas sneakers to the Nike's favored by New York gangsters. Although Run DMC's "My Adidas" made the three striped shoes a staple of hip hop fashion everywhere, Boston clung to its identification with the brand longer and more tightly than other towns. Within the city, there was no more prominent demonstration of that loyalty than the Intervale Posse's Adidas Tree.

Sitting in a wooded lot between Devon and Intervale streets, the Adidas Tree was adorned with dozens of pairs of Adidas sneakers and became a striking symbol of Boston's gang culture. "People used to come from far and wide to throw their Adidas up there," Ennis says. "It was a ritual. It was beautiful for us in the 'hood. We would go there, smoke weed, throw the Adidas up there like you marked your territory. Of course if you weren't cool with Intervale you couldn't do it." The gang soon outfitted Adidas Park with couches, a barbeque and televisions powered from local abandoned homes. On some Sunday afternoons gang members were in the lot under the Adidas Tree holding guns and watching football games.

The strict codes Intervale held their members to gave the gang a chance to expand beyond its neighborhood, says George Festa, the DEA Special Agent in Charge at the time. "The Intervale Posse was a violent, disruptive force that had the biggest chance to expand because they had that tight discipline."

By 1996, the gang's discipline and violence made them a target of the DEA. Authorities wanted an example made of the Posse before the new school year started. On August 29, an interagency task force swept onto Intervale Street and charged fifteen Posse members in federal court and another eight in state court.

"State or federal?" Intervale's boss Sam (Sam Goody) Patrick asked when the task force took him. Federal; he hung his head. Back on Intervale Street, the Massachusetts National Guard rolled combat earthmoving equipment into Adidas Park and leveled the Adidas Tree.

Tony Johnson: Gangland Guru

The Intervale Street Posse might have been one of the most feared crews in Boston but one individual towered over the city's streets. Tony Johnson, an acclaimed high school athlete and reputed gang leader, was called "a gangland guru" by the Boston Globe for the hold he had on the city.

"That kid had more respect on the street than Jesus Christ," said a Boston lawyer. "He was on top of his crew, he was making money, he had enormous gold and the trappings of wealth, and he was completely outside of law enforcement. Tony had no dealings with cops. They could grab him and search him, but he was too smart for that. He was a world unto himself."

A popular athlete and college student, police claimed there was more to the charming Johnson than his achievements on the field and in the classroom. He was a cousin of Boston's original gangsters – the Johnson Brothers and Corbet Street Crew. Further, police alleged that Tony Johnson was angling to become the godfather of Boston's street gangs by organizing each crew into one unstoppable force.

However, people who knew Johnson said he was more likely to use his street status to mediate disputes than start them. "When dudes couldn't go to guys and get their stuff back or even walk through other neighborhoods, Tony was the one that made it safe to go to other people's neighborhoods. He was like Cyrus in the Warriors. He had the biggest and wildest gang in the city," says Cool Gzus, a pioneering Boston rapper and part of noted hip hop groups TDS Mob, Wiseguys and Made Men.

Boston Police believe that in 1987 Johnson organized the largest gangs into a loose association in order to keep New York drug dealers from gaining a foothold in Boston. The same year he appeared on the cover of Boston's first gangsta rap record The Almighty RSO's "Notorious." Johnson did not rap but he was an official member of the group based on his friendship with members Marco Antonio Ennis a.k.a. E Devious and Raymond (Ray Dog) Scott. Ennis says police theories of Johnson as a gang overlord are exaggerations.

"Tony did his thing with the drugs in the streets its true. But in that era drugs played a part in all our lives. The Franklin Hill Giants were his crew and they were getting money."

Even police officers, who Johnson often managed to outwit if not evade, admitted to a grudging respect for the young man. Police said Johnson earned his spurs when he was charged with murder at age 16. Even then, what would become a curious ability to stay ahead of law enforcement appeared to be at work. Johnson was committed to the state Department of Youth Services for murder on Dec. 12, 1984, when he was 17. But three months later he was back on the street, thanks to a technicality.

There was another side to Tony Johnson though, he was one of the best athletes in the city, a two-sport star in football and basketball recruited by Division 1 college programs. He used his big hands and six foot three inch frame to dominate the legendary Boston Neighborhood Basketball League summer games. In high school hallways he was liked by both his teachers and peers.

"He was one of the nicest kids, mannerly, generous," said Abner Logan, Johnson's basketball coach at the Jeremiah Burke High School. "The teachers liked him. He never was a problem here at school."

Johnson completed one year at Hudson Valley Community College in Troy, N.Y., and was apparently being considered for a football scholarship at Syracuse University. "We were so proud that our friend from the hood was on his way to college on a full scholarship," Ennis says. Johnson never made it out of Boston though. The night before he planned to leave for college, as he parked one of his two cars, he was shot twice in the head and killed. "COOL, ARTICULATE AND SAVVY – AND DEAD AT 21" – read the headline in the Boston Globe, detailing Johnson's death.

When Johnson died, the unity he'd been trying to build among the city's gangs was shattered. A Boston police officer who knew Johnson well looked around at the increase in shootings and said, "There was no trouble when Tony was around. He was the Godfather. Castlegate, Intervale, Franklin Hill, they didn't fight when Tony was around. After he got killed, all hell broke loose."

Tony Johnson was the closest thing to a cult figure that many city teen-agers had ever encountered. And for many of them, the streets were a more dangerous place after he was gone. "They thought he was God," said Billy Stewart, a probation officer in Dorchester District Court. "For a while we had kids putting up Tony Johnson statues, you know, little pictures of him. Tony Johnson," he paused, "was smooth."

The Franklin Hill Giants gang did not die with Johnson. In fact, members say, after Johnson's death they were determined to prove they were the toughest gang in the city. "When Tony Johnson died, the Franklin Hill Giants were too big, it got too powerful. When Tony died we said, 'Fuck Corbet. Fuck everybody it's just all about us right now. Tony's gone and if you don't respect us then fuck you," says Franklin Hill Giant and Boston rapper Tangg the Juice.

After Johnson died, Tangg's cousin Rigoberto Godfrey took over as the gang's leader. Tangg says the project's location helped the gang build a reputation as one of the toughest in the city. "We had a nice project in Franklin Hill, one way in and one way out. We shot at the police from rooftops and they couldn't do shit," Tangg says. "We weren't the projects that a bunch of New York [drug dealers] are going to run in and take over. That was never going to happen. Our project was more organized. We had more shooters. Everyone had guns but Franklin Hill had more seriousness as far as killings and making money."

Another piece of Tony Johnson's legacy would live on after his death. Johnson was an integral member of the Almighty RSO. He served as security at stage shows and reportedly put up the initial money for recording sessions. More importantly he represented the hard edge the music was trying to capture as the crack epidemic worsened. As the years passed and Tony Johnson's grip on Boston teens was lost, hip hop took over as the voice of the streets.

The Almighty RSO Saga

Hip hop music came to Boston in 1979 when Skippy White, the owner of the Boston music chain of the same name, ordered 50 copies of "Rapper's Delight" by the Sugarhill Gang. Within a few years, Boston groups were releasing their own records and by the mid-1980s hip-hop was the rage in Boston's inner city neighborhoods of Roxbury, Dorchester, Mattapan, Jamaica Plain and the South End.

For the neighborhood gangbangers there was a thin line between street life and music. "We were rapping about the people we had shot the night before," Tangg the Juice says. "This was before [seminal rap group] NWA. We were like, 'Fuck it let's rap about those dudes we robbed yesterday.'"

Of all the local hip hop upstarts, the Almighty RSO had the most dedicated street following – and the strongest rap industry connections thanks to founder Raymond (Benzino) Scott aka Ray Dog. Tony Rhome and E-Devious rapped with Scott while DJ Def Jeff handled production. Benzino made an important connection when he met Dave Mays, a Harvard student and hip hop enthusiast who started a one page newsletter called The Source distributed at local music shops Skippy White's, Nubian Notion and Spin City. The publication rapidly grew in popularity and by 1990 moved to New York City and expanded into a full magazine. In New York City, The Source seized a dominant position in hip hop media, eventually boasting a circulation over 500,000. As The Source moved to the top of the hip hop world, Boston gangbangers followed as security and muscle.

Even though the Source moved out of Boston, Mays remained closely associated with RSO who, by 1992, had parlayed their independent releases into a deal with major label Tommy Boy Records. Their first release, "One in the Chamba" directly addressed the Boston Police Department over two recent police killings of unarmed men Nathaniel Lackland and Christopher Rogers. Over a sample of the 1977 Blackbirds song "Misterious Vibes", the song pulled no punches in advocating armed resistance to violent police tactics.

"One in the Chamba that was just news reporting," E Devious says. "[A police officer] shot Christopher Rogers under the car. We were just reporting about an incident that happened. Back then rap was more political but it was political with a hard edge."

The song was soon swept up in the national controversy about the messages in gangsta rap. To the Boston Police Patrolman Association it was a taunt from a group that had a long history of encounters with the law. With the backing of Oliver North, the patrolman's association announced they would sue Tommy Boy Records. Soon, RSO was dropped from the label.

"Oliver North was coming at us and look at all the bullshit he was doing. We down here just trying to survive and he's looking at us like we're some fucking terrorists," E Devious says.

Another setback was the murder of group member Rock (Rodney Pitts). Rock was the group's youngest and most charismatic emcee. "He was instrumental in us getting signed to Tommy Boy Records. They liked what he brought to the group," E Devious says. Rock was killed at the old Gallery nightclub in Roxbury. The man charged with the murder, Michael Adams, was acquitted after the jury found he acted in self-defense. Adams was gunned down two years later in an unsolved murder.

Plagued by violence and written off as thugs, the Almighty RSO's next role would be its most shocking move yet - street leaders in a peace movement recognized worldwide as the Boston Miracle.

CHAPTER NINETEEN

HOW THE WISEGUYS SAVED BOSTON

TO MOST OF the hip hop world, Boston's Almighty RSO crew is infamous for violent drama and controversy. Connected to high profile beat downs and attacks on industry figures, RSO's music and image have always included more than a hint of violence. Soon after losing a deal with Tommy Boy Records due to the controversy of "One in the Chamba," RSO recorded an album for RCA. But the group was dropped after members brutally beat two critics from *The Source*. "After that we were really blackballed," said Marco Ennis who along with Raymond (Ray Dog) Scott, formed the backbone of the crew.

In the studio one day reminiscing about "Colors" and how Boston's gang culture had begun, they recalled their friend Tony Johnson's efforts to bring the city's gangbangers together in peace. "The cops think we're just fucked up dudes, interested in killing each other and continuing the bull shit," E-Devious said. "Let's do what they can't do."

The result was the Wiseguys – a collection of rappers from gangs across Boston coming together to make music with former enemies. "The whole Wiseguys project was really an extension of what Tony was doing in [the 1980s]," E-Devious says. "Tony would always say we have more in common with each other than we got differences."

Even as the worst years of the crack epidemic passed, murder rates in Boston remained stubbornly high at about 100 a year. Gang activity was increasing and by 1995 Boston Police said there were 61 gangs and 1,300 members. On Boston-police issued maps of gang activity, RSO appears as a gang in the Four Corners area of Dorchester. Now, as the Wiseguys, they were on the front lines fighting gang violence.

And despite decades of feuding, Boston's gang members did have one strong bond in common: hip hop music had only grown in popularity to inner city youth in the years since RSO started. It wouldn't be easy, however, since Wiseguy founders Scott and Ennis were approaching each gang's impact players – in some cases after recent murders.

"We were going to blocks that were beefing with each other just a few days before. There might have been a shooting the week before and a couple of murders in between," Ennis said. "We went up in these spots trying to find the dopest rappers and telling them, 'We need ya'll to chill we're going to put you on to some music opportunities."

"These young men had been killing each other for the last six and seven years so there's deep rooted resentments towards one another," Scott said.

"You were either part of the group because you were a good rapper and part of a gang or because you were one of the leaders of your gang. [The group] was made of well respected shooters from the hood," said Tangg the Juice, a lead rapper in the Wiseguys.

Ennis and Scott told the group they had to leave their guns behind before entering recording sessions but few listened. "They just were not going to come around without their guns," Ennis said. "Everyone was strapped, you could smell the gunsmoke in the air. These are the cats that represent their different sets and they're all fierce and they're all impact players."

Feuds between the twelve rappers of the Wiseguys could have been endless. The group brought together representatives from gangs engaged in deadly violence for decades. But now, in the studio with rap stars from the Almighty RSO, the competition to write the best verse and stand out lyrically was easing the tension. "Now, [the gang members who make up the Wiseguys] are exercising a different type of competition. If their crew had just been shot at, they couldn't lose in rapping too. It was too competitive for bullshit, if you slipped you didn't make it onto the song and that was everything for them," Ennis.

Ennis and Scott knew if they stayed in Boston, local gang conflicts would interfere. Funded by *The Source* magazine, the Wiseguys went on a national tour promoting their music. "We knew if we took airplanes they wouldn't be able to bring guns with them but if we took buses they'd find a way to bring their guns. So we tried to take as many planes as possible," Ennis said.

At hotels, the group's fiercest rivals were forced to room with each other. The out of town trip was giving perspective to the local feuds that had plagued Boston for more than a decade. "When we left Boston, there was no Heath Street versus Academy or Academy versus Orchard Park beef. We were identified as Boston guys," Mann Terror said. "When we're in California around Bloods and Crips do you think they care that Orchard Park and Academy have problems?"

At the same time, murder rates in Boston were falling rapidly. After racking up 152 homicides in 1990, the murder rate remained stubborn at about 100 per year. The Wiseguys started in 1996 and toured and built relationships throughout 1997 and 1998. By 1999, there were only 31 murders in Boston and none of them were juveniles. For two and a half years during the Wiseguys' efforts no juvenile was killed by a gun in Boston. President Bill Clinton even came to Boston to use the success as a backdrop for a major policy speech on his juvenile-crime platform.

"The impact players were playing in the studio, they were on the road [touring as the Wiseguys]. You take the main dude, then the next three components out of the crew [buy in to the strategy] and the rest of the gang is back home chilling: they're not authorized [by gang leaders] to do anything anyway," Ennis says. "And that was something the cops couldn't do. No matter how much they want to say we're gang members, give us credit for saving lives those two years."

"It's the trickle down effect," Mann Terror says of why the Wiseguys were able to decrease the violence. "My neighborhood sees me doing good they want me to keep doing good because that means they can do good too. [Wiseguys] had a strategy. They came after dudes who had influence in their neighborhoods. They didn't just want rappers. They wanted people in the hood who's word meant something."

There have been many narratives to explain the historic plunge in violence in Boston in the late 1990s – police, probation, politicians, local clergy and anti-gun activists have each claimed a share of the credit. But none of those professionals were actively involved in gangs and crime. Only the Wiseguys brought every gang together to pledge peace.

"We watched the police take all the credit for it, we watched the police get grants. The president came but we did it ourselves," says Tangg. "RSO put it together, The Source magazine put it together but [the Wiseguys] were the ones who got on the phone and squashed beefs [between rival gangs]."

The Wiseguys street credibility would be tested at their opening show in the heart of Boston's gang territory at the Skycap Plaza. Gangs from Orchard Park and Academy projects had been feuding in the street for months shooting at one another, now the two crews would be in the same small space.

"Academy came in they were like 20, 30 deep," Mann Terror says. "[Orchard Park] Trailblazers came in we were like 20, 30 deep. It was an active problem between both crews."

"Half of the show we were on stage. The other half we had to jump off and regulate the crowd, hand to hand," says Tangg. "Nobody else could've controlled that crowd. The police couldn't have done that. We had to do it. It was like we weren't just rappers. When we told the streets to stand down, the streets were going to stand down. That Wiseguys project may not have meant much to the world but in Boston and in Massachusetts it was everything."

The Inside Story of the Stop Snitching Movement

In 1999, disputes over money were dividing the Wiseguys. The group finally broke up when two of the group's many affiliates were found to be police informants – a cardinal sin in hip hop.

After the break up, Wiseguys lead rapper Tangg the Juice was thinking about a gangster influenced domain name he could register on the Internet. "It was still early and nobody was thinking about gangster shit on the Internet," he says. He thought of StopSnitching.com and bought it. Next, he told Ennis about another idea: t-shirts with stop signs and the words Stop Snitching. "Stop snitching t-shirts," Ennis said slowly as he nodded, thinking it over.

Graphic designer Proph Bundy designed the web site and Ennis' clothing company, Antonio Ansaldi, helped design the shirts. After being worn by Harlem rappers The Diplomats in a music video, the shirts took off and sold about 50,000 units.

The message hit a nerve across the country but particularly in Boston where the last half century of organized crime had been dominated by the federal government's dubious deals with criminal informants. "The informant system, as it has evolved in Boston and all over the country, has produced such a large number of false convictions that it's a perfectly appropriate political point of view to say that the snitch system has to be reformed or abolished," civil rights attorney Harvey Silverglate said.

In particular, Boston's inner city communities of Roxbury and Dorchester had suffered from the arbitrary police tactics concerning criminal informants. The misuse and manipulation of informants led Boston police to arrest the wrong people for the murders of Tiffany Moore and Carol Stuart.

In *Snitching: Criminal Informants and the Erosion of American Justice*, legal scholar Alexandra Natapoff says one in 18 young male inner city residents is a criminal informant whose crimes have been excused by authorities because they are providing information on their co-conspirators, friends or neighbors.

That means in Boston's inner city communities, as many as six percent of the young male population could be committing new crimes while working with the police at the same time. These informants exist in a gray world of continuing criminal activity, in which some crime is openly encouraged by the government, some crime is tolerated and some is never discovered. Among criminals, the snitch system seems to go against fair play. Stop Snitching essentially advocated a particular code of the street: those who choose to make their living by breaking the law should not be permitted to escape the costs of that choice by turning in their criminal associates.

However, the shirts became a symbol for increasing violence in Boston when two gang members wore them to a courtroom during the trial of a man accused of killing 10-year-old Trina Persad. Persad had been hit by stray gunfire between two gangs while playing in the daytime at Jermaine Goffigan Park - named for another young victim of Boston gun violence.

Tangg the Juice and E Devious say they disagreed with the shirts being worn to intimidate witnesses. "People started doing stupid shit like wearing it to courthouses and I was like 'damn I didn't mean for it to be used like that,'" says Tangg. "After it started picking up wind we didn't get ahead of it and say we're talking about criminal informants. We're not talking about witnesses like old ladies calling the police. We're talking about people who are shooting guys, saying it was someone else and then going back out and shooting more people."

Boston Mayor Thomas Menino targeted Ennis' clothing store in Dorchester saying the shirts encouraged witness intimidation. As the controversy swirled for the next eight months and the shirts were featured in media across the country including *America's Most Wanted* and *60 Minutes*, sales increased. Eventually though, Ennis and Menino struck a deal to take the shirts off the shelves. Ennis even designed a new shirt with a similar logo and the words, Start Peace. It was another positive endeavor for Ennis who was beginning to be known as much for his community activism as his crime rhymes. But before he could be fully accepted in Boston's anti-violence circles, his old crew would be implicated in a shocking and violent attack on one of the city's most prominent athletes.

Big Roscoe and the Paul Pierce Stabbing

In 2000, tension between the city's top rap crew and Celtics star Paul Pierce boiled over in shocking violence. Pierce had been drafted by the Celtics tenth overall in 1998. By 2000, he was a young millionaire still years away from maturing into a team leader and Celtics officials were privately worrying about Pierce's work ethic and night life activity.

On the night of Sept. 25, 2000 Pierce was out partying again with teammate Tony Battie and Battie's brother Derrick at the Buzz Club in the city's Theater District. Pierce was no stranger to Boston nightlife. A few nights earlier he was out on the town and exchanged words with RSO's entourage.

Tonight, members of the crew were in the same club. RSO had recently changed their name to Made Men to get away from the old controversies but in many ways they were the same old crew. Along with Ennis and Scott, former Wiseguy and RSO affiliate William Ragland was also in the club.

Ragland had rapped on RSO's major label releases but his spot in the group was due to his fearsome reputation as a killer not as an emcee. Since he was 13, Ragland never went more than eight months without being arrested except when he was already locked up. At 14, he walked up to a crowd standing on a Dorchester street and opened fire. A 17-year-old woman was killed and Ragland spent under four years in a juvenile facility.

"He has an explosive temper, which combined with access to firearms and a clear willingness to shoot without hesitation…creates an unacceptable risk to the community. He simply cannot be deterred," a prosecutor once said of him.

That wild streak didn't make him less popular with Made Men. When he was charged with carrying a gun and resisting arrest in the summer of 2000, Benzino put up $25,000 bail to keep Big Roscoe on the streets. One month later, Ragland was at the same Theater District nightclub as Paul Pierce. Ennis and Scott were in a different part of the club, but Ragland was eyeing Pierce suspiciously as the star player spoke to two women Ragland knew.

Ragland walked over and said one of the women was his sister. When Pierce told the man he wasn't trying to hit on the women or disrespect the man he was greeted with a cold stare. Pierce never saw the punch coming but soon he was being attacked from all directions. Something hard and heavy hit him above his right eye.

"It felt like a big blow, like a rock was coming at my head," he said, describing the bottle that was smashed on his forehead. The blow stunned him, he said, and he tried to wipe away the blood that was streaming down his face. The hits kept coming included "stinging blows" he later learned came from stabs in the chest and upper back. "Everything was happening so fast. So many people were on me. I was just trying to get them off me."

A knife ripped a hole in Pierce's diaphragm and punctured his lung, causing it to partially collapse. According to witnesses, Ragland knifed Pierce in the neck and chest while he was pinned against a pool table. "Fuck Paul Pierce!" Ragland reportedly shouted. "Who wants to be the next victim?"

Pierce was short of breath and groggy, almost passing out at one point. The Battie brothers pushed through the crowd and found Pierce leaning against a table wiping blood from his head. "They jumped me," he mumbled. The bleeding from the head subsided but Tony Battie noticed Pierce's shirt was still soaked with blood. "The shirt was sticking to his chest," he said. Battie lifted the shirt and saw eight stab wounds.

"They shanked you, they shanked you," Battie said to Pierce who was frantic and panicking as they drove around the corner to New England Medical Center. Pierce underwent surgery for a collapsed lung and was released three days later. The Battie brothers and a heavy leather jacket he was wearing saved his life.

The assault on Pierce immediately reminded one police officer of an earlier, more violent era. "The beating had all the elements of the original Corbet Street gang [Made Men] descended from. They aren't doing anything too differently today. They get someone in public, beat them and leave people in fear. At the same time, they get people to respect them… Their circumstances have changed but their M.O. hasn't at all. That night with Paul Pierce says a lot."

Ragland and two other Made Men associates were arrested within days. The case against them was weakened though when the women who witnessed the attack recanted their statements – reportedly out of fear. One woman even fainted on the witness stand. Ragland, however, was convicted and sentenced to ten years in prison in addition to a twenty year sentence for being an armed career criminal.

Pierce, of course, recovered and in 2008 led the Celtics to their seventeenth NBA championship. For the Wiseguys, the incident was a violent end to the movement they built during Boston's most peaceful years. For Ennis, the Paul Pierce stabbing convinced him to leave the group he had been with for almost twenty years and start a new chapter of activism and protest.

Boston's Last Chance For Peace

By 2005, Boston had returned to pre-Wiseguy levels of street violence, recording its highest murder rate in a decade. In December, a 19-year-old Dorchester man shot and killed four of his friends in a makeshift basement recording studio after stealing one of the men's handguns. Three of the four victims had formed a rap group, and the weapon was used as a prop in a music video. One of the victims, Edwin Duncan, had worked in Ennis's clothing store. The tragedy, dubbed the Boston Rap Massacre by reporters, and the recent fallout from the Stop Snitching controversy, inspired Ennis – Boston's first gangsta rapper - to push his career in a new direction.

To do so, he abandoned a long running feud with another Boston rap legend, Edo G. (Edward Anderson). In 1991, Edo released Boston rap's signature hit "I Got to Have It." But Ennis says, "I just didn't like him," and one night the rappers clashed in a nightclub brawl between their crews. By 2005, though, the men were close friends and formed the anti-violence group 4Peace with artists Deric Quest (DQuest) and Wyatt (Mo Gee) Jackson. Their first song, "Start Peace," was a catchy call to stop the violence.

They received an immediate positive response including support from Mayor Tom Menino and the gun control group Stop Handgun Violence. The music video was screened at a police chiefs convention and Reverend William Dickerson of the Greater Tabernacle Church regularly played the song at funerals of murdered teenagers.

"When funerals were over Rev. Dickerson would say, 'When you go back in these streets don't seek violence, start peace.' And they would play that song as people viewed the body for the last time. He created a buzz for that song at funeral homes like a DJ would at a club," Ennis says.

Even with the success of 4 Peace, Ennis' next venture showed him a raw side of activism he had never seen. After his clothing store closed in 2009 and his tenants lost their jobs in the recession, Ennis found himself in danger of foreclosure. A neighbor told him about City Life/Vida Urbana and their successful efforts fighting big banks. Ennis cautiously attended a class.

"My first time there I sat in the back and didn't say anything," Ennis told Boston Phoenix reporter Chris Faraone. "I had to learn more, so I went back the next week. The week after that they asked for volunteers, and I said that if I'm going to be in this fight, then I need to do more than just sit here in a chair. From that point I went out with them, and I saw a family get evicted, babies crying, and a grandmother have a heart attack right in the driveway. I'm not scared to say that tears ran down my eyes. It was some real shit, and it was the day when I knew that I had to really get involved."

In the next six months, Ennis occupied US Senator Scott Brown's offices in Washington and he manned the bullhorn for a massive march on Bank of America's Boston offices. "At first I was worried about people driving by and seeing me. But after a few times leading the pack, I said, 'Fuck it — this is bigger than me.' I don't care if anybody finds it corny — right now this is what I feel like I was put here to do. These banks are some tough motherfuckers, and I know I have a voice that this movement needs."

Ennis says he could not have achieved what he has in politics, philanthropy and activism without overcoming the struggles of Boston's crack epidemic, the murder of his friend Tony Johnson, the Stop Snitching controversy and violent rap drama. "Negativity and positivity go hand in hand.

There's not two positives on a battery, not two negatives. You need both to function. I think you need negativity to grow and learn because if that Stop Snitching controversy didn't happen there would be no 4 Peace."

Boston Streets Today

The challenges in Boston's streets today are greater than ever, says Police Superintendent Paul Joyce. In 1988, Boston had 15 gangs with 500 members. Today, Boston gang culture includes over 120 gangs with 3,500 teenagers involved in gang activity in some way.

"The motivations of the first group of young men - accessing the economy and making money in the drug trade - it's not there anymore," Joyce said. "We have young men who are now motivated by violence and the threat of violence. We have a lack of organization, a lack of structure and feuds and alliances that change daily. We have a much more chaotic picture and we have a much higher level of dysfunction among young men we're dealing with today. This is a bigger challenge than what we took on in the 80s."

On September 28, 2010, four people were killed; including a two-year-old boy and his mother, and a fifth man paralyzed in what became known as the Mattapan Massacre. In 2011, accused shooter Dwayne Moore's murder prosecution ended in a mistrial and an acquittal for his co-defendant, Edward Washington. [It was not an exception – Boston Phoenix reporter David Bernstein looked at clearance rates for homicides involving black victims and found that for twenty-two killings in 2002, by 2005, not a single one had resulted in a homicide conviction.]

Moore met his two alleged coconspirators during a state prison sentence he served for a manslaughter conviction. He had only been out of prison for six months the night he allegedly committed the quadruple slaying.

The most frightening aspect of the Mattapan Massacre might be this: there are many Dwayne Moore's in Massachusetts. In 2009, 2,772 prisoners were released to the streets, up from a then record high of 1,933 in 1999. These inmates face increased obstacles in employment and housing as get tough laws narrow their options. Boston Police Superintendent Paul Joyce and Massachusetts Governor Deval Patrick have acknowledged that the violence on the streets is a direct result of what is happening in the state prisons.

While it is true that prisons have perpetuated violent trends in Boston, a select group of prisoners are banding together to use their street credibility to promote peace. Since the days of Malcolm X, Massachusetts prisoners have been part of progressive movements and social change. Today, an inmate named Darrell Jones carries on that tradition. Jones is serving a life sentence for a murder he says he did not commit. That has not stopped him from becoming a well-known figure in Boston politics, activism and media.

Jones and a group of other lifers worked together to produce a 40 minute video, Voices From Behind the Wall, with Roxbury-based youth advocates Teen Empowerment. In emotional and sincere tones, the nine inmates featured in the video blow up the myths of gang life and prison.

"These young cats need to see, you grow old in prison," says inmate Mark Thomas in the video. "I was 22 years old when I came to prison. I'm going on 51 now and it's not funny anymore. I want guys watching this video to see: this could be you."

The film was made with the DOC's permission, but inmates claim the effort angered Old Colony staffers. Boston City Councilor Chuck Turner later suggested officers were dismayed that the film "linked [inmates] to the community in a positive way."

Soon, officer harassment of inmates was at an "all time high," Jones said. When Jones met with an elected official to discuss conditions in state prisons, prison officials leaked false information to news outlets the Boston Herald and WHDH-TV7, claiming Fox had snuck Jones' girlfriend in to see him. A lawsuit filed against the Herald will examine whether prison officials manipulated the media to retaliate against Jones but within days it became clear much of the Herald's reporting was false.

As Department of Corrections officials in Massachusetts frustrated and opposed Jones and the lifers' anti-violence work, at least one prison guard at MCI-Norfolk was involved in a scheme to smuggle pounds of heroin into the facility. In other prisons across the state, guards are regularly busted for smuggling in drugs.

Peaceful movements, such as the one led by Jones and the lifers, are needed more than ever as gun violence in Boston continues to kill kids. Since Tiffany Moore was killed sitting on that blue mailbox in the summer of 1988 many more Boston children have been murdered by gun violence. The horrific list of victims includes Korey Grant, Cedirick Steele, Herman Taylor III, Nicholas Fomby Davis, Steven Odom, Trina Persad, Robert Jones, Germaine Goffigan, Jaewon Martin and Soheil Martin.

Shrines mark where children died. There are so many shrines in Boston now, the city considered regulating them. One marked where Robert Perry was shot and killed in 2002. His killing has never been solved, though the man the streets thought did it was shot and killed almost immediately. His killing has never been solved. Four years to the day after Robert Perry was killed, as his sister Analicia, a twenty-year-old mother, knelt at his shrine to light a candle to his memory, she was shot and killed. She got a shrine. Her killing has never been solved.

What's happening in Boston should be an outrage to its citizens, however, few people outside the Roxbury, Mattapan and Dorchester neighborhoods seem to care. In 2010, Boston and Massachusetts hosted two vigorously contested elections for mayor and governor. Yet even as murder rates in Boston rose dramatically, neither race featured any substantial discussion on inner city violence.

In the years since the Boston Miracle, the coalitions that once worked together have fallen apart due to bickering over who deserves most of the credit. Cooperation turned to competition and control, said activist and streetworker Teny Gross in a Boston Globe op-ed.

"There is no polite way to say it: Boston's regression into its old territorial self has translated directly into death. A decade ago a young man in Dorchester told me, 'You adults are the real gang members, easy to feel slighted, fighting petty beefs, vying for attention and credit.' It is the beefs on the streets that get the headlines. But the beefs in the offices and agencies are now equally to blame for what is happening."

As murder rates increase, Mayor Menino has responded by proposing an avalanche of programs – and then abandoning them soon after to jump on a new trend. Since 2005 Menino has launched more than twenty different police efforts to combat violence. The sheer number of community-policing initiatives — new ones are introduced each year, sometimes each month — has left community leaders befuddled. Many of them muddle if not contradict others. With leaders caught up in petty feuds and indecision, the chances for a return to peace in Boston seem slim. However, Wiseguy leader E Devious (Marco Antonio Ennis) remains hopeful.

"Could we do it again?" Ennis asks. "Yeah I think we could do it, me and EdO G. are attempting to do it now. We're trying to put the proper pieces together for our program 4Peace to duplicate that now. This time if we can get some political power behind it we can do it, because [when the Wiseguys decreased violence in the city in the 1990s] it was just street power, street cred, street knowledge and industry knowledge. We could change a lot of lives." Ennis pointed around the streets surrounding the Dorchester park he sat in. "Because the common thread to all these kids is music, fashion, arts and social media - that's their life. We have to teach them what's really real out here; and teach them how to survive in these streets without out getting caught up in these streets."

The story of community activist Darrin Howell offers insight into why Boston youths choose to carry guns. Howell, an ex-gun offender making a transition to a college student at UMass-Boston, conducted a comprehensive study of Boston murders between 1988 and 2008. Howell found that nearly half of all homicide victims were between the ages of 14 and 25 and the overwhelming majority of victims were killed in the neighborhoods of Dorchester, Mattapan and Roxbury. He also relates his own experience on why he chose to arm himself as a child in Boston's inner city community.

"I carried a firearm for protection. I was not out to hurt anyone but I wanted to project a clear message that I was not going to be hurt either. I believe the youth of today have taken that message and through the glamorization of violence have adopted a philosophy that it is better to be caught with a firearm than without one." Howell also described his own transformation from gun offender to a well-known activist. He said although his peers did not accept this change initially, in time he has gained their support – suggesting that even the most hard core street figures in Boston know it is time for change.

The problem of violence in Boston is too big for any one activist though. Twenty-five years have passed since crack and guns were introduced to Boston's inner city community and children have inherited the hopelessness of previous generations. For real change to occur, powerful figures such as Mayor Menino must listen to voices such as Darrell Jones, Antonio Ennis and Darrin Howell and find a balanced approach to making streets safe for children, families and, yes, even the Gangsters of Boston.

EPILOGUE

BY 2011, WHITEY Bulger was a legend enshrined on the big screen as inspiration for Jack Nicholson's character in The Departed. But holed up in a small, dirty apartment in California, the man who survived the Irish Gang War, corrupted the FBI and murdered at least nineteen people on his way to the all-time top of Boston's gangland had outlived that legend.

Now, he was Charles Gasko, a retiree living with his wife Carol. He'd been in the same rent control apartment for thirteen years staying up late into the night watching television with black curtains drawn. When he finally went to bed the aging gangster slept alone in the master bedroom while his loyal girlfriend used the guest room.

To fellow residents of the Princess Eugenia apartment complex Bulger and Catherine Grieg were a nice couple who valued their privacy. Bulger once overruled his girlfriend's request to have a maintenance crew repaint the chipped walls in their apartment; perhaps because they would have discovered the holes he cut to hide an arsenal of weapons and $800,000 in cash.

Bulger became even more reclusive after the May 1 killing of Osama Bin Laden, the only other person on the FBI's Top 10 Most Wanted List more notorious than the gangster himself. His girlfriend Catherine Grieg began telling people that his Alzheimer's was progressing – even as his mind remained sharp – putting up an additional barrier to the outside world.

The Gasko's ordinary existence helped Bulger live undetected, according to a former Boston police detective who worked six years with the FBI trying to track Bulger down. "We were looking for a gangster and that was part of the problem," said Charles (Chip) Fleming. "He wasn't a gangster anymore."

No one, it seemed, would ever get an answer to the question, "Where's Whitey?" That is, until he was identified by the ex-beauty queen.

The Gangster, the Beauty Queen and the Cat

When Bulger fled Boston with Grieg, he had a rock solid fake identity in his pocket. Posing as Thomas Baxter, he bought a car in New York and traveled the country with Greig from Chicago to a resort town in Louisiana's Cajun country. But when Bulger's ex-girlfriend Theresa Stanley started helping the FBI in 1996 she told agents about the Baxter alias and where Bulger had been staying, allowing them to track him to Louisiana. She quickly regretted what she had done and told a Bulger associate who warned the gangster and sent him scrambling to find a new identity.

Property records indicate Whitey Bulger and Catherine Grieg moved into their two bedroom unit at the Princess Eugenia complex, two blocks from the Pacific Ocean, in April 1998. By that time they were using the Gasko aliases they invented. It worked for paying bills with cash and cashier's checks. But if they planned to drive, bank or get health care they would need identification in the form of driver's licenses or social security numbers.

Sometime between 1998 and 2000, Bulger was walking in the Los Angeles area when he saw James William Lawlor, an alcoholic army veteran living on the streets. Bulger was apparently struck by how much they resembled one another. Both men had white beards, were bald on top, were of Irish descent and had the same ruddy complexion. Bulger immediately devised a plan to take the man's identity. "He took care of [Lawlor] and got him off the booze. They became friends," said an investigator on the case.

Bulger told Lawlor he had entered the country illegally and needed to use his identification to remain in the United States. Bulger took Lawlor's social security number, driver's license and birth certificate, information he used to pick up medicine at a Santa Monica facility and dip into a bank account to buy clothes and health products.

In return, Bulger agreed to pay the rent on Lawlor's home, a one-room apartment at the West End Hotel. It was in that tiny apartment that hotel employees found Lawlor dead of heart disease on Aug. 8, 2010. He had been dead for days. Bulger was devastated by the news but grief didn't prevent him from continuing to use the man's identity.

Beginning around May 1 when Navy SEALS killed bin Laden, Bulger began spending more time inside. Boston Police Detective Chip Fleming said the bin Laden killing was a turning point in the search for Whitey. "Once bin Laden was killed that freed up money to go after Whitey." He added that Bulger was familiar with the inner workings of the FBI and may have expected more resources to shift to his search.

On a Monday morning in June 2011, the FBI launched a publicity campaign focused on Grieg. Thirty-second television spots ran in commercial breaks of popular daytime shows in fourteen cities nationwide. The FBI said the tip came into the Los Angeles office shortly after 8 p.m. the next day and was relayed to the Bulger task force in Boston, which by that time had shrunk to a few investigators.

Just before 4 p.m. on June 22, the FBI began surveillance on the Princess Eugenia complex. A couple of agents met the building's property manager who identified the couple "100 percent." Hoping to draw Bulger outside peacefully the FBI instructed the manager to call Bulger's apartment and tell them someone had broken into their storage unit in the garage. At 5:45 p.m. when Bulger came to inspect his unit he was immediately surrounded by FBI agents and Boston police.

FBI agents ordered Bulger to get down on his knees but he refused. "He looked old, he looked dejected," said a neighbor who witnessed the scene. "He looked at me and he was sort of ashamed. He looked down."

Agents instructed Bulger to call Greig on the phone. "Carol, stay in the apartment. I've been arrested."

News of Bulger's arrest shocked Boston but few believed the story of an anonymous tipster. The FBI knew where he was the whole time, the speculation went. The Boston Globe, however, revealed the identity – Icelandic beauty queen and former model Anna Bjornsdottir.

A 1980 People magazine profile of Bjornsdottir described her "as one of the world's most beautiful and successful models" who earned more than $2,000 a day for appearing in commercials for Noxzema and Vidal Sassoon. By the 2000s Bjornsdottir and her husband were renting an apartment two blocks from where Bulger and Grieg were staying.

Bjornsdottir first noticed the elderly couple for their devotion to an abandoned local cat. At least twice a day Catherine Grieg would crouch on the sidewalk in front of the building and feed Tiger as Bulger looked on. Their devotion caught Bjornsdottir's attention. "Isn't she nice," the beauty queens said of Greig.

Bjornsdottir and Grieg would speak each morning around 6 a.m. as Grieg fed the cat and Bjornsdottir walked the neighborhood. When the FBI launched a series of ads for Bulger's capture, Bjornsdottir recognized the elderly couple as she watched television in Reykjavik, Iceland.

With a phone call to the FBI Bjornsdottir ended one of the longest and most expensive manhunts in American history and brought Bulger home to Boston to face charges that he had killed nineteen people over a thirty year reign of terror. The Icelandic beauty collected the $2 million reward but the fact remains that Whitey Bulger – the man who outwitted the underworld, the FBI and the entire city of Boston – was brought down by a cat.

Locked away in the Plymouth County House of Corrections, Bulger has communicated with family, his girlfriend Grieg and actor Mark Wahlberg about a possible movie deal. He has even promised to testify at his March 2013 trial – a final opportunity for the longtime informant to try and talk his way out of trouble. Until then, Bulger is alone with his memories – of Southie, of Alcatraz, of murder – and staring into the abyss.

BIBLIOGRAPHY

BOOKS

Legends of Winter Hill by Jay Atkinson

Cradle of Violence: How Boston's Waterfront Mobs Ignited the Revolution by Russell Bourne.

Hitman: The Untold Story of Johnny Martorano by Howie Carr

The Brothers Bulger by Howie Carr

Paddy Whacked by TJ English

Double Cross by Sam and Chuck Giancana

The Dark Side of Camelot by Seymour M. Hersh

Black Mass by Dick Lehr and Gerard O'Neill

Underboss by Dick Lehr and Gerard O'Neill

Liberty's Chosen Home by Alan Lupo

Common Ground by J. Anthony Lukas

The Napoleon of Crime by Ben Macintyre

Malcom X: A Life of Reinvention by Manning Marable

Don't Shoot by David M. Kennedy

Citizen Somerville by Bobby Martini and Elayne Keratsis

All Souls by Michael Patrick MacDonald

Snitching by Alexandra Natapoff

A Criminal and An Irishman by Patrick Nee

Deadly Alliance by Ralph Ranalli

The Knave of Boston by Francis Russell

The Crime of the Century: How the Brink's Robbers Stole Millions and the Hearts of Boston by Stephanie Schorow

The Cocoanut Grove Fire by Stephanie Schorow
Brutal by Kevin Weeks
The Autobiography of Malcolm X by Malcolm X and Alex Haley

NEWS ARTICLES

'Daddy' Black Slain By Gang In His Home, Providence Sunday Journal, September 25, 1932.

20,000 File By Bier of "Daddy" Black, Boston Chronicle, Oct. 1, 1932.

Lombardi Surrenders in Gustin Gang Killings, Daily Boston Globe, Jan. 1, 1932.

Gangster Wins in Police Chase, Daily Boston Globe, Sep. 22, 1933.

Roxbury Volunteers Spread Calm by Janet Riddell, Boston Globe, April 6, 1968.

3 Killed in Roxbury by Robert A. Jordan, Boston Globe, Nov. 14, 1968.

Guido St. Laurent: Feared and Respected by Janet Riddell, Boston Globe, Nov. 14, 1968.

N.E.G.R.O. Leaders Slain by Dan Queen, Bay State Banner, Nov. 17, 1968.

U.S. Probers Cancel Roxbury Jobs Project by William A. Davis, Boston Globe, Dec. 29, 1968.

Raymond Patriarca Dies at 76; Reputedly Ruled N.E. Organized Crime by Richard J. Connolly and Jim Calogero, Boston Globe, July 12, 1984.

Another Day, Another Bullet For Butchy by Kevin Cullen, Boston Globe, Aug. 9, 1989.

'It Ain't Easy Being A Doe in Charlestown' by Kevin Cullen, Boston Globe, Sep. 7, 1989.

Women and crack equal addiction, unequal care by Diane Alters, Boston Globe, Nov. 1, 1989.

"Gang Godfather or Mean Streets Robin Hood?" by Ric Kahn, The Boston Phoenix, April 27, 1990.

Nobody Won by Dan Shaughnessy, Boston Globe, Sep. 30, 1990.

Getting Away With Murder: Charlestown's Code of Silence means most neighborhood killings remain unsolved by Dick Lehr, Boston Globe, Oct. 11, 1992.

Townies' feud lacks boundary, good aim by Kevin Cullen, Boston Globe, Nov. 23, 1993.

'Code of Silence' target of Charlestown arrests by Judy Rakowsky, Boston Globe, June 23, 1994.

A Gang's rise and fall; Drugs, murder, mob machismo led to demise by Ric Kahn, Boston Globe, Sep. 5, 1996.

Pierce recovering as cops eye rappers' pals in attack by Tom Farmer and Jose Martinez, Boston Herald, Sep. 27, 2000.

Pierce Recounts Nightclub Attack by Kathleen Burge, Boston Globe, Sep. 25, 2002.

A Dozen Bloody Years and an Arrest; Pursuing the case that tore at Boston's Cape Verdeans By Kevin Cullen, Boston Globe, July 20, 2007.

Angiulo's funeral draws hundreds; Honoring an infamous native son by Shelley Murphy, Sep. 4, 2009.

"Two Accused Killers Return To A Very Different Chinatown" by Tara H. Arden-Smith and Kathleen Burge, Boston Globe Dec. 27, 2001.

Guilty Plea Ends Gang Terror Spree: Vietnamese boss hunted down after years of violence by Anne E. Kornblut. Boston Globe. Jan 13, 1998.

Fall of leader, gang leaves a power void in Asian underworld by Judy Rakowsky, Boston Globe, Jul 28, 1996.

"6 gunned down at Chinatown club; 5 are dead" by Peter J. Howe, Boston Globe, Jan. 13, 1991.

"The last king of Chinatown" by Daniel Golden, Boston Globe, Nov 3, 1991.

"He Will Not Be Moved" by Chris Faraone, The Boston Phoenix, Feb. 3, 2012.

ACKNOWLEDGMENTS

There are many people who helped me with *Gangsters of Boston*. Thank you to the following people and places who directly made this book happen: staff at the Boston Public Library, Muck Rock News and Emerson College Library. Everyone who sat down with me for interviews: Professor Robert Cvornyak at Rhode Island College, legendary television reporter Sarah Ann Shaw, Mel King, Gaspar Vetrano, Darryl Whiting, the DEA, Marco Ennis, Cool Gzus, Tangg the Juice, Derrick Tyler, innocent man Darrell Jones, Raymond (Benzino) Scott, Dave Mays, Mann Terror, Rodney Draffen and all those who cannot be named. Thank you to Ron Chepesiuk and everyone at Strategic Media Books.

A big thank you to all my journalism mentors for their guidance and kindness in a doomed industry: Neil McCabe, Andrea Gregory, Kat Powers, David Harris, Joe Keohane, Chris Faraone, and everyone at the Somerville News, Somerville Journal, Cambridge Chronicle, Wellesley Townsman, FEDS magazine and Boston Phoenix. Thank you to the great writer and editor Winelle Felix for her help on this book

This book is dedicated to the memory of my father George Hassett Sr. but also to the memory of my grandparents – Mary Hassett, Robert Hassett, Buddy Francis and my Nana, Kathryn Francis. Most of all, though, this book is dedicated to my mother Diane Francis Hassett who instilled in me the love of reading and learning. Thank you Mom, I love you.